BANKING AND BANKING DEVELOPMENTS SERIES

FINANCIAL INSTITUTIONS IN TURMOIL

BANKING AND BANKING DEVELOPMENTS SERIES

Financial Institutions in Turmoil
Carl D. Aspelin (Editor)
2010. ISBN: 978-1-60692-044-2

BANKING AND BANKING DEVELOPMENTS SERIES

FINANCIAL INSTITUTIONS IN TURMOIL

CARL D. ASPELIN
EDITOR

Nova Science Publishers, Inc.
New York

For permission to use material from this book please contact us:
Telephone 631-231-7269; Fax 631-231-8175
Web Site: http://www.novapublishers.com

Library of Congress Cataloging-in-Publication Data

Aspelin, Carl D.
Financial institutions in turmoil / editor, Carl D. Aspelin.
p. cm.
Includes index.
ISBN 978-1-60692-044-2 (hbk.)
1. Banks and banking--United States. 2. Financial services industry--United States. 3. Finance--Government policy--United States. I. Title.
HG2491.A77 2009
332.10973--dc22

2009041022

Published by Nova Science Publishers, Inc. ✦ New York

CONTENTS

PREFACE

This book discusses the profitability of minority banks, regulators' support and assessment efforts, and the views of minority banks on the regulators' efforts. Potential limitations in the regulators' support efforts are identified that would likely be of significance to agency managers and warrant follow-up analysis. In addition, this book reviews how U.S. financial regulators were overseeing dealers' credit derivative operations, including the security and resiliency of the information technology systems used for these products. Furthermore, various trends in both the physical and futures markets have affected energy prices. This book focuses on trends and patterns in the future and physical energy markets and their effects on energy prices, the scope of CFTC's regulatory authority and the effectiveness of CFTC's monitoring and detection of abuses in energy markets.

This book consists of public documents which have been located, gathered, combined, reformatted, and enhanced with a subject index, selectively edited and bound to provide easy access.

Chapter 1 - Federal Reserve Banks fulfill the coin demand of the nation's depository institutions—which include commercial banks, savings and loan associations, and credit unions—by ordering new coins from the U.S. Mint and managing coins held in inventory at the Reserve Banks and in coin terminals. Reliably estimating the demand for coins and efficiently managing the inventory of circulated coins is important to ensure that depository institutions have enough coins to meet the public's demand and to avoid unnecessary coin production costs. Since late 2006, rising metal prices have driven the costs of producing pennies and nickels above the face values of the coins. This chapter addresses (1) the Reserve Banks' process for ordering and distributing coins to the nation's depository institutions and (2) the extent to which this process meets depository institutions' demand for coins.

GAO interviewed officials responsible for coin distribution at each of the 12 Reserve Banks and met with representatives of 4 large operators of Federal Reserve coin terminals, 2 banking associations, the U.S. Mint, and the nation's largest coin recycling company. GAO also analyzed Reserve Bank data for fiscal years 1993 through 2007.

Federal Reserve and U.S. Mint officials generally agreed with GAO's findings in the report and provided technical comments, which were incorporated as appropriate.

Chapter 2 - Minority banks can play an important role in serving the financial needs of historically underserved communities and growing populations of minorities. For this reason, the Financial Institutions, Reform, Recovery, and Enforcement Act of 1989 (FIRREA) established goals that the Federal Deposit Insurance Corporation (FDIC) and the Office of Thrift Supervision (OTS) must work toward to preserve and promote such institutions (support efforts). While not required to do so by FIRREA, the Board of Governors of the Federal Reserve System (Federal Reserve) and Office of the Comptroller of the Currency (OCC) have established some minority bank support efforts.

This testimony, based on a 2006 GAO report, discusses the profitability of minority banks, regulators' support and assessment efforts, and the views of minority banks on the regulators' efforts as identified through responses from a survey of 149 such institutions.

Chapter 3 - Over-the-counter (OTC) credit derivatives are privately negotiated contracts that allow a party to transfer the risk of default on a bond or loan to another party without transferring ownership. After trading in these products grew dramatically in recent years, backlogs of thousands of trades developed for which dealers had yet to formally confirm the trade terms with end-users—such as hedge funds, pension funds, and insurance companies—and other dealers. Not confirming these trades raised the risk that losses could arise.

GAO was asked to review (1) what caused the trade confirmation backlogs and how they were being addressed and (2) how U.S. financial regulators were overseeing dealers' credit derivative operations, including the security and resiliency of the information technology systems used for these products. GAO analyzed data on credit derivatives operations that dealers submitted to regulators, reviewed regulatory examination reports and work papers, and interviewed regulators, dealers, end-users, and industry organizations.

Chapter 4 - Energy prices for crude oil, heating oil, unleaded gasoline, and natural gas have risen substantially since 2002, generating questions about the role derivatives markets have played and the scope of the Commodity Futures Trading Commission's (CFTC) authority. This testimony focuses on (1) trends and patterns in the futures and physical energy markets and their effects on energy prices, (2) the scope of CFTC's regulatory authority, and (3) the effectiveness of CFTC's monitoring and detection of abuses in energy markets. The testimony is based on the GAO report, *Commodity Futures Trading Commission: Trends in Energy Derivatives Markets Raise Questions about CFTC's Oversight* (GAO-08-25, October 19, 2007). For this work, GAO analyzed futures and large trader data and interviewed market participants, experts, and officials at six federal agencies.

Chapter 5 – This chapter is a letter written to the U. S. Securities and Exchange Commission.

Chapter 6 – This chapter is a letter written to the Federal Deposit Insurance Corporation.

Chapter 7 - As the U.S. workforce has become increasingly diverse, many private and public sector organizations have recognized the importance of recruiting and retaining minority and women candidates for key positions. However, previous congressional hearings have raised concerns about a lack of diversity at the management level in the financial services industry, which provides services that are essential to the continued growth and economic prosperity of the country.

This testimony discusses findings from a June 2006 GAO report and more recent work on diversity in the financial services industry.

Specifically, GAO assesses (1) what the available data show about diversity at the management level from 1993 through 2006 and (2) steps that the industry has taken to promote workforce diversity and the challenges involved.

To address the testimony's objectives, GAO analyzed data from the Equal Employment Opportunity Commission (EEOC); reviewed select studies; and interviewed officials from financial services firms, trade organizations, and organizations that represent minority and women professionals.

In: Financial Institutions in Turmoil
Editor: Carl D. Aspelin

ISBN: 978-1-60692-044-2

Chapter 1

U.S. COINS: THE FEDERAL RESERVE BANKS ARE FULFILLING COIN DEMAND, BUT OPTIMAL INVENTORY RANGES ARE UNDEFINED*

U. S. Government Accountability Office

WHY GAO DID THIS STUDY

Federal Reserve Banks fulfill the coin demand of the nation's depository institutions—which include commercial banks, savings and loan associations, and credit unions—by ordering new coins from the U.S. Mint and managing coins held in inventory at the Reserve Banks and in coin terminals. Reliably estimating the demand for coins and efficiently managing the inventory of circulated coins is important to ensure that depository institutions have enough coins to meet the public's demand and to avoid unnecessary coin production costs. Since late 2006, rising metal prices have driven the costs of producing pennies and nickels above the face values of the coins. This chapter addresses (1) the Reserve Banks' process for ordering and distributing coins to the

* This is an edited, reformatted and augmented version of a U. S. Government Accountability Office publication dated March 2008.

nation's depository institutions and (2) the extent to which this process meets depository institutions' demand for coins.

GAO interviewed officials responsible for coin distribution at each of the 12 Reserve Banks and met with representatives of 4 large operators of Federal Reserve coin terminals, 2 banking associations, the U.S. Mint, and the nation's largest coin recycling company. GAO also analyzed Reserve Bank data for fiscal years 1993 through 2007.

Federal Reserve and U.S. Mint officials generally agreed with GAO's findings in the report and provided technical comments, which were incorporated as appropriate.

To view the full product, including the scope and methodology, click on GAO-08-401. For more information, contact Susan Fleming at (202) 512-2834 or flemings@gao.gov.

What GAO Found

The Reserve Banks' process for ordering and distributing coins uses new coins ordered from the U.S. Mint, circulated coins in inventory, and transfers of circulated coins to meet depository institutions' demand for coins. New coin orders begin each month with a recommendation generated by a forecasting tool. Each Reserve Bank office then refines this recommendation in light of its current inventory holdings and its knowledge of local factors that may affect demand, such as changes in a transit authority's use of coins. Each office next submits a request for coins to the Reserve Banks' national Cash Product Office (CPO). CPO seeks to fill the request with transfers of circulated coins from other offices before it consolidates the requests and submits a monthly order for new coins to the U.S. Mint. In fiscal years 2006 and 2007, CPO used transfers to reduce its new coin orders by approximately 10 percent.

The Reserve Banks' process for ordering and distributing coins has met depository institutions' demand since fiscal year 2000, but the process does not define optimal coin inventory ranges. Currently, each Reserve Bank office sets and manages its own inventory levels, resulting in varying levels of inventory held relative to demand. Overall, inventory levels for most denominations have generally been decreasing since fiscal year 2001, yet inventory levels are more likely to be high than low relative to demand, because, for the Reserve Banks, the risk of not meeting depository institutions' demand for coins far exceeds the risk of holding too many coins in inventory. However, holding coins in inventory that could be used to fulfill demand elsewhere can be inefficient, resulting in new coin production costs that could have been avoided if coins held in inventory had been used instead. To increase the efficiency of the Reserve Banks' process, CPO plans this year to begin implementing a new approach to inventory management that it piloted in 2006 and found effective. Under this approach, CPO will determine the number of circulated and new coins each district will receive monthly and will be responsible for ensuring that the Reserve Bank offices maintain appropriate inventory levels.

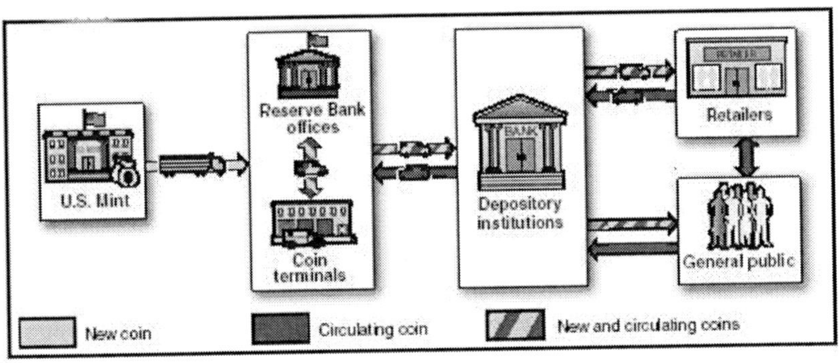

Source: GAO.

Coin Supply and Distribution Process

March 21, 2008
The Honorable Luis V. Gutierrez
Chairman
The Honorable Ron Paul
Ranking Member
Subcommittee on Domestic and International
Monetary Policy, Trade, and Technology
Committee on Financial Services
House of Representatives

The Federal Reserve Banks (Reserve Banks) and the U.S. Mint both play a role in ensuring that the economy has an adequate supply of coins for trade and commerce. The Reserve Banks fulfill the coin demand of the nation's depository institutions—which include commercial banks, savings and loan associations, and credit unions—by ordering new coins from the U.S. Mint and managing an inventory of circulated coins stored in Reserve Banks and coin terminals throughout the nation. In 2007, the U.S. Mint produced 15.4 billion coins, with a value of about $2 billion. According to the Department of the Treasury, as of November 30, 2007, coins worth approximately $37 billion were in circulation throughout the country. Reliably estimating the demand for new coins and efficiently managing the inventory of circulated coins is important—first, to ensure that the depository institutions have enough coins to meet the public's demand and, second, to avoid unnecessary coin production costs. During the fourth quarter of 2006, rising metal prices drove the costs of producing pennies and nickels above the face values of these coins.[1] According to the U.S. Mint's 2007 annual report, the penny costs 1.7 cents to produce and the nickel costs 9.5 cents.[2]

The Federal Reserve System is composed of a central, governmental agency—the Board of Governors (Board)—and 12 regional Reserve Banks, each of which is located in a Federal Reserve district. The Reserve Banks are the operating arms of the central banking system. They carry out a variety of Federal Reserve System functions, including operating a nationwide payment system and distributing the nation's currency and coin. The Reserve Banks have 30 offices that, among other responsibilities, provide coins to depository institutions. The Reserve Banks' national Cash Product Office (CPO), located at the Federal Reserve Bank of San Francisco, coordinates coin distribution from a national perspective as one of its responsibilities. The Reserve Banks store coins on-site and at about 180 coin terminals located throughout the country. The coin terminals provide additional storage space for coins and help to facilitate their distribution. You asked us to examine the processes for ordering and distributing all denominations of coins without creating excess inventory. Accordingly, this chapter addresses (1) the Reserve Banks' process for ordering and distributing coins and (2) the extent to which this process meets the depository institutions' demand for coins.[3]

To determine the Reserve Banks' process for ordering and distributing coins, we reviewed relevant reports and research papers on how the Reserve Banks and the U.S. Mint determine the number of coins to be produced and distributed. We interviewed Federal Reserve economists and Board and Reserve Bank officials representing the 30 Reserve Bank offices to understand how the Reserve Bank offices develop orders for new coins from the U.S. Mint and manage their coin inventory levels. We also interviewed key stakeholders—including officials from the U.S. Mint, operators of coin terminals with agreements to store Reserve Bank coin inventory, and representatives of banking associations—to determine how the Reserve Banks work in collaboration with others to identify and fulfill the depository institutions' requests for coins. We analyzed information on the costs paid by the U.S. Mint to transport circulated coins and analyzed the number of transfers between Reserve Banks from fiscal years 2002 through 2007.

To determine the extent to which the Reserve Banks' process meets the demand for coins, we obtained data on the Reserve Banks' coin payments to depository institutions, receipts for coins deposited by the depository institutions, orders for new coins, and inventory levels for fiscal years 1993 through 2007 for each coin denomination and Reserve Bank.[4] We analyzed these data to identify the demand for coins, the extent to which the Reserve Banks order new coins to meet demand, and the amount of inventory available to meet demand. We presented our data on a fiscal year (October through September) basis because the U.S. Mint operates on a fiscal year; however, the Reserve Banks operate on a calendar year. To assess the reliability of the Reserve Banks' coin data, we talked with agency officials about data quality control procedures and reviewed relevant documentation. We determined that these data were sufficiently reliable for the purposes of this chapter. We interviewed Reserve Bank officials to discuss factors affecting trends in the data and the Reserve Banks' approach to coin inventory management. We also interviewed two banking associations and the four coin terminal operators with the most agreements to store Reserve Bank coin inventory to obtain their views on the Reserve Banks' process for fulfilling depository institutions' demand for coins. We conducted this performance audit from April 2007 through March 2008 in accordance with generally accepted government auditing standards. Those standards require that we plan and perform the audit to obtain sufficient, appropriate evidence to provide a reasonable basis for our findings and conclusions based on our audit objectives. We believe that the evidence obtained provides a reasonable basis for our findings and conclusions based on our audit objectives. More details about our objectives, scope, and methodology appear in appendix I.

RESULTS IN BRIEF

The Reserve Banks' process for ordering and distributing coins uses new coins ordered from the U.S. Mint, circulated coins held in inventory, and transfers of circulated coins between Reserve Bank offices to meet the depository institutions' demand. To develop orders for new coins, the Reserve Bank offices combine coin demand forecasts, local information, and CPO's assessment of opportunities to redistribute circulated coins between Reserve

Bank offices. Every month, the Reserve Bank offices receive recommended coin orders generated by a forecasting tool that is maintained by the Economic Research Group at the Federal Reserve Bank of San Francisco. Each office then compares its current inventory levels with the inventory levels it wants to hold to meet demand and considers factors that may affect demand within its jurisdiction to refine the recommended coin order. Such factors may include coin recycling activity (i.e., the extent to which the public uses coin-counting machines, such as Coinstar, to trade in coins for currency or some form of credit, such as a gift card); the issuance of a commemorative circulating coin; and transit authorities' or casinos' use of coins. Once a Reserve Bank office has considered these factors, it adjusts the tool's recommended coin order and then sends a request for coins to CPO. CPO reviews the offices' requests for coins from a national perspective and looks for opportunities to fill those requests by transferring circulated coins between Reserve Bank offices, rather than ordering new coins. Reserve Bank data show that CPO reduced orders for new coins by approximately 10 percent in fiscal years 2006 and 2007 by fulfilling the Reserve Bank offices' requests with transfers of circulated coins from other offices. Once CPO has identified circulated coins that can be transferred to fulfill the Reserve Bank offices' requests for coins, CPO reduces the offices' orders for new coins, consolidates all of the orders, and sends the final order to the U.S. Mint.

The Reserve Banks' process for distributing coins has met depository institutions' demand since fiscal year 2000, but the process does not define optimal coin inventory ranges for Reserve Bank offices to hold to meet demand. Our analysis of the Reserve Banks' coin order, inventory, payment, and receipt data showed that the Reserve Banks maintained enough inventory to meet demand, even when demand was greater than anticipated. In addition, our analysis showed that overall inventory levels for most denominations have generally been decreasing since fiscal year 2001. However, the Reserve Banks have taken a decentralized approach to inventory management that allows the Reserve Bank offices to determine what inventory levels they should keep on hand to meet future demand and avoid the risk of shortages. Specifically, each Reserve Bank office sets and manages its own inventory levels, resulting in varying levels of inventory being held by the Reserve Banks relative to demand. Reserve Bank officials expressed no concern about holding too many coins and told us that excess inventory is an issue only when coin inventories approach storage capacity limits. However, with rare exceptions, the Reserve Banks have more storage capacity than they need to maintain their current inventory levels; therefore, storage capacity limits do not create an incentive to determine and manage to optimal coin inventory ranges. CPO and Reserve Bank officials noted that the risk of not meeting depository institutions' demand for coins far exceeds the risk of having too many coins in inventory, and that it is easier to deplete coin inventories than to build them up. However, holding coins in inventory that could be used to fulfill demand elsewhere can be inefficient, resulting in new coin production costs that could have been avoided if coins held in inventory had been used instead to fulfill demand. To increase the efficiency of the Reserve Banks' process, CPO received approval from the Reserve Banks in October 2007 to centralize the development and placement of coin orders. Starting in three districts, CPO will determine the final numbers of circulated and new coins that will be shipped monthly to the Reserve Bank offices. CPO will also be responsible for ensuring that the offices maintain appropriate inventory levels. Results of a pilot program suggest that these changes could reduce inventories and smooth the U.S. Mint's production schedule. Federal Reserve and U.S. Mint officials generally agreed with the findings of the report and provided technical comments which were incorporated as appropriate.

BACKGROUND

One of the functions of the Reserve Banks is to fulfill the coin demand of the nation's depository institutions—which include commercial banks, savings and loan associations, and credit unions—by distributing coin inventories stored in the Reserve Banks' vaults and at coin terminals, including circulated coins and new coins ordered from the U.S. Mint. The Reserve Banks have 30 offices that provide coins to depository institutions and are responsible for an area within 1 of the Federal Reserve's 12 districts.[5] Figure 1 shows a map of the Reserve Bank districts (districts) and the locations of the offices that provide coin services.

As figure 2 shows, the Reserve Banks hold and distribute coins from their vaults and contract with armored carrier companies to hold the rest of the Reserve Banks' inventory.

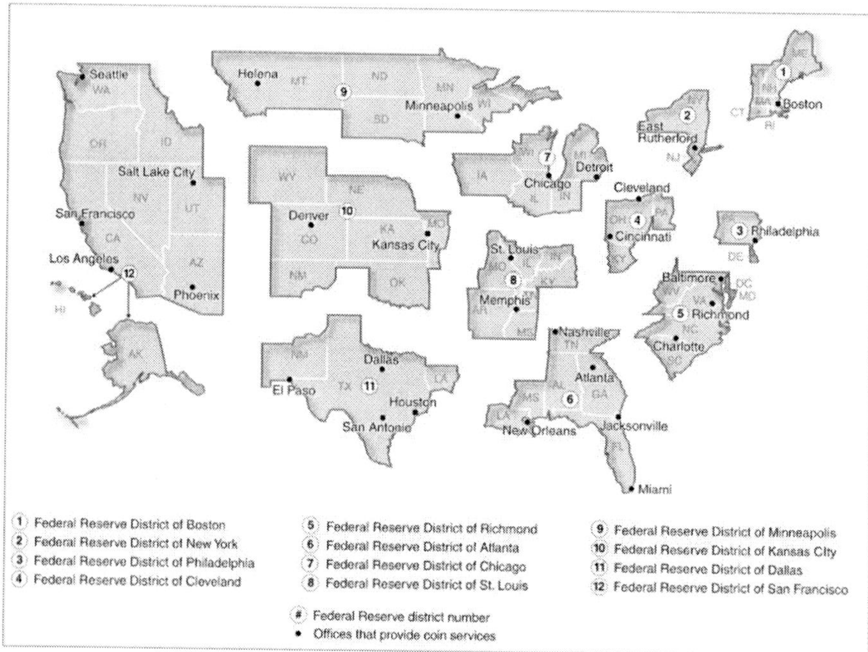

Sources: Federal Reserve (data) and Map Resources (map).

Note: The Phoenix and East Rutherford offices are processing centers that are responsible for distributing coins. The remaining 28 offices are Federal Reserve head offices and branches.

Figure 1. Map of Reserve Bank Districts and Locations of the Offices That Provide Coin Services

As of December 31, 2007, 179 coin terminals held about 61 percent of the Reserve Banks' total coin inventory, in terms of volume. According to Reserve Bank officials, the arrangement between the Reserve Banks and the armored carrier companies that operate these coin terminals began because both parties agreed that having more distribution points would be more cost-efficient from a societal perspective. Federal Reserve officials and coin terminal operators said that, historically, this has been a "win- win" arrangement because it has eliminated the need for armored carriers to haul coins to and from the Reserve Banks before distributing them to the depository institutions. The armored carrier companies store Reserve Banks' coin inventory in their coin terminals at no charge. The agreement between the two entities (1) defines a limit on the value of inventory that a particular coin operator can hold for a Reserve Bank at a particular terminal and (2) requires the coin terminal operator to maintain liability insurance for loss of or damage to the Reserve Bank's coin inventory. The coin terminal agreements can be canceled with prior notice and without cause at any time by either party. The armored carrier companies also maintain depository institutions' coin inventories in the coin terminals at no charge; however, the companies earn revenue from the coin processing, wrapping, and transportation services that they provide to the depository institutions.

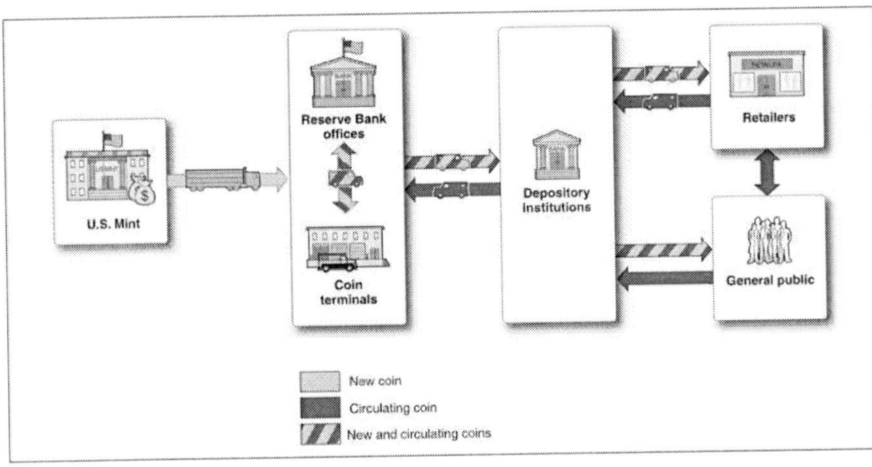

Source: GAO.

Notes: Some depository institutions choose not to receive coins directly from the Reserve Banks. Instead, these banks obtain coins through correspondent banks that have an account with a Reserve Bank. The term "retailers" encompasses any commercial business that uses coins, including retail stores, casinos, restaurants, and vending machine operators.

The new coins produced by the U.S. Mint are a small portion of the total number of coins in circulation. As we have previously mentioned, the U.S. Mint produced about $2 billion worth of coins in fiscal year 2007, while the total value of the coins in circulation was about $37 billion.

Figure 2. Coin Supply and Distribution Process

In addition to the coins held in their inventory, the Reserve Banks purchase new coins at face value from the U.S. Mint to fulfill depository institutions' demand.[6] To develop an annual production schedule and fulfill the Reserve Banks' coin orders, the U.S. Mint uses national coin demand forecasting models[7] to determine how many new coins to produce. U.S. Mint facilities in Philadelphia and Denver then produce the new coins, and the Mint ships the new coins to the Reserve Bank offices or coin terminals. Appendix II shows trends in the U.S. Mint's coin production data for fiscal years 2002 through 2007. The U.S. Mint also may transfer circulated coins between Reserve Bank offices. We discuss this matter in more detail later in the report.

Depository institutions order coins from the Reserve Banks to meet retailers' and the public's demand. These orders include requests for new commemorative circulating coins from congressionally enacted programs, such as the 50 State Quarters and the Presidential $1 Coins Programs, as well as for other coins for day-to-day transactional use.[8] Reserve Bank offices fill these orders with new and circulated coins held in the offices' vaults and at the coin terminals. Depository institutions contract with armored carriers to process and deliver the coins to them; then depository institutions provide coins to retailers and the general public. Depository institutions also return coins to the Reserve Banks when they have more coins in their inventory than they want to hold to meet demand. For example, when the public's demand for coins falls after the holiday season and the depository institutions have accumulated more coins than they want to hold for day-to-day transactions, the depository institutions deposit the extra coins with the Reserve Banks. According to two nationwide banking associations, the depository institutions have an incentive to limit the number of coins they hold in inventory because the institutions do not earn interest on coins held in their own vaults.

THE RESERVE BANKS' PROCESS FOR ORDERING AND DISTRIBUTING COINS USES NEW COINS, COIN INVENTORIES, AND COIN TRANSFERS TO MEET DEMAND

The Reserve Banks' process for ordering and distributing coins uses orders of new coins from the U.S. Mint, the Reserve Bank offices' coin inventories, and transfers of circulated coins between Reserve Bank offices to meet estimates of depository institutions' demand. These estimates are based on coin demand forecasts generated by a forecasting tool. The offices prepare requests for coins on the basis of these estimates and on their own assessments of demand and send the requests to CPO for review. CPO then looks for opportunities to transfer circulated coins between Reserve Bank offices to help fulfill the offices' requests. CPO reduces the offices' requests for coins by the amounts of the transfers, consolidates the adjusted requests, and monthly sends a final consolidated order for new coins to the U.S. Mint.

Coin Demand Forecasts, Inventory Holdings, and Assessments of Local Market Demand Drive Reserve Bank Offices' Requests for New Coins

According to Federal Reserve officials, forecasting coin demand is not an exact science and requires judgment. Therefore, the Reserve Bank offices use both a data-driven process and professional judgment to develop coin orders. Specifically, the offices use an econometric inventory management and forecasting (IMF) tool that the Federal Reserve developed in consultation with the U.S. Mint to forecast coin demand at the Reserve Bank office level and to recommend coin orders for each office. The IMF tool analyzes historical data on coin payments to and receipts from depository institutions and is maintained by the Economic Research Group at the Federal Reserve Bank of San Francisco. According to documentation for the IMF tool, the tool is able to predict the seasonal fluctuations in coin demand fairly accurately because these fluctuations tend to be fairly regular. For example, the demand for coin rises in November in response to the public's demand for coins over the holidays and then decreases in January. While the timing of these fluctuations is fairly regular, their magnitude is more difficult to project, according to Federal Reserve officials. In addition, the IMF tool was developed about the same time that the commemorative circulating coin programs were beginning. Therefore, according to Reserve Bank officials, the tool projects coin demand for economic transactions, but the tool does not estimate demand for collecting commemorative circulating coins. Hence, judgment is involved in estimating both the magnitude of seasonal fluctuations in coin demand and the demand for collecting commemorative circulating coins.

As shown in figure 3, currently, the 30 Reserve Bank offices receive data from the IMF tool each month as a starting point for preparing their coin orders. Most Reserve Bank officials told us that they start the monthly coin ordering process by examining the orders recommended by the IMF tool or their current inventory levels for each denomination.

Reserve Bank officials emphasized that although the IMF tool's analysis is a helpful starting point for the coin ordering process, assessments of local market factors are important because the tool's analysis is based on historical payments and receipts data and may not consider unique factors affecting future coin demand. Coin demand is affected by factors specific to particular districts. For example, five districts noted that local casinos were moving to coinless slot machines, which would reduce coin demand in and coin orders for these districts. Conversely, several districts increase their coin orders to account for collectors' demand when new coins are released for commemorative circulating coin programs, such as the 50 State Quarters Program. Reserve Bank officials noted that changes in the U.S. Postal Service's and local transit authorities' use of coins also affect coin demand. For example, in one district, the local transit authority retrofitted its ticket machines to dispense dollar coins, which resulted in greater demand for dollar coins in that district. Most of the districts cited coin recycling companies, such as Coinstar, as a factor affecting the number of coins returned by the depository institutions and the number of new coins to be ordered from the U.S. Mint. Coin recycling machines found in grocery stores, retail stores, and some depository institutions have made it easier now than it was in the past for the public to trade in coins for currency or some form of credit, such as a gift card. In some districts, coin recycling has returned large volumes of coins to circulation and to the Reserve Banks. Reserve Bank officials said that when more coins are returned than are ordered by the depository institutions, they reduce their orders of new coins from the U.S. Mint. According to data from one major coin recycling company, the value of coins returned to circulation through recycling grew from approximately $1 billion in 2000 to $2.6 billion in 2006.

To obtain information on local market factors, officials at the Reserve Bank offices talk with coin terminal operators and sometimes with officials at depository institutions in their districts. The coin terminal operators provide the Reserve Bank offices with daily inventory data on the Reserve Bank coins held by the terminals. The coin terminal operators hold inventory for both the depository institutions and the Reserve Banks and may provide the Reserve Banks with insight into changes in the depository institutions' coin demand. Some Reserve Bank officials also obtain information on coin demand through conversations with depository institution officials, usually in the course of discussing currency issues. During these conversations, the depository institutions can provide advance notice of any circumstances that may change coin demand, such as upcoming festivals or state fairs, which typically would increase their demand for coins. The conversations with coin terminal operators and depository institutions are important because officials at the Reserve Bank offices can obtain information on potential coin requests or deposits back with the Reserve Banks, which could affect the Reserve Banks' inventory levels or orders for new coins.

According to the Reserve Bank officials with whom we spoke, before the offices finalize and send their orders to CPO, they look for opportunities to transfer coins within their district to meet projected demand. For example, one

Reserve Bank office may want additional coins, while another office may have more coins than it wants to hold to meet short-term demand. The Reserve Bank office works with the coin terminal operators to move the coins as needed. According to Reserve Bank and coin terminal officials, as part of their normal business, the coin terminal operators transport coins to and from the Reserve Banks and are able to absorb the costs of the transfers by combining them with previously scheduled pickups and deliveries for their depository institution customers.

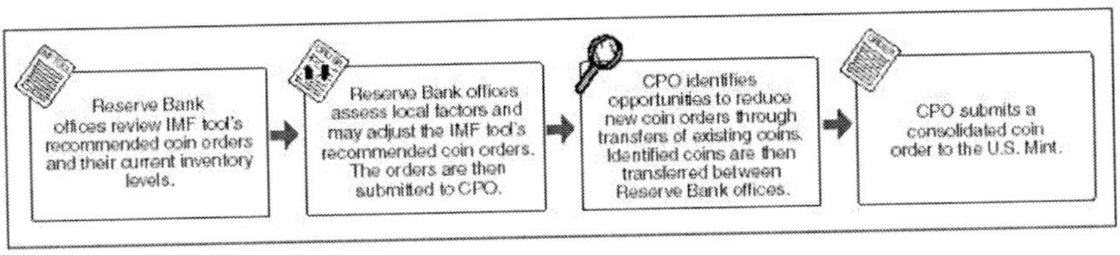

Source: GAO.

Figure 3. Reserve Banks' Current Monthly Coin Ordering Process

CPO Coordinates the Reserve Banks' Coin Order and Identifies Opportunities for Reducing the Order through Transfers

In 2001, CPO began coordinating coin distribution from a national perspective on behalf of the Reserve Banks to enhance coordination with the U.S. Mint and look for opportunities to redistribute coin inventories. Historically, the Reserve Banks individually developed and submitted their own coin orders to the U.S. Mint without any insight into coin inventories in other districts or consideration of whether coins could be transferred from other districts to meet demand, rather than ordering new coins.[9] In 1999, shortages of pennies occurred in some regions of the country because some depository institutions were hoarding pennies and the U.S. Mint could not fulfill the Reserve Banks' increased orders for pennies. During this time, the Reserve Banks moved coins from one district to another to satisfy demand but did not have a centralized coordination process in place to facilitate these transfers, according to Federal Reserve officials. Following this experience, the Reserve Bank of San Francisco assumed responsibility for coordinating coin operations at Reserve Banks through its CPO. CPO is now the Reserve Banks' primary liaison with the U.S. Mint and is responsible for finalizing and submitting a monthly consolidated coin order for the Reserve Banks.

According to Federal Reserve officials, CPO has focused on achieving system efficiencies by implementing more centralized coin management strategies, including enhancing coordination with the U.S. Mint; improving distribution channels by increasing the number of Reserve Bank coin terminals; and redistributing national inventories of coins, as appropriate, to meet demand, thereby reducing the need for new coins from the Mint.

With the exception of new releases of commemorative circulating coins, CPO determines whether the Reserve Banks' requests for coins can be filled with circulated coins in Reserve Banks' inventories or whether new coins need to be ordered from the U.S. Mint. CPO compares the Reserve Bank offices' requests for coins with the IMF tool's recommended orders and the offices' current inventory levels. According to CPO officials, if an office's request differs significantly from the order recommended by the IMF tool, CPO contacts the Reserve Bank office to discuss the reasons for the difference. CPO also compares current inventory levels with historic inventory data to determine whether the Reserve Banks have enough coins to meet seasonal changes in demand. While the Reserve Bank offices make the final decision on how many coins they request, a recent agreement will allow CPO, with input from the Reserve Bank offices, to make the final decision. We discuss this agreement in more detail later in the report.

CPO looks for opportunities to reduce the new coin order to the U.S. Mint by transferring coins from one district to another. CPO officials noted that using circulated inventory rather than purchasing new coins reduces the number of new coins that the U.S. Mint produces and the Mint's costs of production. Yet according to a U.S. Mint official, continuing demand for new coins means that using circulating inventory does not avoid the production of coins, but merely delays it. To determine whether coins can be transferred, CPO considers such things as constraints on storage space, the distance between the office or terminal that requests additional coins and the one that has available inventory, and insurance limits at the coin terminals. CPO then works with the U.S. Mint to transfer circulated coins between Federal Reserve offices that are more than 100 miles apart.[10] The U.S. Mint paid about $1.3 million for 638 coin transfers in fiscal year 2006 and about $915,000 for 404 coin transfers in fiscal year 2007.[11] According to U.S. Mint officials, the Mint contracts and pays for these coin transfers because balancing inventories among the Reserve Banks helps to lower the volatility of production for the Mint and the Mint has ongoing contracts for shipping large quantities of coins. However, according to a U.S. Mint official, the U.S. Mint is looking to phase out the practice of paying for transfers. The official recognizes that coin inventories may occasionally expand in some areas or regions, but believes that such conditions are temporary. Therefore, transferring coins from existing inventories may only temporarily delay the production of additional coins to meet the demands of commerce.[12] See appendix V for data on the number of transfers and the corresponding budget for fiscal years 2002 through 2007. Our analysis of Reserve Banks' order data shows that CPO reduced orders by about 10 percent in fiscal years 2006 and 2007 by fulfilling Reserve Bank offices' coin requests with circulated inventory. Specifically, the Reserve Banks submitted requests to CPO for approximately 18 billion coins in fiscal year 2006 and for approximately 16 billion coins in fiscal year 2007, and CPO was able to reduce these requests through transfers by over 2.2 billion coins in fiscal year 2006 and by over 1.5 billion coins in fiscal year 2007.

Once CPO makes adjustments and consolidates the Reserve Bank offices' orders, CPO submits a final new coin order to the U.S. Mint 1 month before the coins are scheduled to be delivered. The order includes a shipping schedule outlining when and where the coins should be shipped as well as a 5-month coin order forecast. Upon receiving the order from CPO, the U.S. Mint ensures that it will have the coins to fulfill the order and then distributes coins to the Reserve Banks and coin terminals from its production facilities in Philadelphia and Denver. Both U.S. Mint and Federal Reserve officials said that they continually communicate throughout the month on the coin order, and that the Reserve Banks have the flexibility to adjust the coin order and delivery destination.

CPO has several working groups of coin stakeholders, including depository institutions, vending machine operators, and armored carriers, to help address any potential or current coin distribution issues. For example, CPO interacts with depository institutions through its Customer Advisory Council, which currently consists of the 16 largest depository institutions in the country in terms of cash volume. Coins are typically not the primary focus of the council's meetings, but the meetings give the depository institutions an opportunity to discuss any concerns about coins, such as the distribution of newly released commemorative circulating coins. As mandated by law, the Secretary of the Treasury and the Federal Reserve's Board of Governors are taking steps to ensure that an adequate supply of dollar coins is available for commerce and collectors.[13] The U.S. Mint and the Federal Reserve are consulting with coin users and holding forums to identify stakeholders' ideas for the efficient distribution and circulation of dollar coins as well as other circulating coins.

THE RESERVE BANKS' PROCESS FULFILLS COIN DEMAND, BUT OPTIMAL INVENTORY RANGES ARE UNDEFINED

The Reserve Banks' process for ordering and distributing coins has fulfilled depository institutions' demand for the coins, but does not define optimal ranges for the Reserve Banks to hold in inventory to meet demand. Our analysis of Reserve Bank data showed that the Reserve Banks maintained enough inventory to meet demand, even when demand was greater than anticipated. Coin stakeholders confirmed that the Reserve Banks' process has fulfilled depository institutions' demand for coins in recent years. However, the Reserve Banks have taken a decentralized approach to inventory management that allows the Reserve Bank offices to use their own judgment to set inventory levels that they think are appropriate to meet future demand and avoid the risk of shortages. Reserve Bank officials expressed no concern about holding too many coins and told us that excess inventory is an issue only when coin inventories approach storage capacity limits. However, with rare exceptions, the Reserve Banks have more storage capacity than they need to maintain their current inventories, and, therefore, storage capacity does not serve as an incentive for the banks to evaluate and manage to optimal coin inventory ranges. To increase the efficiency of the distribution process, CPO has received approval from the Reserve Banks to centralize the development and placement of coin orders, and CPO will be responsible for ensuring that the offices maintain appropriate inventory levels.

The Reserve Banks' Ordering and Distribution Process Has Met Demand for Coins

The Reserve Banks' process has ensured that enough coins are available through orders of new coins and the Reserve Banks' inventories of circulated coins to meet the depository institutions' demand for coins. In each year since 1993, the number of coins demanded by the depository institutions has generally exceeded the number of coins deposited back to the Reserve Banks for all denominations, except the half-dollar. For example, as figure 4 shows, in fiscal year 2007, the Reserve Banks paid out 76 billion coins to the depository institutions (payments) and received 62 billion coins back from the depository institutions (receipts). This difference between payments and receipts is called “net pay.” For example, net pay for fiscal year 2007 was about 14 billion coins. See appendix III for payments and receipts data, by denomination, for fiscal years 1993 through 2007.

Since the number of coins received by the Reserve Banks is less than the number of coins sent to the depository institutions to meet their demand, the Reserve Banks have to order new coins or use circulated inventory to meet demand. When depository institutions demand more coins than they return over a month or a year, net pay is positive for that period and additional coins have to be ordered or coin inventory has to be used to meet the demand. When depository institutions return more coins to the Reserve Banks than they order over a month or a year, net pay is negative for that period and the Reserve Banks’ inventory of coins can grow. Net pay fluctuates throughout the year, depending on the public’s spending patterns. Specifically, Reserve Bank data show that net pay was generally positive for all denominations, except the half-dollar, throughout the year, except in January when the demand for coins declines. Net pay for the half-dollar has been negative since fiscal year 2004 because the Reserve Banks received more half-dollars back than they paid out. Understanding and predicting net pay is critical to the Reserve Banks’ ability to meet coin demand. According to Federal Reserve officials, net pay is positive for many reasons. For example, the public stores coins that it receives in jars and dresser drawers and sometimes discards coins. Collectors’ demand for coins can also increase the Reserve Banks’ payments for commemorative circulating coins, while limiting the Reserve Banks’ receipts because the coins are kept out of circulation. When coins leave “active” circulation— that is, the coins are stored and not deposited or used for commerce—they are not available to meet depository institutions’ demand.

During fiscal years 1993 through 2007, the Reserve Banks’ aggregate orders for new coins tracked together with net pay fairly closely. For example, in fiscal year 2002, total orders for new coins—14.72 billion coins—were a little lower than the total net pay for all coins—15.11 billion coins—and resulted in a decrease in inventory for some denominations. In fiscal year 2007, total orders for new coins—14.63 billion coins—were a little higher than the total net pay for all coins—14.02 billion coins, suggesting the Reserve Banks ordered enough coins to fulfill net pay for the year and increased total inventory. Federal Reserve officials suggest that this aggregate annual increase of nearly 600 million coins can, in part, be explained by the introduction of the Presidential $1 Coin Program. After the first year of the program, the Reserve Banks report inventories of at least 300 million Presidential dollar coins. Orders for the penny constituted over half of the total orders for new coins. In fiscal year 2007, orders for the penny were 7.76 billion coins, while net pay was 7.79 billion coins. According to Reserve Bank officials, the difference between orders for new pennies and net pay resulted in an aggregate decline of about 30 million pennies in Reserve Banks' inventories.

The Reserve Banks strive to maintain sufficient inventories of coins to fulfill demand, despite seasonal and unanticipated changes and potential interruptions in the supply of new coins. First, inventory is important in handling the seasonal fluctuations in demand for coins. According to documentation on the IMF tool and Reserve Bank officials, this fluctuating demand can be met by either (1) adjusting the number of coins ordered to keep pace with known seasonal changes in demand or (2) keeping orders constant and allowing inventory to fluctuate in response to these changes in demand. The Reserve Banks place orders to keep the U.S. Mint's production schedule fairly consistent and allow inventories to fluctuate with the seasonality of coin demand. For example, Reserve Bank officials said they ensure that they have enough coins on hand to meet the high coin demand leading into the summer and holiday months. According to Federal Reserve officials, a Reserve Bank office may not transfer coins out of its area if the office knows that those coins will be needed in the next week or month. Federal Reserve officials also noted that although the Reserve Banks can predict the timing of seasonal changes in demand for coins, it is more difficult for them to predict the magnitude of the changes from one year to the next. Predicting demand is important because the U.S. Mint may not be able to produce enough coins within a short time frame to keep up with heavy demand.[14] Second, since there is some uncertainty in the actual demand for coins in any given month, the Reserve Banks' coin inventory provides a buffer against any changes in demand that may occur between the times the coins are ordered and received. Third, the Reserve Banks want to hold enough inventory to handle disruptions in supply from the U.S. Mint. For example, when the U.S. Mint's production facilities in Philadelphia shut down, starting in March 2002, for 7 weeks to correct safety concerns, the Mint worked with the Reserve Banks to ensure that coins were available to fulfill demand.

Figure 5 shows that when compared with expected demand, expressed as days of payable inventory, the Reserve Banks' overall inventory for the penny, nickel, dime, and quarter has generally decreased since fiscal year 2001.[15] For example, the penny inventory declined from an average of 32 days of payable inventory, or 3.0 billion coins, in fiscal year 2001 to an average of 16 days of payable inventory, or 2.2 billion coins, in fiscal year 2007. The nickel inventory declined from 37 days of payable inventory in fiscal year 2001 to 25 days of payable inventory in fiscal year 2007. Inventory levels throughout the year vary around these averages because of fluctuations in the public's spending patterns.

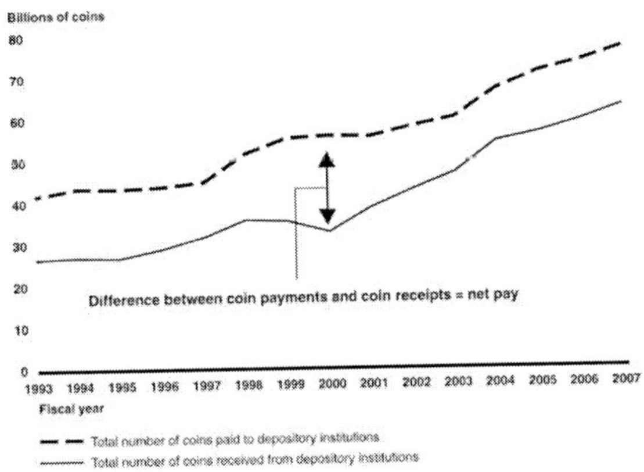

Source: Federal Reserve.

Figure 4. Number of Coins the Reserve Banks Paid to and Received from Depository Institutions, Fiscal Years 1993-2007

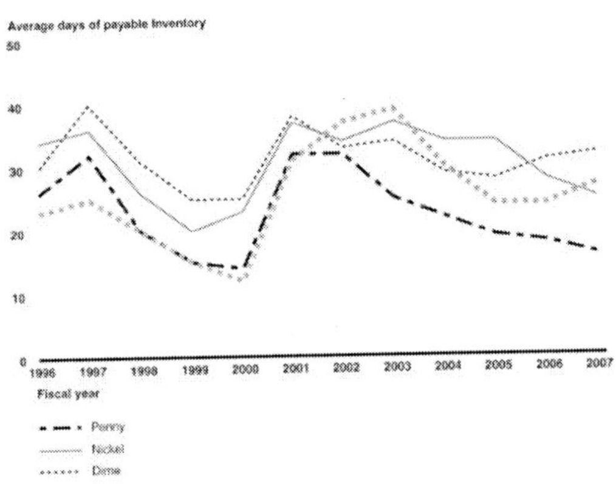

Source: Federal Reserve.

Note: The inventory data are represented in terms of average days of payable inventory. A day of payable inventory is the level of inventory needed by the Reserve Banks to meet 1 day's expected payments to depository institutions.

Figure 5. Average Days of Payable Inventory for the Reserve Banks for the Penny, Nickel, Dime, and Quarter, Fiscal Years 1996-2007

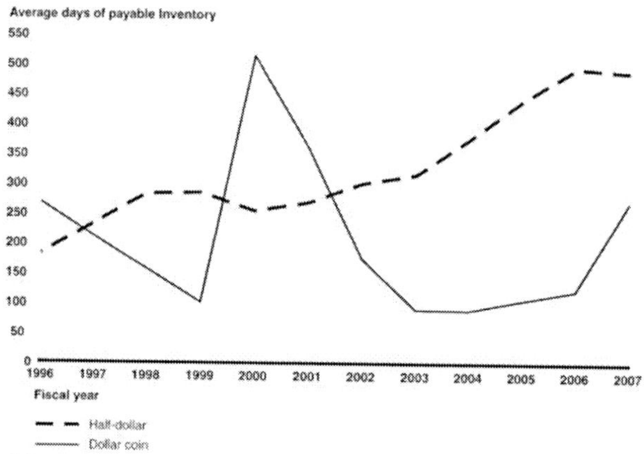

Source: Federal Reserve.

Figure 6. Average Days of Payable Inventory for the Reserve Banks for the Half-Dollar and Dollar Coin, Fiscal Years 1996-2007

Figure 6 shows that the days of payable inventory for the half-dollar and dollar coins greatly exceed the levels for the other denominations and have generally increased in recent years. According to Federal Reserve officials, there is little demand for these denominations. Federal Reserve officials said that dollar coin inventories have also grown as a result of the Presidential $1 Coin Program, which requires the Federal Reserve to ensure that, during an introductory period, an adequate supply of each newly minted design (there are four new coins each year) is made available for commerce and collectors.

Several factors affected trends in the Reserve Banks' inventory levels during fiscal years 1993 through 2007. For example, inventory levels for all denominations dropped from fiscal years 1997 to 1999. Reserve Bank officials said that the demand for all coin denominations grew in 1999 in anticipation of the new millennium (Y2K). In fiscal year 2001, inventory levels for all denominations increased. According to the U.S. Mint's 2001 annual report, the economy, which is directly related to the demand for coins, took a downturn in the middle of fiscal year 2000, resulting in a decrease in coin demand and a buildup of coin inventories. According to Reserve Bank officials, the inventory trends for the quarter and dollar coin reflect the challenges posed by the commemorative circulating programs associated with these coins. The officials noted that commemorative circulating coin programs, such as the Presidential $1 Coin Program, create uncertainty about the demand for those denominations. These programs involve the distribution of multiple coin designs and require the Reserve Banks to order enough commemorative circulating coins to meet the normal demand for coins for commercial transactions as well as the potential demand from collectors when the coins are first introduced. According to Reserve Bank officials, the Reserve Banks did not initially have experience in working with commemorative circulating coins and placed large orders for state quarters to ensure that they would have enough on hand to meet both normal transactional demand and potential collector demand. As a result, more quarters flowed back to the Reserve Banks than Reserve Bank officials expected for the first several releases. Reserve Bank officials noted that their forecasts of demand for state quarters have improved, and that their inventory of quarters has declined. The officials also noted that even with more experience, however, programs, such as the Presidential $1 Coin Program, require the Reserve Banks to order more coins than they would otherwise use for transactional purposes, thereby increasing Reserve Banks' coin inventory levels beyond the levels they would ordinarily hold.

The coin terminal operators, banking associations, and Reserve Bank officials with whom we spoke confirmed that the Reserve Banks' process has fulfilled the depository institutions' demand for coins in recent years. Reserve Bank and CPO officials told us that they have been able to fill all depository institutions' requests for coin. The four coin terminal operators that we spoke with also noted that the Reserve Banks have been able to meet the demand of the depository institutions in their terminals. Finally, representatives from two banking associations said that constituent banks across the country have voiced no concern about the Reserve Banks' ability to distribute coins to the depository institutions.

Optimal Inventory Ranges Are Undefined, but the Reserve Banks Are Taking Steps to Manage Coin Inventory More Efficiently

The Reserve Banks have taken a decentralized approach to managing coin inventory, under which the Reserve Bank offices have decided what inventory levels are appropriate to keep on hand to meet forecasted demand and avoid the risk of coin shortages. Each Reserve Bank office has defined its own inventory levels on the basis of professional judgment and historical data, to meet demand and avoid running out of coins, and has used the capacity of its storage facilities as the key determinant of its maximum inventory levels. According to Reserve Bank officials, insurance limits at the coin terminals also help to define maximum inventory levels, but they can be adjusted, if necessary. Reserve Banks we spoke with had no specific levels for maximum inventory other than storage capacity and coin terminal insurance limits.

Because each Reserve Bank sets its own inventory levels, the districts manage to different inventory levels and hold varying levels of inventory relative to demand. For example, according to Reserve Bank officials, 3 of the 12 Reserve Banks generally try to hold at least 10 days of payable inventory for all denominations, while 6 of the 12 districts generally try to hold at least 20 or more days of payable inventory. Table 1 shows that for fiscal year 2007, the districts held varying levels of inventory relative to demand for the different denominations. For example, the penny inventories ranged from an average of 8 days in the Boston district to 26 days in the San Francisco district, while the quarter inventories ranged from 17 days in the St. Louis district to 40 days in the Philadelphia district.

Table 1. Average Days of Payable Inventory for the Penny, Nickel, Dime, and Quarter for the Reserve Banks, by District, in Fiscal Year 2007

	Average days of payable inventory, fiscal year 2007			
District	**Penny**	**Nickel**	**Dime**	**Quarter**
Boston	8	16	20	19
New York	10	17	19	21
Chicago	13	19	27	29
Dallas	13	24	30	28
Cleveland	14	25	36	38
Kansas City	14	28	30	32
St. Louis	16	21	32	17
Philadelphia	17	23	25	40
Richmond	17	22	27	21
Atlanta	19	30	40	20
Minneapolis	23	41	42	33
San Francisco	26	35	44	31
Range across the Reserve Banks	**8 – 26**	**16 – 41**	**19 – 44**	**17 – 40**

Source: GAO analysis of Reserve Bank data.

Note: The inventory data are represented in terms of average days of payable inventory. A day of payable inventory is the level of inventory needed by the Reserve Banks to meet 1 day's expected payments to depository institutions.

Table 2. Range of Average Days of Payable Inventory for Penny, Nickel, Dime, and Quarter across Reserve Banks, Fiscal Years 1996-2007

	Range of average days of payable inventory			
Fiscal	Penny	Nickel	Dime	Quarter
1996	16 – 33	18 – 49	19 – 66	14 – 68
1997	21 – 52	22 – 50	17 – 101	10 – 137
1998	12 – 34	20 – 34	22 – 45	9 – 132
1999	8 – 24	13 – 31	16 – 42	9 – 55
2000	7 – 22	9 – 43	8 – 39	5 – 17
2001	20 – 49	26 – 64	26 – 60	23 – 51
2002	20 – 46	22 – 54	20 – 51	27 – 57
2003	16 – 40	25 – 61	24 – 63	16 – 78
2004	17 – 37	26 – 51	21 – 51	14 – 68
2005	13 – 32	25 – 50	18 – 42	11 – 55
2006	11 – 28	22 – 40	22 – 43	18 – 33
2007	8 – 26	16 – 41	19 – 44	17 – 40

Source: GAO analysis of Reserve Bank data.

Note: The inventory data are represented in terms of average days of payable inventory. A day of payable inventory is the level of inventory needed by the Reserve Banks to meet 1 day's expected payments to depository institutions.

Table 2 shows how the inventories for the penny, nickel, dime, and quarter have varied across Reserve Banks from fiscal years 1996 through 2007.[16]

According to Federal Reserve officials and documentation of the Reserve Banks' IMF tool, the districts hold varying levels of inventory relative to demand because of the differences in the variability in coin demand and because some offices have more storage capacity. To be able to respond to the variability in demand, some Reserve Bank offices need to hold more coins than other offices relative to demand to ensure that they have enough coins to meet demand at all times. See appendix IV for the inventory levels relative to demand, by district and denomination, for fiscal years 2005 through 2007.

Most Reserve Bank officials said that they were generally comfortable with their current inventory levels and expressed no concerns about having too many coins. Several Reserve Bank officials told us that they ordered conservatively—that is, they erred, if at all, on the side of ordering too many coins—because they were more concerned about not having enough coins to meet depository institutions' demand during high demand periods than about having too many coins at other times. CPO officials said it would be easier to deplete coin inventories than to build them up. Furthermore, most Reserve Bank officials were not concerned about having too many coins because they said they have ample on-site and off- site storage capacity and insurance levels at the coin terminals to store their coin inventory. For example, two districts have new, on-site coin vaults that were built within the last 10 years and were designed to accommodate the entire coin inventory for the district, even without coin terminals. Reserve Bank officials said that if the coin inventory level at a particular location approaches the storage limits, they work to move coins to another Reserve Bank or terminal.

CPO and Reserve Bank officials noted that the risk of not meeting depository institutions' demand for coins far exceeds the risk of having too many coins in inventory, as long as storage capacity exists. For example, Federal Reserve officials told us that in 1999, they had problems fulfilling the depository institutions' demand for pennies. During this time, the U.S. Mint could not produce enough pennies to fill Reserve Banks' orders. In addition, the Reserve Banks were not yet coordinating coin distribution nationally and, therefore, could not easily identify sources of inventory available for redistribution. According to Federal Reserve officials and coin terminal operators, some depository institutions became concerned that coins would not be available to meet their demand and began hoarding coins, which further exacerbated the problem. Federal Reserve officials noted that since 2001, CPO has coordinated Reserve Bank coin distribution from a national perspective to help ensure confidence in the availability of coins, and, since that time, the Reserve Banks have experienced no shortages.

Although we only heard about storage capacity concerns from Reserve Bank officials in one district, some coin terminal operators expressed concerns about coin inventory levels in their terminals. Officials from one Reserve Bank told us that, on rare occasions, they have had to negotiate with depository institutions on when the Reserve Bank could accept coin deposits because storage space was not immediately available. Reserve Bank officials also said that every effort is made to redistribute coins before insurance levels are reached at the coin terminals, and that the Reserve Bank offices work with the coin terminal operators to stay under the insurance limits. However, two of the four coin terminal operators with whom we spoke said that the Reserve Banks maintain higher inventory levels than the operators consider sufficient to respond to changes in demand. CPO and Reserve Bank officials said that they were sensitive to the numbers of coins being held at the coin terminals, but the officials noted that the Reserve Banks work to stay within the limits established in their agreements with the operators. One coin terminal operator noted that it did not have concerns about the Reserve Banks' coin inventory levels or the distribution process. However, this operator noted that high volumes of coin recycling activity posed a challenge in some of its terminals. This operator also said that CPO was helping to move some of the coins out of the terminals, but that the high volumes would continue to be a problem until coin stakeholders—coin terminal operators, depository institutions, and CPO—find a solution to equitably redistribute the recycled coins.

Although we recognize the importance of minimizing the risk of not having sufficient coins to meet demand at all times, the Reserve Banks' current approach to inventory management does not define an optimal range of inventory for the offices to meet demand. Inventory levels that greatly exceed likely future demand could result in the overproduction of new coins and in potential storage concerns for the coin terminal operators. Data show that the Reserve Banks' overall inventory levels relative to demand for all denominations, except the half-dollar and the dollar coins, have generally decreased since 2001. However, the Reserve Banks and coin terminals have sufficient capacity for the Reserve Banks to hold higher levels of inventory for some denominations than are likely to be used to meet demand. Moreover, the storage capacity at the coin terminals is provided to the Reserve Banks at no charge. As a result, the Reserve Banks lack an incentive to evaluate and manage to optimal coin inventory ranges. In addition, the current approach to inventory management could lead to the overproduction of new coins in the short term or to the retention in some districts of coin inventory that could be redistributed to meet demand in another district. Thus, a Reserve Bank may incur few or no charges for storing high inventory levels, but the U.S. Mint may incur costs for producing new coins when circulated coins may be available to fulfill demand.[17] Producing new pennies and nickels when circulated coins could be used instead is particularly inefficient, since these denominations cost more to produce than they are worth. According to Federal Reserve officials, to mitigate this risk, CPO has been working with the Reserve Banks to manage inventories from a national perspective by transferring, where appropriate, inventories from one Reserve Bank to another one. According to a U.S. Mint official, a continuing demand for new coins means that producing coins when there is production capacity is not a concern because these coins will eventually be needed. In fact, he indicated that delaying production when there is production capacity may actually increase costs in the long run because production costs, like other costs, tend to increase over time.

CPO has recognized the importance of further centralizing and increasing the efficiency of the Reserve Banks' approach to coin inventory management and has identified opportunities for doing so. In 2006, the Reserve Banks and the U.S. Mint co-chartered a 6-month pilot of a new inventory management approach in one district. During the pilot, CPO (1) managed the inventory using vendor software that forecasts coin demand at the Reserve Bank office or terminal level[18] to provide consistent upper and lower bounds for inventory levels at each terminal site in the district and (2) used this information to maintain inventory levels to meet demand in the district. The Reserve Bank office was then responsible for moving coins among the coin terminals to meet demand. The Reserve Banks and the U.S. Mint assessed the results of the pilot and found that the new approach reduced the risk of shortages, transportation expenses, and inefficiencies associated with the U.S. Mint' s production volatility as well as increased stakeholders' confidence in the coin distribution system. According to CPO officials, the pilot also demonstrated that the district's inventory levels could be reduced. As a result of the pilot, CPO received approval from the Reserve Banks in October 2007 to implement a more centralized approach to managing coin orders and inventories.[19] According to CPO officials, they are expecting to phase in this new approach, beginning with three districts in the second quarter of 2008.

When the new approach is implemented, CPO will have the final authority to determine orders on behalf of the Reserve Bank offices and will be responsible for managing inventory levels that are maintained at the office level. According to CPO officials, CPO will continue to provide the Reserve Bank offices with a recommended monthly order. The Reserve Bank offices will be able to review this order and suggest revisions, but ultimately CPO will decide on the final order for each office. Although Reserve Bank officials told us that under the current approach, their adjustments to the IMF tool's recommended coin orders were minimal, over the past 3 years the combined impact of these adjustments was sometimes substantial. For example, the IMF tool recommended a total order of $52 million in pennies for all of the Reserve Bank offices in fiscal year 2007. Following the offices' assessment of local market factors and the availability of transfers of circulated coins to fulfill the offices' requests, CPO submitted a total order of $77.6 million for new pennies to the U.S. Mint. CPO's ability to now decide on the number of coins each district will receive monthly could potentially result in decreased orders for new coins from the U.S. Mint. CPO is considering establishing inventory ranges for the Reserve Bank offices on the basis of factors such as historical trends in coin payments and receipts, the amount of time taken to transport coins to a Reserve Bank office, and storage capacity limits to better define the level of inventory to be held to meet demand. We believe that the establishment of inventory ranges could help CPO and the Reserve Banks evaluate and report on the effectiveness of CPO's inventory management approach. CPO officials believe that these changes will improve the Reserve Banks' inventory management because CPO can provide a national perspective on where inventory can be used to meet demand, including where coins can be moved when necessary to meet demand in one district, while freeing space for coin deposits in storage facilities that are approaching capacity in another district. U.S. Mint officials said that the new approach could allow the U.S. Mint to further smooth its production schedule, thereby lowering costs associated with unpredictable changes in production.

AGENCY COMMENTS

We provided a draft of this chapter to the Board of Governors of the Federal Reserve System and to the Department of the Treasury for their review and comment. The Director of the Division of Reserve Bank Operations and Payment Systems provided written comments, which are reproduced in appendix VI. Overall, the Federal Reserve agrees with the findings in our report and believes that the data in the report reflect the Reserve Banks' efficient and effective management of coin inventories. The Federal Reserve also provided technical comments, which we have addressed in this chapter as appropriate. The Acting Deputy Director of the U.S. Mint provided oral comments stating that the agency agrees with the information in this chapter as it pertains to the U.S. Mint and provided technical comments, which we have also incorporated as appropriate.

Susan A. Fleming
Director, Physical Infrastructure Issues

APPENDIX I: OBJECTIVES, SCOPE, AND METHODOLOGY

The objectives of this chapter were to examine (1) the Reserve Banks' process for ordering and distributing coins and (2) the extent to which this process meets the depository institutions' demand for coins.

To describe the Reserve Banks' process for supplying coins throughout the country, we obtained and reviewed relevant articles, reports, economic studies, and technical documentation on how the Reserve Banks and the U.S. Mint determine the number of coins to be produced and distributed. We also interviewed Federal Reserve and U.S. Mint economists who were involved in the development of economic models used to predict coin demand. During these interviews, we reviewed how the national coin forecast models are used by both the Reserve Banks and the U.S. Mint and discussed the accuracy of these models in predicting net pay at the national level. We interviewed officials from the Federal Reserve's Board of Governors (Board), each of the 12 Reserve Bank districts, and the national Cash Product Office (CPO) to determine how coin orders are developed and submitted to the U.S. Mint. In addition, we reviewed statutes related to the Federal Reserve and U.S. Mint.

We also interviewed key stakeholders, including officials from the U.S. Mint, operators of coin terminals with agreements to store Reserve Bank coin inventory, and representatives of banking associations, to determine how the Reserve Banks work in collaboration with others to identify and fulfill the depository institutions' requests for coins. We obtained and analyzed information on the costs paid by the U.S. Mint to transport existing coins and analyzed the number of transfers between Reserve Bank districts since fiscal year 2002. To determine how CPO was able to reduce orders for new coins through transfers of existing coin inventory, we reviewed Reserve Bank data documenting actual coin demand and compared these data with the Reserve Banks' actual order to the U.S. Mint for new coins and the number of circulated coin transfers processed by CPO.

To determine the extent to which the Reserve Banks' coin distribution process meets the depository institutions' demand for coins throughout the country, we obtained data on the Reserve Banks coin payments to depository institutions, receipts for coins deposited by the depository institutions, orders for new coins, and inventory levels for fiscal years 1993 through 2007 for each coin denomination and for each Reserve Bank. We analyzed these data using Excel and SAS statistical analysis software. To calculate Reserve Banks' number of coins paid to the depository institutions and Reserve Banks' number of coins received from the depository institutions at the national and district level for all coin denominations, we converted the data from value of coins to volume of coins and then calculated fiscal year totals for each denomination at the national and district level. We created line charts to compare the total number of coins that Reserve Bank paid to depository institutions with the total number of coins that the Reserve Bank received from the depository institutions. To calculate net pay and the Reserve Banks' coin order to the U.S. Mint, we converted the data from value of coins to volume of coins and calculated fiscal year totals at the national and district level. We created line charts to compare the net pay data with the Reserve Banks' coin order data.

To calculate the Reserve Banks' days of payable inventory, we consulted with officials at the Board and CPO to determine an appropriate methodology. CPO and Reserve Banks calculate payable inventory information several different ways, depending upon what they are assessing. For the purposes of our review, we determined that a comparison of inventory relative to a 3-month daily average of payments for 3 years was the most appropriate calculation to determine the Reserve Banks' inventory position, because it compares inventory relative to what the Reserve Banks could reasonably have expected coin payments to be in the future. This methodology captures coin inventory levels relative to what Reserve Banks expected to need to meet future payments to depository institutions. For the numerator, we used end-of-month inventory levels for a given month. For the denominator, for the 3 previous years, we used the quarter following the inventory month used in the numerator to assess inventory levels relative to demand in the following quarter. For example, when we calculated days of payable inventory for December 2006, we used data for January, February, and March, 2004; January, February, and March, 2005; and January, February, and March, 2006, in the denominator. To calculate the average daily payment rate, we took the monthly payments data from each month of the quarter from the previous 3 years and divided by 21 business days to obtain an average daily payment rate for each month. We then totaled the daily payment rates for the 9 months and divided by 9 to obtain an average payment rate of the 3 quarters for the 3 years. To calculate the annual average days of payable inventory, by denomination, for each Reserve Bank, we averaged the monthly figures on days of payable inventory that we computed as we have previously described. Because of the methodology we used to calculate days of payable inventory, 1996 is the earliest year for which we can present the data. We used statistical analysis software to complete this analysis for each coin denomination at the national and Reserve Bank level.

We also interviewed officials at the Board and Reserve Banks to discuss factors affecting trends in the data, the level of inventory that each district tries to hold, and the Reserve Banks' approach to coin inventory management. To describe the Reserve Banks' new centralized approach to coin inventory management and how it might address concerns about inventory management, we interviewed officials at CPO and the Board about a 2006 pilot to test a new inventory management approach at the Reserve Bank of Cleveland.

To assess the reliability of the coin data we received from the Reserve Banks and U.S. Mint, we talked with agency officials about data quality control procedures and reviewed relevant documentation. For example, we reviewed audit reports for fiscal years 2006 and 2007 prepared by the Department of the Treasury's Office of Inspector General, which reported that the U.S. Mint's data were accurately presented and in conformity with generally accepted accounting principles. The U.S. Mint has received approximately 15 consecutive unqualified opinions. These internal control audits found no material weaknesses and found that the U.S. Mint is in compliance with the Federal Manager's Financial Integrity Act. For the Federal Reserve data, we reviewed an independent auditor's reports on the Federal Reserve's financial statements for fiscal years 1995 through 2006, and found that the Federal Reserve's data were accurately presented and in conformity with generally accepted accounting principles. We also performed advanced electronic testing to assess the reliability of the computer-processed data, and determined that these data were accurate, complete, and consistent and, therefore, sufficiently reliable for the purposes of this chapter.

We conducted this performance audit from April 2007 through March 2008 in accordance with generally accepted government auditing standards. Those standards require that we plan and perform the audit to obtain sufficient, appropriate evidence to provide a reasonable basis for our findings and conclusions based on our audit objectives. We believe that the evidence obtained provides a reasonable basis for our findings and conclusions based on our audit objectives.

APPENDIX II: COIN PRODUCTION TRENDS, BY DENOMINATION

Figures 7 through 13 show trends in the U.S. Mint's coin production data for fiscal years 2002 through 2007. These data represent all of the "circulating" coins produced by the U.S. Mint; they do not include the "proof" or "uncirculated" quality coins produced by the Mint.

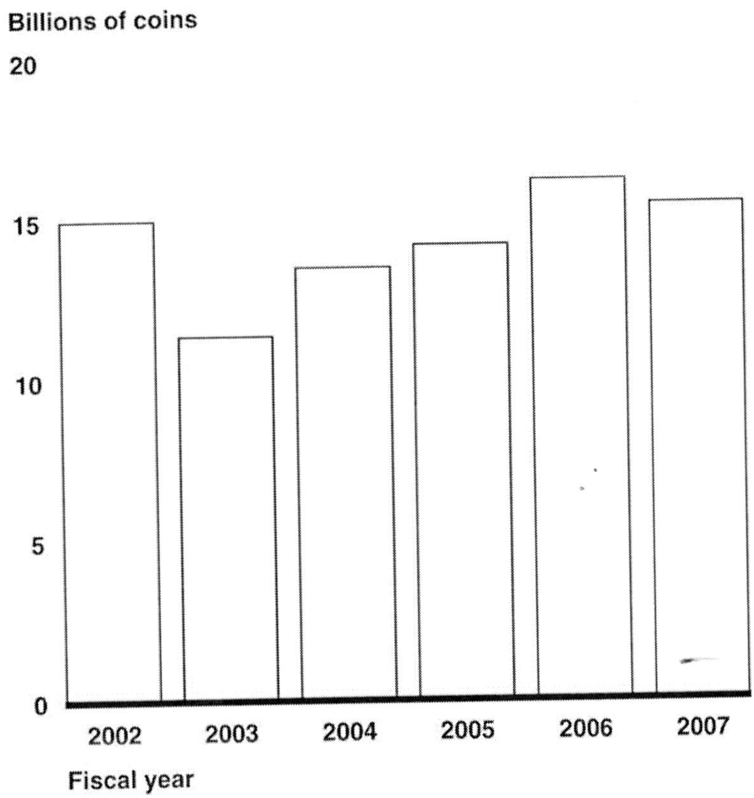

Source: U.S. Mint.

Figure 7. U.S. Mint's Coin Production for Fiscal Years 2002-2007, Total Coins (Penny, Nickel, Dime, Quarter, Half-Dollar, and Dollar)

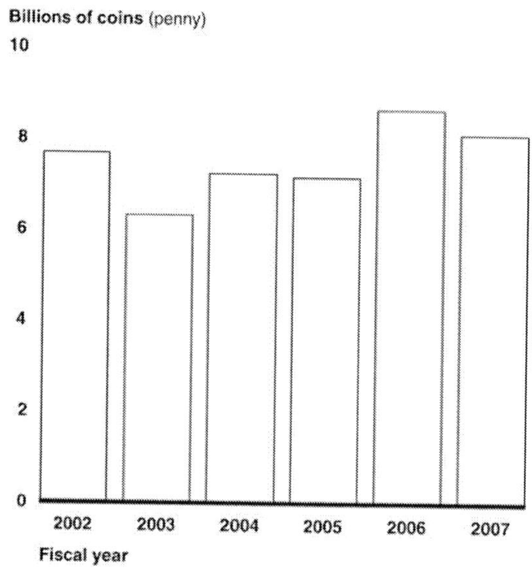

Source: U.S. Mint.

Figure 8. U.S. Mint's Coin Production for Fiscal Years 2002-2007, Penny

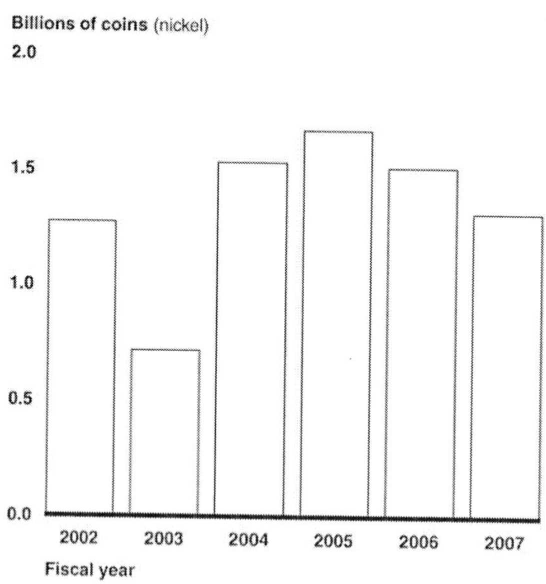

Source: U.S. Mint.

Figure 9. U.S. Mint's Coin Production for Fiscal Years 2002-2007, Nickel

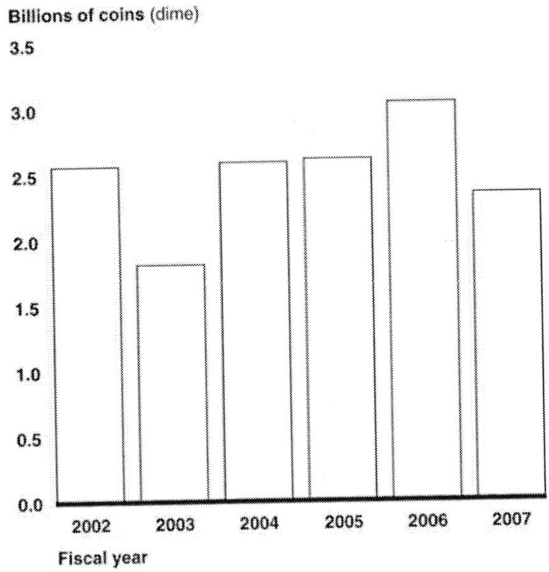

Source: U.S. Mint.

Figure 10. U.S. Mint's Coin Production for Fiscal Years 2002-2007, Dime

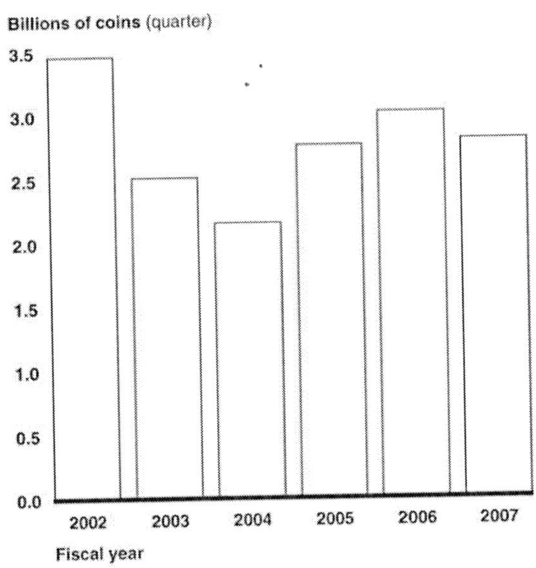

Source: U.S. Mint.

Figure 11. U.S. Mint's Coin Production for Fiscal Years 2002-2007, Quarter

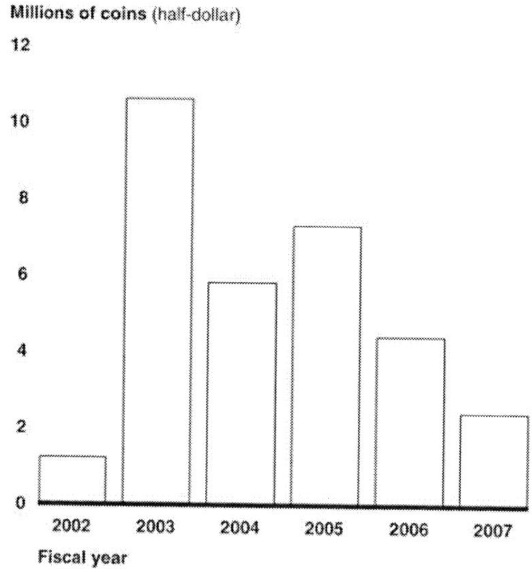

Source: U.S. Mint.

Figure 12. U.S. Mint's Coin Production for Fiscal Years 2002-2007, Half-Dollar

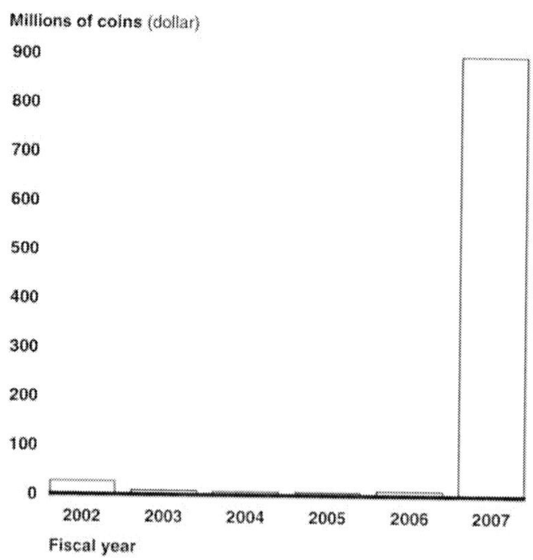

Source: U.S. Mint.

Figure 13. U.S. Mint's Coin Production for Fiscal Years 2002-2007, Dollar Coin

APPENDIX III: NATIONAL PAYMENTS AND RECEIPTS DATA, BY DENOMINATION

The Reserve Banks make coin payments to depository institutions and accept coin deposits from depository institutions on a daily basis. Figures 14 through 19 show total payments and receipts for each coin denomination for all 12 Reserve Banks for fiscal years 1993 through 2007.

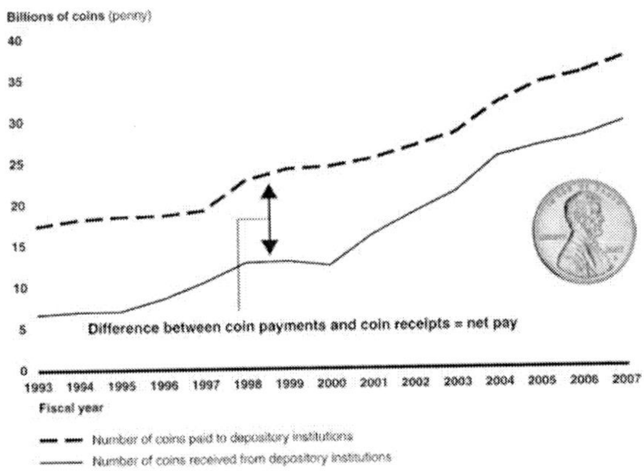

Sources: Federal Reserve and U.S. Mint.

Figure 14. Number of Pennies the Reserve Banks Paid to and Received from Depository Institutions, Fiscal Years 1993-2007

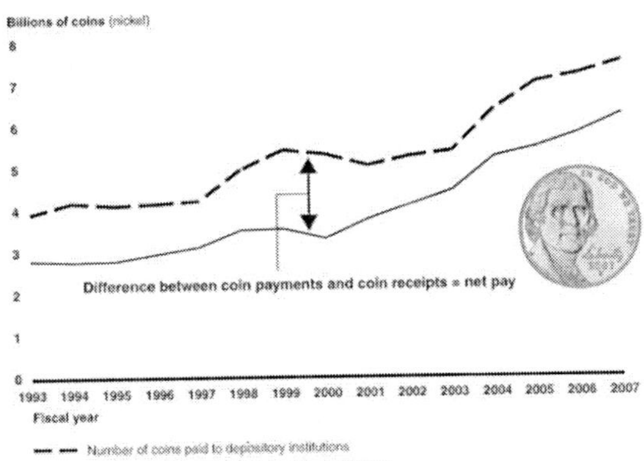

Sources: Federal Reserve and U.S. Mint.

Figure 15. Number of Nickels the Reserve Banks Paid to and Received from Depository Institutions, Fiscal Years 1993-2007

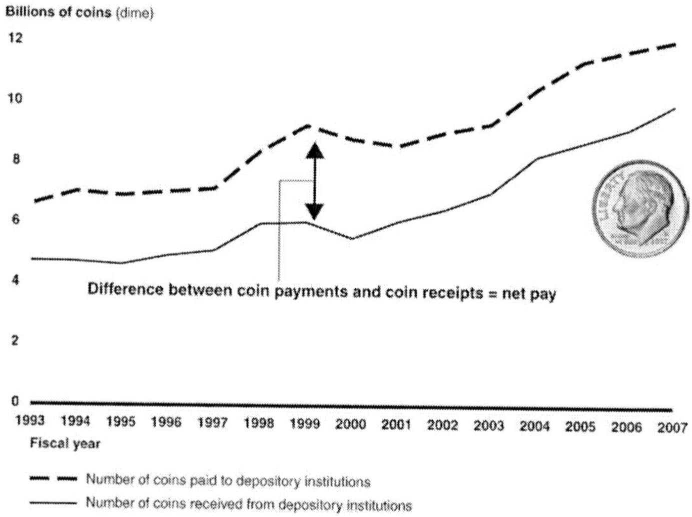

Sources: Federal Reserve and U.S. Mint.

Figure 16. Number of Dimes the Reserve Banks Paid to and Received from Depository Institutions, Fiscal Years 1993-2007

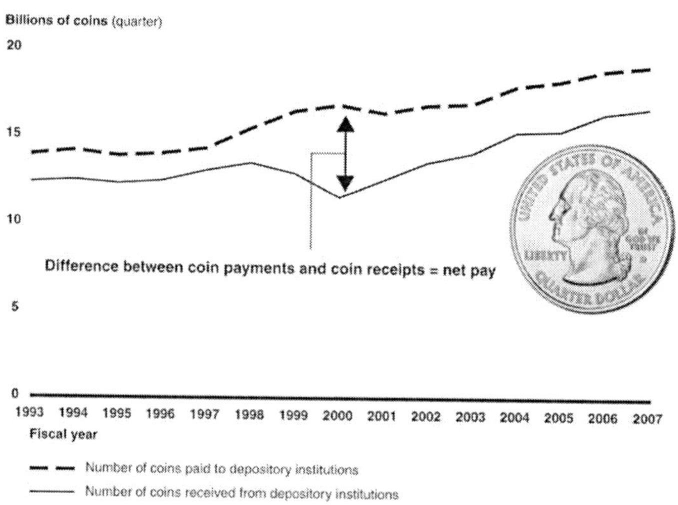

Sources: Federal Reserve and U.S. Mint.

Figure 17. Number of Quarters the Reserve Banks Paid to and Received from Depository Institutions, Fiscal Years 1993-2007

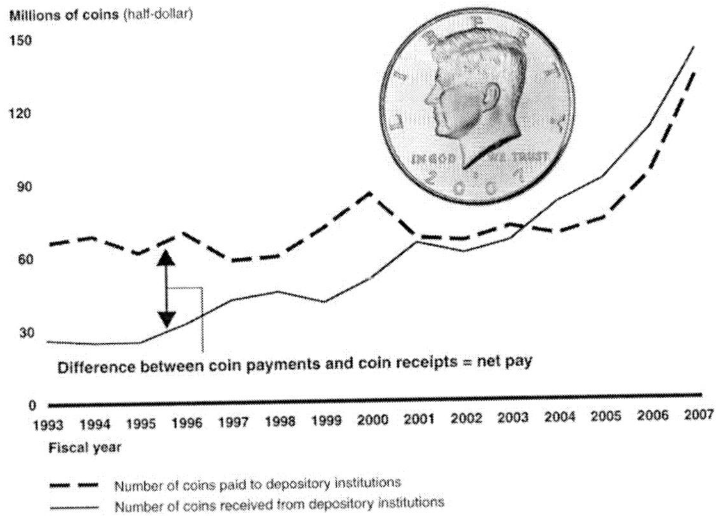

Sources: Federal Reserve and U.S. Mint.

Figure 18. Number of Half-Dollars the Reserve Banks Paid to and Received from Depository Institutions, Fiscal Years 1993-2007

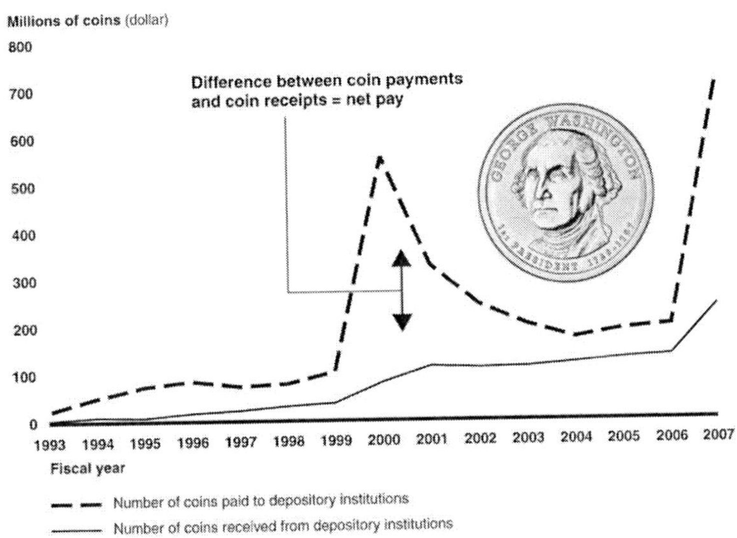

Sources: Federal Reserve and U.S. Mint.

Figure 19. Number of Dollar Coins the Reserve Banks Paid to and Received from Depository Institutions, Fiscal Years 1993-2007

APPENDIX IV: AVERAGE DAYS OF PAYABLE COIN INVENTORY, BY RESERVE BANK DISTRICT AND COIN DENOMINATION

The Reserve Banks strive to maintain sufficient inventories of coins to fulfill demand, despite seasonal and unanticipated changes in demand for coins and potential interruptions in the supply of new coins. Tables 3 through 14 show the days of payable inventory maintained at each of the 12 Reserve Banks from fiscal years 2005 through 2007. Payable inventory represents the amount of inventory needed to meet expected demand for coins and is calculated by comparing inventories with average payment data over a 3-month period for the preceding 3 years.

Table 3. Average Days of Payable Inventory, by Denomination, for the Reserve Bank District of Boston, Fiscal Years 2005-2007

Fiscal	Penny	Nickel	Dime	Quarter	Half-dollar	Dollar
2005	20	28	18	11	1,044	217
2006	17	29	35	27	1,087	181
2007	8	16	20	19	1,268	446

Source: GAO analysis of Federal Reserve data.

Table 4. Average Days of Payable Inventory, by Denomination, for the Reserve Bank District of New York, Fiscal Years 2005-2007

Fiscal year	Penny	Nickel	Dime	Quarter	Half-dollar	Dollar
2005	20	48	29	16	1,682	49
2006	11	25	22	18	1,745	87
2007	10	17	19	21	1,573	84

Source: GAO analysis of Federal Reserve data.

Table 5. Average Days of Payable Inventory, by Denomination, for the Reserve Bank District of Philadelphia, Fiscal Years 2005-2007

Fiscal year	Penny	Nickel	Dime	Quarter	Half-dollar	Dollar
2005	25	27	25	55	1,026	118
2006	23	27	29	33	1,261	95
2007	17	23	25	40	1,180	344

Source: GAO analysis of Federal Reserve data.

Table 6. Average Days of Payable Inventory, by Denomination, for the Reserve Bank District of Cleveland, Fiscal Years 2005-2007

Fiscal year	Penny	Nickel	Dime	Quarter	Half-dollar	Dollar
2005	17	46	30	25	551	115
2006	15	33	34	33	695	155
2007	14	25	36	38	771	490

Source: GAO analysis of Federal Reserve data.

Table 7. Average Days of Payable Inventory, by Denomination, for the Reserve Bank District of Richmond, Fiscal Years 2005-2007

Fiscal year	Penny	Nickel	Dime	Quarter	Half-dollar	Dollar
2005	19	29	19	15	538	119
2006	17	24	22	19	582	124
2007	17	22	27	21	550	355

Source: GAO analysis of Federal Reserve data.

Table 8. Average Days of Payable Inventory, by Denomination, for the Reserve Bank District of Atlanta, Fiscal Years 2005-2007

Fiscal year	Penny	Nickel	Dime	Quarter	Half-dollar	Dollar
2005	16	25	25	20	390	103
2006	19	27	34	19	549	152
2007	19	30	40	20	612	264

Source: GAO analysis of Federal Reserve data.

Table 9. Average Days of Payable Inventory, by Denomination, for the Reserve Bank District of Chicago, Fiscal Years 2005-2007

Fiscal year	Penny	Nickel	Dime	Quarter	Half-dollar	Dollar
2005	16	26	32	34	338	67
2006	14	22	30	23	389	74
2007	13	19	27	29	399	200

Source: GAO analysis of Federal Reserve data.

Table 10. Average Days of Payable Inventory, by Denomination, for the Reserve Bank District of St. Louis, Fiscal Years 2005-2007

Fiscal year	Penny	Nickel	Dime	Quarter	Half-dollar	Dollar
2005	13	29	21	21	344	88
2006	17	27	28	20	547	100
2007	16	21	32	17	539	296

Source: GAO analysis of Federal Reserve data.

Table 11. Average Days of Payable Inventory, by Denomination, for the Reserve Bank District of Minneapolis, Fiscal Years 2005-2007

Fiscal year	Penny	Nickel	Dime	Quarter	Half-dollar	Dollar
2005	23	50	30	18	281	106
2006	20	40	43	27	215	174
2007	23	41	42	33	234	391

Source: GAO analysis of Federal Reserve data.

Table 12. Average Days of Payable Inventory, by Denomination, for the Reserve Bank District of Kansas City, Fiscal Years 2005-2007

Fiscal year	Penny	Nickel	Dime	Quarter	Half-dollar	Dollar
2005	18	38	27	21	288	100
2006	23	29	27	29	225	93
2007	14	28	30	32	208	237

Source: GAO analysis of Federal Reserve data.

Table 13. Average Days of Payable Inventory, by Denomination, for the Reserve Bank District of Dallas, Fiscal Years 2005-2007

Fiscal year	Penny	Nickel	Dime	Quarter	Half-dollar	Dollar
2005	13	32	27	30	530	177
2006	17	25	28	25	392	167
2007	13	24	30	28	250	441

Source: GAO analysis of Federal Reserve data.

Table 14. Average Days of Payable Inventory, by Denomination, for the Reserve Bank District of San Francisco, Fiscal Years 2005-2007

Fiscal year	Penny	Nickel	Dime	Quarter	Half-dollar	Dollar
2005	32	46	42	29	235	159
2006	28	37	42	29	229	164
2007	26	35	44	31	203	275

Source: GAO analysis of Federal Reserve data.

Appendix V: Number of Coin Transfers and Related Costs, Fiscal Years 2002-2007

CPO looks for opportunities to reduce orders for new coins to the U.S. Mint by transferring circulating coins from one Reserve Bank district to another. The U.S. Mint pays for the cost for transfers over 100 miles. Table 15 shows the number and cost of transfers paid by the U.S. Mint from fiscal years 2002 through 2007.

Table 15. U.S. Mint Coin Transfers and Cost Information, Fiscal Years 2002-2007

Fiscal year	Number of transfers	U.S. Mint transfer cost
2002	299	$479,707
2003	496	744,823
2004	640	1,239,128
2005	677	1,350,698
2006	638	1,273,481
2007	404	914,769

Source: U.S. Mint data.

APPENDIX VI: COMMENTS FROM THE BOARD OF GOVERNORS OF THE FEDERAL RESERVE SYSTEM

BOARD OF GOVERNORS
OF THE
FEDERAL RESERVE SYSTEM
WASHINGTON, D.C. 20551

LOUISE L. ROSEMAN
DIRECTOR
DIVISION OF
RESERVE BANK OPERATIONS
AND PAYMENT SYSTEMS

March 18, 2008

Richard J. Hillman
Managing Director
Financial Markets and Community Investment
U.S. Government Accountability Office
441 G Street, N.W.
Washington, D.C. 20548

Dear Mr. Hillman:

Thank you for the opportunity to comment on the GAO's draft report titled *U.S. Coins: The Federal Reserve Banks Are Fulfilling Coin Demand, But Optimal Inventory Ranges Are Undefined.* We agree with the GAO's conclusion that the Reserve Banks are fulfilling depository institutions' coin demand while generally reducing orders for new coin from the U.S. Mint and inventory levels at the Reserve Banks. We believe that the data presented in the report reflect the Reserve Banks' efficient and effective management of coin inventories.

As the report suggests, the Reserve Banks have made material improvements in coin distribution in recent years. The Federal Reserve will continue to evaluate ways to improve the efficiency and effectiveness of the coin distribution process.

We have provided some technical comments under separate cover.

Sincerely,

End Notes

[1] The costs of producing other coins, such as the quarter and dollar coins, are below the face values of these coins. For example, in fiscal year 2007, the quarter cost the U.S. Mint 9.8 cents to produce and the dollar coin cost 15.7 cents, according to the Mint's annual report.

[2] Proposed legislation—Coin Modernization and Taxpayer Savings Act of 2008, H.R. 5512, 110th Cong. (2008); Coin Modernization and Taxpayer Savings Act of 2007, H.R. 3956, 110th Cong. (2007); and Coinage Materials Modernization Act of 2007, H.R. 3330, 110th Cong. (2007)—would give the Secretary of the Treasury the authority to change the weight and content of circulating coins, which could reduce the U.S. Mint's production costs. Currently, the weight and composition of U.S. coins is set forth in law. See 31 U.S.C. § 5112.

[3] Although one of the Reserve Banks' responsibilities is to ensure that enough coins and currency are available to meet depository institutions' demand, we discuss in this report only the coin services provided by the Reserve Banks.

[4] The Reserve Bank data represent data for all 30 offices that provide coins to depository institutions.

[5] The Reserve Banks and their offices also perform other functions and services unrelated to coins, such as supervising member banks and bank holding companies.

[6] As we have previously mentioned, the production costs of most coins are below their face values. This difference between production cost and face value is called "seigniorage," or the profit earned by the U.S. government from making coins. Seigniorage reduces the government's requirement to borrow money from the public to finance the government's debt.

[7] The forecasting models take into account several factors, including historical data on coin demand and economic variables, such as the inflation rate as measured in the Consumer Price Index and the federal funds rate, which is the interest rate that banks charge each other for overnight loans. According to U.S. Mint officials, until recently, the Mint averaged the results of five national coin demand forecasting models—two models maintained by the Mint and three models maintained by the Federal Reserve—to estimate demand and plan a long-term production schedule. In late 2007, the U.S. Mint stopped using its models and now uses only the three models supported by the Federal Reserve. According to U.S. Mint officials, they made this change as part of the Mint's efforts to increase the efficiency of its operations.

[8] Depository institutions can order Presidential dollar coins directly from their Reserve Bank for a specified period of time before the public release date for the coin. This advance ordering helps the depository institutions to have the coins on hand on the public release date to meet their customers' demand.

[9] The Reserve Banks are separate legal entities that, before 2001, managed their own coin inventories to meet demand within their districts. The Board exercises general supervision over the Reserve Banks.

[10] The Reserve Banks pay for transfer between offices that are less than 100 miles apart.

[11] According to 31 U.S.C. § 5136, all expenses incurred by the Secretary of the Treasury for operations and programs of the U.S. Mint that are determined to be ordinary and reasonable incidents of Mint operations and programs are authorized to be paid out of the U.S. Mint Public Enterprise Fund. The statute defines "Mint operations and programs" as the activities concerning and assets used in the distribution of coinage.

[12] The official also noted that delaying production, when the U.S. Mint has production capacity, may actually increase costs in the long run because production costs, like other costs, tend to increase over time.

[13] The Presidential $1 Coin Act of 2005, § p, 31 U.S.C. § 5112(p).

[14] In fiscal year 2007, the U.S. Mint had an average cycle time of 61 days. The cycle time starts when the order for the raw materials is placed and ends when the coin order is filled.

[15] The inventory data are represented in terms of days of payable inventory. A day of payable inventory is the level of inventory needed to meet 1 day's expected payments to depository institutions. See appendix I for additional information on this calculation.

[16] Because of our methodology in calculating average days of payable inventory data, 1996 is the earliest year for which we can present the data. See appendix I for more details.

[17] Even though the production costs of other coins are less than their face values, resulting in a financial gain to the government (called seigniorage), there are still societal costs associated with producing these coins, such as the metal resources used to make the coins.

[18] According to the Reserve Bank officials, the IMF tool forecasts coin demand for an area covered by the Reserve Bank office, which could include several coin terminals.

[19] The Federal Reserve has chosen in the past to manage payments services on a systemwide basis for reasons of efficiency and to ensure effective operations of Reserve Bank programs. For example, the Federal Reserve consolidated the management of some payment services, such as check clearing and direct deposits, provided by the individual Reserve Banks. Federal Reserve committees worked with payments industry officials to develop standards to facilitate increased use of electronic check processing and to foster technical change on the basis of the preference of most payment system participants. As a result of these efforts, the Federal Reserve was able to consolidate check processing operations and apply emerging technologies to the Reserve Banks' business processes that led to improvements in quality and a reduction in costs. See GAO, *Federal Reserve System: Update on GAO's 1996 Recommendations*, GAO-02-774 (Washington, D.C.: Sept. 25, 2002), for more information.

In: Financial Institutions in Turmoil
Editor: Carl D. Aspelin

ISBN: 978-1-60692-044-2

Chapter 2

MINORITY BANKS: REGULATORS' ASSESSMENTS OF THE EFFECTIVENESS OF THEIR SUPPORT EFFORTS HAVE BEEN LIMITED*

U. S. Government Accountability Office

WHY GAO DID THIS STUDY

Minority banks can play an important role in serving the financial needs of historically underserved communities and growing populations of minorities. For this reason, the Financial Institutions, Reform, Recovery, and Enforcement Act of 1989 (FIRREA) established goals that the Federal Deposit Insurance Corporation (FDIC) and the Office of Thrift Supervision (OTS) must work toward to preserve and promote such institutions (support efforts). While not required to do so by FIRREA, the Board of Governors of the Federal Reserve System (Federal Reserve) and Office of the Comptroller of the Currency (OCC) have established some minority bank support efforts.

This testimony, based on a 2006 GAO report, discusses the profitability of minority banks, regulators' support and assessment efforts, and the views of

* This is an edited, reformatted and augmented version of a U. S. Government Accountability Office publication dated October 2007.

minority banks on the regulators' efforts as identified through responses from a survey of 149 such institutions.

WHAT GAO RECOMMENDS

In the 2006 report, GAO recommended that the regulators review the effectiveness of their support efforts by such means as (1) surveying minority banks and/or (2) establishing performance measures.

Since the report, all of the regulators have reported taking steps to survey or obtain information from minority banks on their support efforts. However, it is too soon to evaluate the effectiveness of these assessment efforts.

To view the full product, including the scope and methodology, click on GAO-08-233T. For more information, contact George Scott at (202) 512-7215 or scottg@gao.gov.

WHAT GAO FOUND

GAO reported in 2006 that the profitability of most large minority banks (assets greater than $100 million) was nearly equal to that of their peers (similarly sized banks) in 2005 and earlier years, according to FDIC data. However, many small minority banks and African-American banks of all sizes were less profitable than their peers. GAO's analysis and other studies identified some possible explanations for these differences, including relatively higher loan loss reserves and operating expenses and competition from larger banks.

Bank regulators had adopted differing approaches to supporting minority banks, but no agency had regularly and comprehensively assessed the effectiveness of its efforts. FDIC—which supervises over half of all minority banks—had the most comprehensive support efforts and leads interagency efforts. OTS focused on providing technical assistance to minority banks. While not required to do so by FIRREA, OCC and the Federal Reserve had taken some steps to support minority banks. Although FDIC had recently sought to assess the effectiveness of its support efforts through various methods, none of the regulators comprehensively surveyed minority banks or had developed performance measures. Consequently, the regulators were not well positioned to assess their support efforts.

GAO's survey of minority banks identified potential limitations in the regulators' support efforts that would likely be of significance to agency managers and warrant follow-up analysis. Only about one-third of survey respondents rated their regulators' efforts for minority banks as very good or good, while 26 percent rated the efforts as fair, 13 percent as poor or very poor, and 25 percent responded "don't know" (see figure). Banks regulated by FDIC were more positive about their agency's efforts than banks regulated by other agencies. However, only about half of the FDIC-regulated banks and about a quarter of the banks regulated by other agencies rated their agency's efforts as very good or good. Although regulators may have emphasized the provision of technical assistance to minority banks, less than 30 percent of such institutions have used such agency services within the last 3 years and therefore may be missing opportunities to address problems that limit their operations or financial performance.

Mr. Chairman and Members of the Subcommittee:

I am pleased to be here to discuss the findings of a report that we issued last year on the efforts of federal bank regulators to support minority banks.[1] As described in our report, minority banks are a small community within the banking industry, accounting for 2 percent of all financial institutions and total industry assets. Despite their small numbers, minority banks can play an important role in serving the financial needs of historically underserved communities, such as African-Americans, and growing populations of minorities, such as Hispanic-Americans and Asian- Americans.

For this reason, Section 308 of the Financial Institutions Reform, Recovery, and Enforcement Act of 1989 (FIRREA) established goals toward which federal regulators must work to preserve and promote such institutions.[2] For example, the Federal Deposit Insurance Corporation (FDIC) and the Office of Thrift Supervision (OTS), in consultation with the Department of the Treasury (Treasury), are required to provide minority banks with technical assistance and training and educational programs and work toward preserving the character of minority banks in cases involving mergers or acquisitions of these institutions (I will refer to such activities as minority bank support efforts in my testimony today).[3] While the other bank regulators—the Board of Governors of the Federal Reserve System (Federal Reserve) and the Office of the Comptroller of the Currency (OCC)—are not subject to Section 308 of FIRREA, they also have engaged in efforts to support minority banks over the years.

You and other members of the House Financial Services Committee, including the Chairman, requested in 2005 that we review the efforts of all of the regulators to support minority banks out of concerns about the effectiveness of those efforts. We had previously reported in 1993 that while FDIC and OTS had taken steps to comply with Section 308, minority banks had mixed views on the effectiveness of the agencies' efforts.[4] In particular, minority banks were concerned that the regulators did not provide adequate technical assistance, and, more generally, that agency safety and soundness examiners did not understand the unique challenges that their institutions faced. We recommended in the 1993 report that FDIC and OTS periodically survey minority banks to assess the effectiveness of their support efforts. Given the passage of time between 1993 and 2005, you requested that we follow up on minority bank issues and the efforts of all bank regulators to support such institutions.

In my testimony today, I will discuss the key findings of our 2006 report, which included steps to (1) review the profitability of minority banks over time; (2) identify the regulators' minority bank support efforts and determine whether the regulators were evaluating the effectiveness of those efforts; and (3) obtain the views of minority banks on the support efforts and related regulatory issues. Additionally, in the last section of this testimony, I will provide a brief update on some of the steps the regulators have taken in response to recommendations in our 2006 report.

To address the first objective, we obtained and analyzed financial data for minority banks from FDIC for 1995, 2000, and 2005. We also reviewed background literature and conducted interviews with minority banks to discuss the business environment in which these banks operate. For the second objective, we interviewed officials from Treasury, FDIC, the Federal Reserve, OCC, and OTS and reviewed regulators' documentation addressing their efforts to support minority banks and assess the effectiveness of these efforts. We also compared the regulators' efforts to our standards for program assessment and performance measures and those established in the Government Performance and Results Act.[5] To address the third objective, we surveyed all institutions identified by the banking regulators as minority institutions. The Web-based survey, which was conducted from March through April 2006, asked about the banks' awareness and use of the regulators' minority bank support efforts and also asked the banks to rate these efforts. We received 149 survey responses out of a total population of 195 minority banks, for a response rate of 76 percent. Finally, in preparation for this testimony, we contacted the regulators in order to obtain information on any efforts they may have undertaken in response to the recommendations in our 2006 rcport.

We conducted our work in Washington, D.C., and New York in accordance with generally accepted government auditing standards.

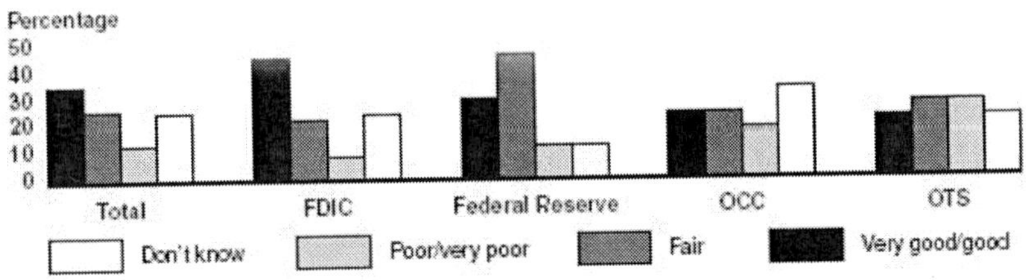

Source: GAO.

Minority Banks' Ratings of Support Efforts, by Regulator

IN BRIEF

Our analysis of FDIC data showed that while the profitability of most minority banks with assets greater than $100 million nearly equaled the profitability of all similarly sized banks (peers), the profitability of smaller minority banks and African-American banks of all sizes did not.[6] Profitability is commonly measured by return on assets (ROA), or the ratio of profits to assets, and ROAs are typically compared across peer groups to assess performance.[7] Many small minority banks (those with less than $100 million in assets) had ROAs that were substantially lower than those of their peer groups in 2005 as well as in 1995 and 2000. Moreover, African- American banks of all sizes had ROAs that were significantly below those of their peers in 2005 as well as in 1995 and 2000 (African-American banks of all sizes and other small minority banks account for about half of all minority banks). Our analysis of FDIC data identified some possible explanations for the relatively low profitability of some small minority banks and African-American banks, such as relatively higher reserves for potential loan losses and administrative expenses and competition from larger banks. Nevertheless, the majority of officials from banks across all minority groups were positive about their banks' financial outlook, and many saw their minority status as an advantage in serving their communities (for example, in providing services in the language predominantly used by the minority community).

The bank regulators have adopted differing approaches to supporting minority banks, and, at the time of our review, no agency had assessed the effectiveness of its efforts through regular and comprehensive surveys of minority banks or outcome-oriented performance measures.[8] FDIC— which supervises more than half of all minority banks—had the most comprehensive program to support minority banks and led an interagency group that coordinates such efforts. Among other things, FDIC has designated officials in the agency's headquarters and regional offices to be responsible for minority bank efforts, held periodic conferences for minority banks, and established formal policies for annual outreach to the banks it regulates to make them aware of available technical assistance. OTS also designated staff to be responsible for the agency's efforts to support minority banks, developed outreach procedures, and focused its efforts on providing technical assistance. OCC and the Federal Reserve, while not required to do so by Section 308 of FIRREA, undertook some efforts to support minority banks, such as holding occasional conferences for Native American banks, and were planning additional efforts. FDIC proactively sought to assess the effectiveness of its support efforts; for example, it surveyed minority banks. However, these surveys did not address key activities, such as the provision of technical assistance, and the agency had not established outcome-oriented performance measures for its support efforts. Furthermore, none of the other regulators comprehensively surveyed minority banks on the effectiveness of their support efforts or established outcome-oriented performance measures. Consequently, the regulators were not well positioned to assess the results of their support efforts or identify areas for improvement.

Our survey of minority banks identified potential limitations in the regulators' support efforts that likely would be of significance to agency managers and warrant follow-up analysis. About one-third of survey respondents rated their regulators' efforts for minority banks as very good or good, while 26 percent rated the efforts as fair, 13 percent as poor or very poor, and 25 percent responded "do not know." FDIC-regulated banks were more positive about their agency's efforts than banks that other agencies regulated. However, only about half of the FDIC-regulated banks and about a quarter of the banks regulated by other agencies rated their agency's efforts as very good or good. Although regulators may emphasize the provision of technical assistance to minority banks, less than 30 percent of such institutions said they had used such agency services within the last 3 years. Therefore, the banks may have been missing opportunities to address problems that limited their operations or financial performance. As we found in our 1993 report, some minority bank officials also said that examiners did not always understand the challenges that the banks may face in providing services in their communities or operating environments. Although the bank officials said they did not expect special treatment in the examination process, they suggested that examiners needed to undergo more training to improve their understanding of minority banks and the customer base they serve.

To allow the regulators to better understand the effectiveness of their support efforts, our October 2006 report recommended that the regulators review such efforts and, in so doing, consider employing the following methods: (1) regularly surveying the minority banks under their supervision on all efforts and regulatory areas affecting these institutions; or (2) establishing outcome-oriented performance measures to evaluate the extent to which their efforts are achieving their objectives. Subsequent to the report's issuance, the regulators have reported taking steps to better assess or enhance their minority bank support efforts. For example, all of the regulators have developed surveys or are in the process of consulting with minority banks to obtain feedback on their support efforts. I also note that some regulators plan to provide additional training to their examiners on minority bank issues. These initiatives are positive developments, but it is too soon to evaluate their effectiveness. We encourage agency officials to ensure that they collect and analyze relevant data and take steps to enhance their minority bank support efforts as may be warranted.

BACKGROUND

Many minority banks are located in urban areas and seek to serve distressed communities and populations that financial institutions traditionally have underserved. For example, after the Civil War, banks were established to provide financial services to African-Americans. More recently, Asian-American and Hispanic-American banks have been established to serve the rapidly growing Asian and Hispanic communities in the United States. In our review of regulators' lists of minority banks, we identified a total minority bank population of 195 for 2005 (see table 1).

Table 2 shows that the distribution of minority banks by size is similar to the distribution of all banks by size. More than 40 percent of all minority banks had assets of less than $100 million.

Table 1. Number and Percentage of Minority Banks, by Type, 2005

Type of minority bank	Number of banks	Percentage of all minority banks
Asian-American[a]	73	37
African-American	46	24
Hispanic-American	38	19
Native American	20	10
Women-owned	13	7
Other[b]	5	3
Total	**195**	**100**

Source: GAO analysis of Treasury and federal banking regulators' data.

Note: We identified the total minority bank population by obtaining and reviewing the most current lists (available at the time the population was compiled) from the federal banking regulators and Treasury. We reviewed FDIC and the Federal Reserve's publicly available lists, which were current as of September 30, 2005. We also reviewed OCC's list from December 31, 2005, Treasury's most recent list from 2004, and OTS's from January 2006.

[a] Asian-American includes individuals of Pacific Island descent.

[b] The "other" category includes banks considered to have minority status that are not covered by the listed minority categories. "Other" also includes banks that are owned or managed by more than one minority group in accordance with a banking regulator's definition.

Table 2. Percentage of Minority Banks and Total Banking Industry, by Asset Size, 2005

Asset size	Percentage of minority banks	Percentage of total banking industry
< $100 million	42	44
$100 million to $300 million	32	33
$300 million to $500 million	9	9
$500 million to $1 billion	7	7
$1 billion to $10 billion	7	6
> $10 billion	3	1
Total	**100**	**100**

Source: GAO analysis of FDIC data.

Each federally insured depository institution, including each minority bank, has a primary federal regulator. As shown in table 3, FDIC serves as the primary federal regulator for more than half of minority banks—109 of the 195 banks, or 56 percent—and the Federal Reserve regulates the fewest.

The federal regulators primarily focus on ensuring the safety and soundness of banks and do so through on-site examinations and other means. Regulators may also close banks that are deemed insolvent and posing a risk to Deposit Insurance Fund[9] FDIC is responsible for ensuring that the deposits in failed banks are protected up to established deposit insurance limits.

Table 3. Number of Minority Banks, by Regulator, 2005

Regulator	Number of minority banks	Percentage
FDIC	109	56
OCC	43	22
OTS	22	11
Federal Reserve	21	11
Total	**195**	**100**

Source: GAO analysis of Treasury and the federal banking regulators' data.

Note: Treasury and the banking regulators have different criteria for the banks they consider to be eligible to participate in their minority bank efforts. In accordance with our request, in our population of minority banks we included any bank considered by at least one regulator to be eligible to participate in its efforts. However, in some cases minority banks not considered by their primary regulator to be minority institutions were considered to be eligible for participation in another regulator's efforts. We identified 10 FDIC-regulated banks, 4 Federal Reserve-regulated banks, 3 OCC-regulated banks, and 1 OTS-regulated bank fitting this description.

While the regulators' primary focus is bank safety and soundness, laws and regulations can identify additional goals and objectives. Recognizing the importance of minority banks, Section 308 of FIRREA outlined five broad goals toward which FDIC and OTS, in consultation with Treasury, are to work to preserve and promote minority banks. These goals are:

- preserving the present number of minority banks;
- preserving their minority character in cases involving mergers or acquisitions of minority banks;
- providing technical assistance to prevent insolvency of institutions that are not currently insolvent;
- promoting and encouraging the creation of new minority banks; and

- providing for training, technical assistance, and education programs.

Technical assistance is typically defined as one-to-one assistance that a regulator may provide to a bank in response to a request. For example, a regulator may advise a bank on compliance with a particular statute or regulation. Regulators also may provide technical assistance to banks that is related to deficiencies identified in safety and soundness examinations. In contrast, education programs typically are open to all banks regulated by a particular agency or all banks located within a regulator's regional office. For example, regulators may offer training for banks to review compliance with laws and regulations.

Large Minority Banks Showed Profitability Close to That of Their Peers, but Many Small and African-American Banks Have Been Less Profitable

As shown in figure 1, our 2006 report found that, according to FDIC data, most minority banks with assets exceeding $100 million had ROAs in 2005 that were close to those of their peer groups, while many smaller banks had ROAs that were significantly lower than those of their peers. Minority banks with more than $100 million in assets accounted for 58 percent of all minority banks, while those with less than $100 million accounted for 42 percent. Each size category of minority banks with more than $100 million in assets had a weighted average ROA that was slightly lower than that of its peers, but in each case their ROAs exceeded 1 percent.[10] By historical banking industry standards, an ROA of 1 percent or more generally has been considered to indicate an adequate level of profitability. We found that profitability of the larger minority, Hispanic-American, Asian- American, Native American, and women-owned banks were close to, and in some cases exceeded, the profitability of their peers in 2005.

In contrast, small minority banks (those with assets of less than $100 million) had an average ROA of 0.4 percent, and their peers had an average ROA of 1 percent. Our analysis of FDIC data for 1995 and 2000 also indicated some similar patterns, with minority banks with assets greater than $100 million showing levels of profitability that generally were close to those of their peers, or ROAs of about 1 percent, and minority banks with assets of less than $100 million showing greater differences with their peers.

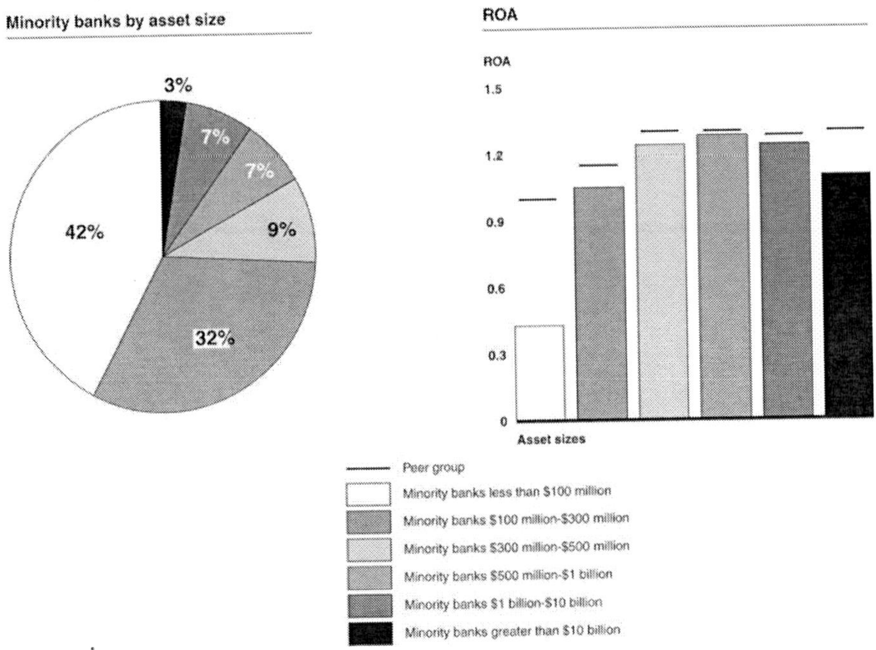

Source: GAO.

Figure 1. Percentage of Minority Banks by Size and Average ROA for Minority Banks and Peer Groups by Asset Size, 2005

The profitability of African-American banks generally has been below that of their peers in all size categories (see figure 2).[11] For example, African-American banks with less than $100 million in assets—which constitute 61 percent of all African-American banks—had an average ROA of 0.16 percent, while their peers averaged 1.0 percent. Our analysis of FDIC data for 2000 and 1995 also found that African-American banks of all sizes had lower ROAs than their peers.

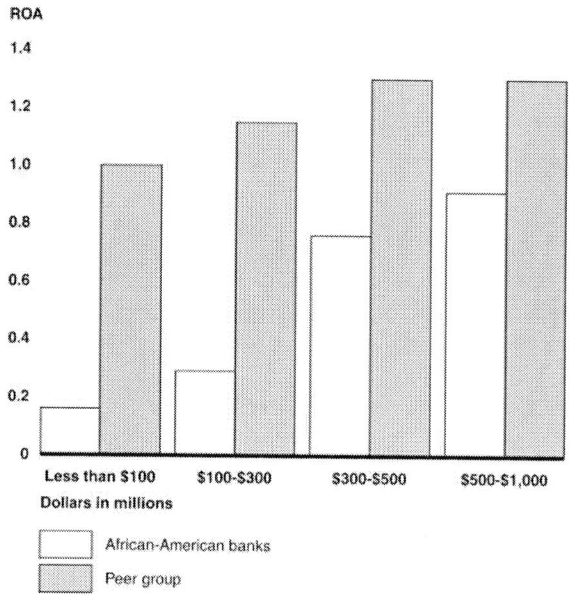

Source: GAO analysis of FDIC data.

Figure 2. Average ROA of African-American Banks and Peer Banks by Asset Size, 2005

Our analysis of 2005 FDIC data also suggests some possible reasons for the differences in profitability between some minority banks and their peers.[12] For example, our analysis of 2005 FDIC data showed that African-American banks with assets of less than $300 million—which constitute 87 percent of all African-American banks—had significantly higher loan loss reserves as a percentage of their total assets than the average for their peers (see figure 3).[13] Although having higher loan loss reserves may be necessary for the safe and sound operation of any particular bank, they lower bank profits because loan loss reserves are counted as expenses.

We also found some evidence that higher operating expenses might affect the profitability of some minority banks. Operating expenses— expenditures for items such as administrative expenses and salaries—typically are compared to an institution's total earning assets, such as loans and investments, to indicate the proportion of earning assets that banks spend on operating expenses. As figure 4 indicates, many minority banks with less than $100 million in assets had higher operating expenses than their peers in 2005. Academic studies we reviewed generally reached similar conclusions.

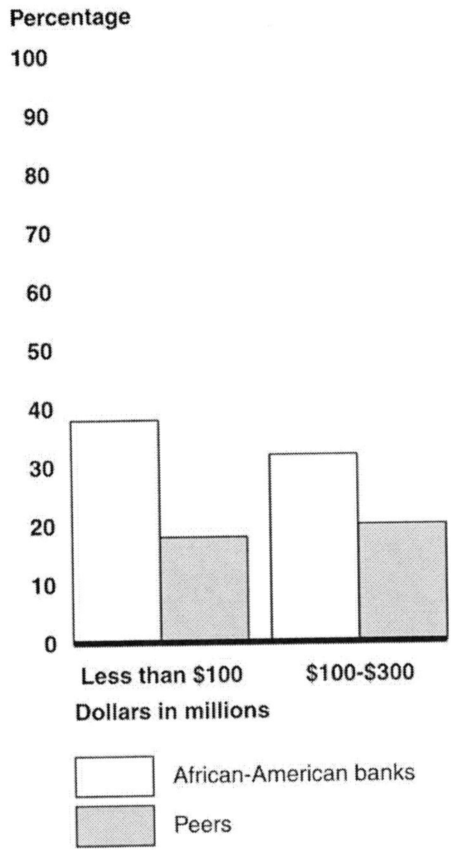

Source: GAO analysis of FDIC data.

Figure 3. Average Loan Loss Reserves as a Percentage of Assets for African-American and Peer Banks, 2005

Officials from several minority banks we contacted also described aspects of their operating environment, business practices, and customer service that could result in higher operating costs. In particular, the officials cited the costs associated with providing banking services in low-income urban areas or in communities with high immigrant populations. Bank officials also told us that they focus on fostering strong customer relationships, sometimes providing financial literacy services. Consequently, as part of their mission these banks spend more time and resources on their customers per transaction than other banks. Other minority bank officials said that their customers made relatively small deposits and preferred to do business in person at bank branch locations rather than through potentially lower-cost alternatives, such as over the phone or the Internet.

Minority bank officials also cited other factors that may have limited their profitability. In particular, in response to Community Reinvestment Act (CRA) incentives, the officials said that larger banks and other financial institutions were increasing competition for minority banks' traditional customer base.[14] The officials said that larger banks could offer loans and other financial services at more competitive prices because they could raise funds at lower rates and take advantage of operational efficiencies. In addition, officials from some African-American and Hispanic banks cited attracting and retaining quality staff as a challenge to their profitability.

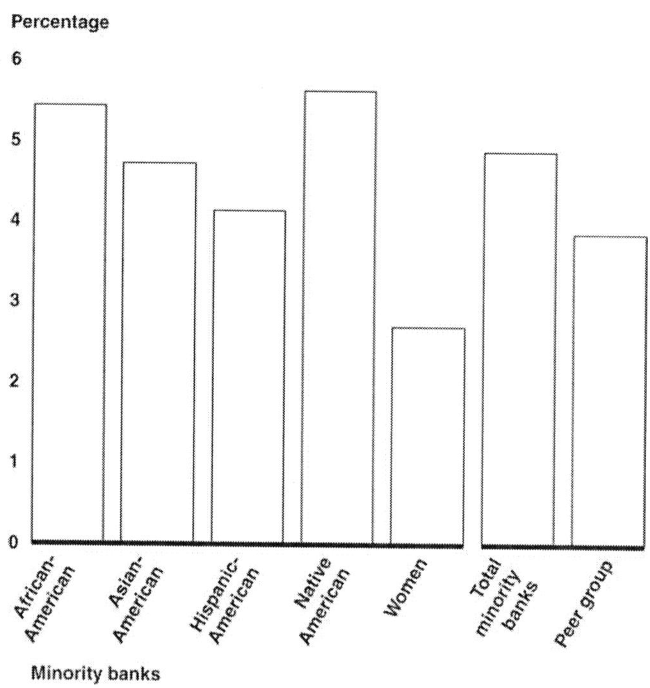

Source: GAO analysis of FDIC data.

Figure 4. Average Operating Expenses Relative to Earning Assets of Banks with Assets Less Than $100 million, 2005

Despite these challenges, officials from banks across minority groups were optimistic about the financial outlook for their institutions. When asked in our survey to rate their financial outlook compared to those of the past 3 to 5 years, 65 percent said it would be much or slightly better; 21 percent thought it would be about the same, and 11 percent thought it would be slightly or much worse, while 3 percent did not know. Officials from minority banks said that their institutions had advantages in serving minority communities. For example, officials from an Asian-American bank said that the staff's ability to communicate in the customers' primary language provided a competitive advantage.

REGULATORS ADOPTED DIFFERING APPROACHES TO SUPPORTING MINORITY BANKS, BUT ASSESSMENT EFFORTS WERE LIMITED

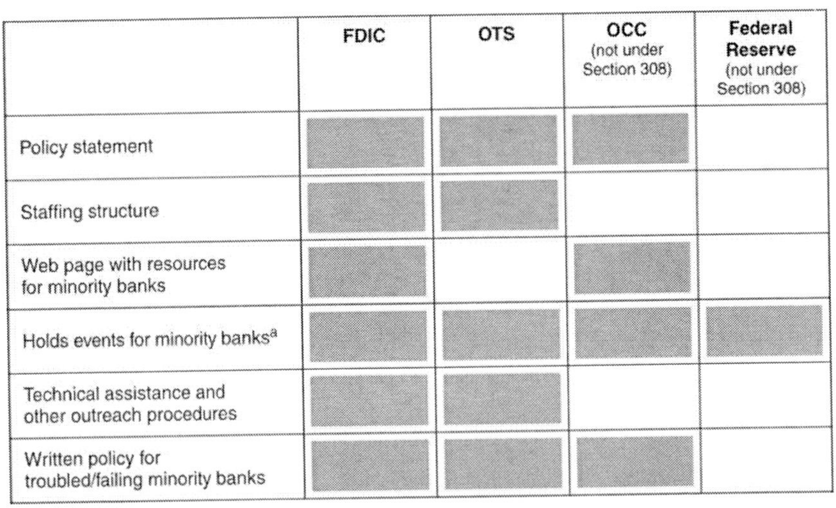

Source: GAO.

[a] FDIC holds conferences for all minority banks on a regular basis. OTS, OCC, and the Federal Reserve have hosted occasional events for some groups of minority banks.

Figure 5. Banking Regulators' Efforts to Support Minority Banks, as of October 2006

Our report found that FDIC—which supervises 109 of 195 minority banks—had developed the most extensive efforts to support minority banks among the banking regulators (see figure 5). FDIC had also taken the lead in coordinating regulators' efforts in support of minority banks, including leading a group of all the banking regulators that meets semiannually to discuss individual agency initiatives, training and outreach events, and each agency's list of minority banks. OTS had developed a variety of support programs, including developing a minority bank policy statement and staffing support structure. OCC had also taken steps to support minority banks, such as developing a policy statement. OCC and the Federal Reserve had also hosted events for some minority banks.

The following highlights some key support activities discussed in our October 2006 report.

Policy Statements

FDIC, OTS, and OCC all have policy statements that outline the agencies' efforts for minority banks. They discuss how the regulators identify minority banks, participate in minority bank events, provide technical assistance, and work toward preserving the character of minority banks during the resolution process. OCC officials told us that they developed their policy statement in 2001 after an interagency meeting of the federal banking regulators on minority bank issues. Both FDIC and OTS issued policy statements in 2002.

Staffing Structure

FDIC has a national coordinator in Washington, D.C. and coordinators in each regional office from its Division of Supervision and Consumer Protection to implement the agency's minority bank program. Among other responsibilities, the national coordinator regularly contacts minority bank trade associations about participation in events and other issues, coordinates with other agencies, and compiles quarterly reports for the FDIC chairman based on regional coordinators' reports on their minority bank activities. Similarly, OTS has a national coordinator in its headquarters and supervisory and community affairs staff in each region who maintain contact with the minority banks that OTS regulates. While OCC and the Federal Reserve did not have similar staffing structures, officials from these agencies had contacted minority banks among their responsibilities.

Minority Bank Events and Training

FDIC has taken the lead role in sponsoring, hosting, and coordinating events in support of minority banks. For example, in August 2006 FDIC sponsored a national conference for minority banks in which representatives from OTS, OCC, and the Federal Reserve participated. FDIC also has sponsored the Minority Bankers Roundtable (MBR) series, which agency officials told us was designed to provide insight into the regulatory relationship between minority banks and FDIC and explore opportunities for partnerships between FDIC and these banks. In 2005, FDIC held six roundtables around the country for minority banks supervised by all of the regulators. To varying degrees, OTS, OCC, and the Federal Reserve also have held events to support minority banks, such as Native American Institutions.

Technical Assistance

All of the federal banking regulators told us that they provided their minority banks with technical assistance if requested, but only FDIC and OTS have specific procedures for offering this assistance. More specifically, FDIC and OTS officials told us that they proactively seek to make minority banks aware of such assistance through established outreach procedures outside of their customary examination and supervision processes. FDIC also has a policy that requires its regional coordinators to ensure that examination case managers contact minority banks from 90 to 120 days after an examination to offer technical assistance in any problem areas that were identified during the examination. This policy is unique to minority banks. OCC and the Federal Reserve provide technical assistance to all of their banks, but had not established outreach procedures for all their minority banks outside of the customary examination and supervision processes. However, OCC officials told us that they were in the process of developing an outreach plan for all minority banks regulated by the agency. Federal Reserve officials told us that Federal Reserve districts conduct informal outreach to their minority banks and consult with other districts on minority bank issues as needed.

Policies to Preserve the Minority Character of Troubled Banks

FDIC has developed policies for failing banks that are consistent with FIRREA's requirement that the agency work to preserve the minority character of minority banks in cases of mergers and acquisitions. For example, FDIC maintains a list of qualified minority banks or minority investors that may be asked to bid on the assets of troubled minority banks that are expected to fail. However, FDIC is required to accept the bids on failing banks that pose the lowest expected cost to the Deposit Insurance Fund.[15] As a result, all bidders, including minority bidders, are subject to competition. OTS and OCC have developed written policies that describe how the agencies will work with FDIC to identify qualified minority banks or investors to acquire minority banks that are failing. While the Federal Reserve does not have a similar written policy, agency officials say that they also work with FDIC to identify qualified minority banks or investors. All four agencies also said that they try to assist troubled minority banks improve their financial condition before it deteriorates to the point that a resolution through FDIC becomes necessary. For example, agencies may provide technical assistance in such situations or try to identify other minority banks willing to acquire or merge with the troubled institutions.

At the Time of Our Report, Regulators Did Not Assess Their Support Efforts through Surveys or Performance Measures

While FDIC was proactive in assessing its support efforts for minority banks, none of the regulators routinely and comprehensively surveyed their minority banks on all issues affecting the institutions, nor have the regulators established outcome-oriented performance measures. Evaluating the effectiveness of federal programs is vitally important to manage programs successfully and improve program results. To this end, in 1993 Congress enacted the Government Performance and Results Act, which instituted a governmentwide requirement that agencies report on their results in achieving their agency and program goals.

As part of its assessment methods, FDIC conducted roundtables and surveyed minority banks on aspects of its minority bank efforts. For example, in 2005, FDIC requested feedback on its efforts from institutions that attended the agency's six MBRs (which approximately one-third of minority banks attended). The agency also sent a survey letter to all minority banks to seek their feedback on several proposals to better serve such institutions, but only 24 minority banks responded. The proposals included holding another national minority bank conference, instituting a partnership program with universities, and developing a minority bank museum exhibition.[16] FDIC officials said that they used the information gathered from the MBRs and the survey to develop recommendations for improving programs and developing new initiatives.

While FDIC had taken steps to assess the effectiveness of its minority bank support efforts, we identified some limitations in its approach. For example, in FDIC's surveys of minority banks, the agency did not solicit feedback on key aspects of its support efforts, such as the provision of technical assistance. Moreover, FDIC has not established outcome- oriented performance measures to gauge the effectiveness of its various support efforts. None of the other regulators had surveyed minority banks recently on support efforts or developed performance measures.

By not taking such steps, we concluded that the regulators were not well positioned to assess their support efforts or identify areas for improvement. Further, the regulators could not take corrective action as necessary to provide better support efforts to minority banks.

Survey of Minority Banks Identified Potential Limitations in Regulators' Support Efforts and Other Regulatory Issues

Minority bank officials we surveyed identified potential limitations in the regulators' efforts to support them and related regulatory issues, such as examiners' understanding of issues affecting minority banks, which would likely be of significance to agency managers and warrant follow-up analysis. Some 36 percent of survey respondents described their regulators' efforts as very good or good, 26 percent described them as fair, and 13 percent described the efforts as poor or very poor (see figure 6). A relatively large percentage—25 percent—responded "do not know" to this question.

Banks' responses varied by regulator, with 45 percent of banks regulated by FDIC giving very good or good responses, compared with about 25 percent of banks regulated by other agencies. However, more than half of FDIC-regulated banks and about three-quarters of the other minority banks responded that their regulator's efforts were fair, poor, or very poor or responded with a "do not know." In particular, banks regulated by OTS gave the highest percentage of poor or very poor marks, while banks regulated by the Federal Reserve most often provided fair marks.

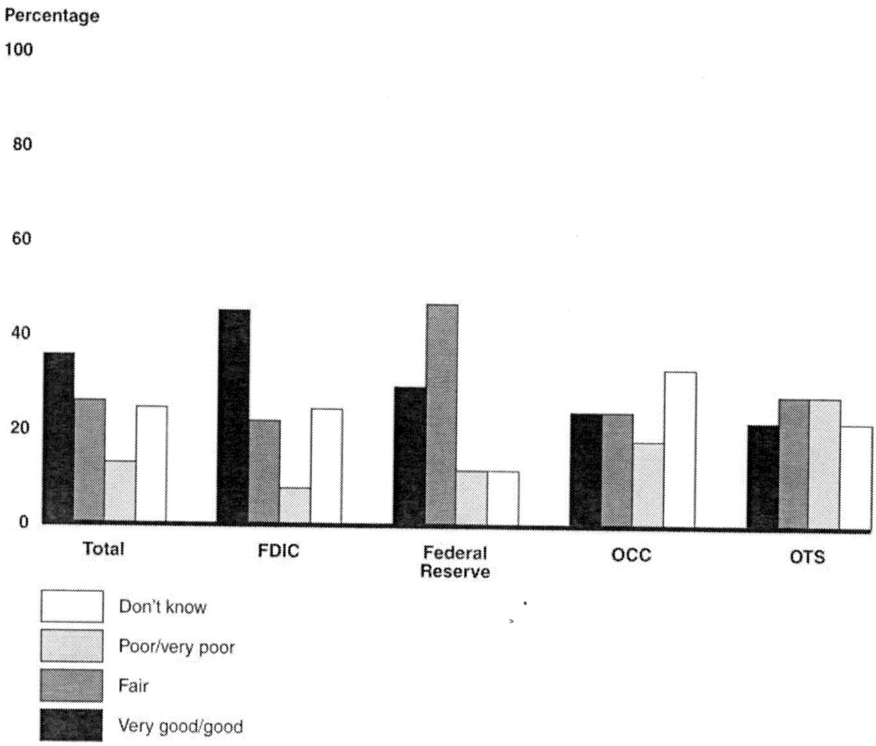

Source: GAO.

Figure 6. Minority Banks' Ratings of Support Efforts, by Regulator

Nearly half of minority banks reported that they attended FDIC roundtables and conferences designed for minority banks, and about half of the 65 respondents that attended these events found them to be extremely or very useful (see figure 7). Almost a third found them to be moderately useful, and 17 percent found them to be slightly or not at all useful. One participant commented that the information was useful, as was the opportunity to meet the regulators. Many banks also commented that the events provided a good opportunity to network and share ideas with other minority banks.

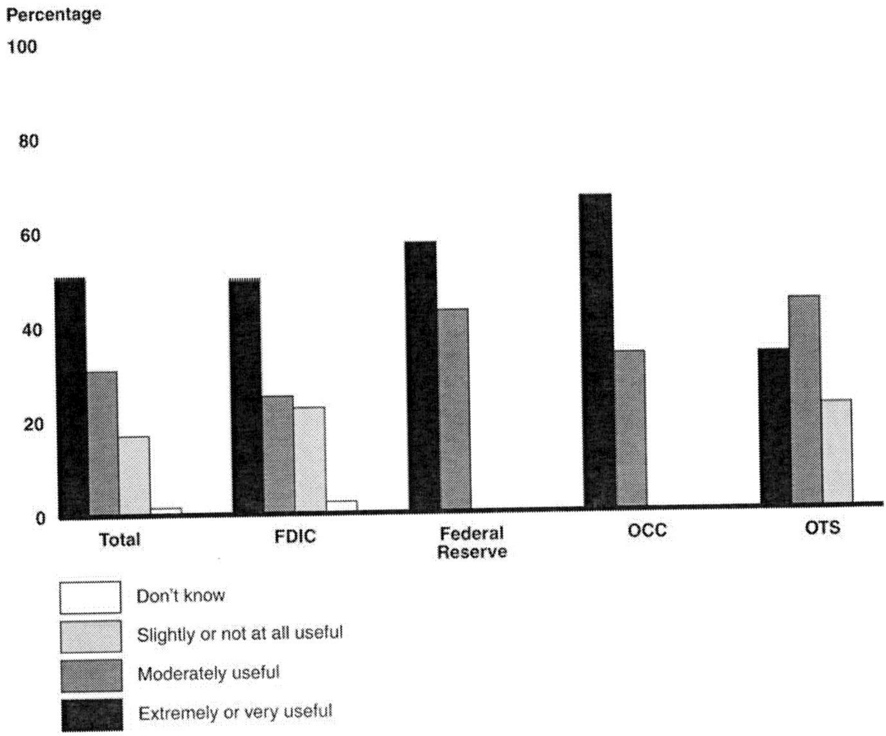

Source: GAO.

Figure 7. Usefulness of FDIC's Roundtables and Conferences, by Regulator

While FDIC and OTS emphasized technical services as key components of their efforts to support minority banks, less than 30 percent of the institutions they regulate reported using such assistance within the last 3 years (see figure 8). Minority banks regulated by OCC and the Federal Reserve reported similarly low usage of technical assistance services. However, of the few banks that used technical assistance—41—the majority rated the assistance provided as extremely or very useful.[17] Further, although small minority banks and African-American banks of all sizes have consistently faced financial challenges and might benefit from certain types of assistance, the banks also reported low rates of usage of the agencies' technical assistance. While our survey did not address the reasons that relatively few minority banks appear to use the technical assistance and banking regulators cannot compel banks under their supervision to make use of offered technical assistance, the potential exists that many such institutions may be missing opportunities to learn how to correct problems that limit their operational and financial performance.

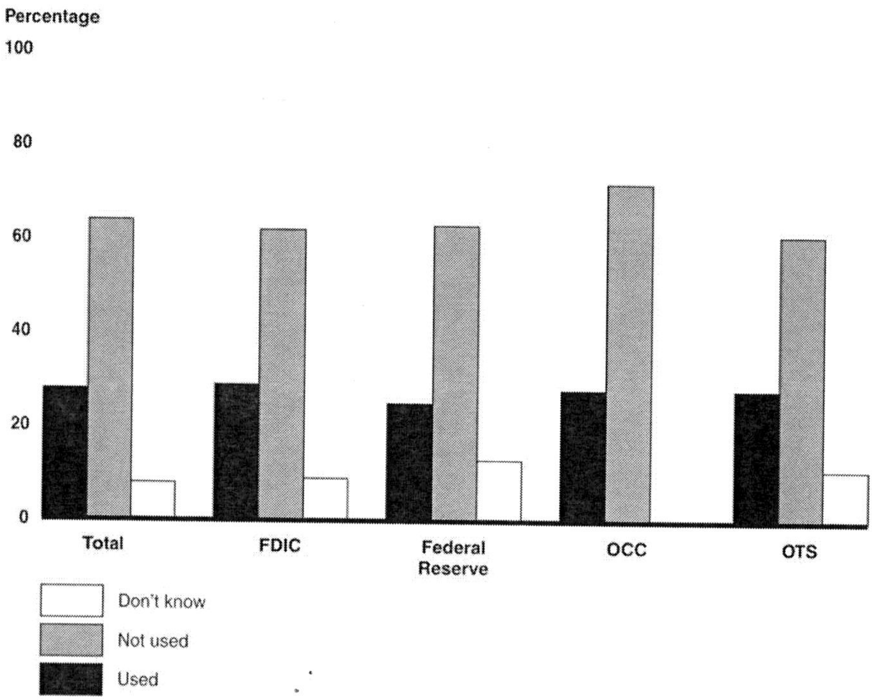

Source: GAO.

Figure 8. Minority Banks' Use of Technical Assistance, by Regulator

Survey Respondents Expressed Concerns about the Examination Process and a Provision of CRA Designed to Assist Minority Banks

More than 80 percent of the minority banks we surveyed responded that their regulators did a very good or good job of administering examinations, and almost 90 percent felt that they had very good or good relationships with their regulator. However, as in our 1993 report, some minority bank officials said in both survey responses and interviews that examiners did not always understand the challenges the banks faced in providing services in their particular communities. Twenty-one percent of survey respondents mentioned this issue when asked for suggestions about how regulators could improve their efforts to support minority banks, and several minority banks that we interviewed elaborated on this topic.

The bank officials said that examiners tended to treat minority banks like any other bank when they conducted examinations and thought such comparisons were not appropriate. For example, some bank officials whose institutions serve immigrant communities said that their customers tended to do business in cash and carried a significant amount of cash because banking services were not widely available or trusted in the customers' home countries. Bank officials said that examiners sometimes commented negatively on the practice of customers doing business in cash or placed the bank under increased scrutiny relative to the Bank Secrecy Act's requirements for cash transactions.[18] While the bank officials said that they did not expect preferential treatment in the examination process, several suggested that examiners undergo additional training so that they could better understand minority banks and the communities that these institutions served. FDIC has conducted such training for its examiners. In 2004, FDIC invited the president of a minority bank to speak to about 500 FDIC examiners on the uniqueness of minority banks and the examination process. FDIC officials later reported that the examiners found the discussion helpful.

Many survey respondents also said that a CRA provision that was designed to assist their institutions was not effectively achieving this goal. The provision allows bank regulators conducting CRA examinations to give consideration to banks that assist minority banks through capital investment, loan participation, and other ventures that help meet the credit needs of local communities. Despite this provision, only 18 percent of survey respondents said that CRA had—to a very great or great extent— encouraged other institutions to invest in or form partnerships with their institutions, while more than half said that CRA encouraged such activities to some, little, or no extent (see figure 9). Some minority bankers attributed their view that the CRA provision has not been effective, in part, to a lack of clarity in interagency guidance on the act's implementation. They said that the interagency guidance should be clarified to assure banks that they will receive CRA consideration in making investments in minority banks.

Regulators Recently Have Taken Steps to Assess and Enhance Their Minority Bank Support Efforts, but It Is Too Soon to Assess Their Effectiveness

Our 2006 report recommended that the bank regulators regularly review the effectiveness of their minority bank support efforts and related regulatory activities and, as appropriate, make changes necessary to better serve such institutions. In conducting such reviews, we recommended that the regulators consider conducting periodic surveys of minority banks or developing outcome-oriented performance measures for their support efforts. In conducting such reviews, we also suggested that the regulators focus on the overall views of minority banks about support efforts, the usage and effectiveness of technical assistance (particularly assistance provided to small minority and African-American banks), and the level of training provided to agency examiners on minority banks and their operating environments.

Over the past year, bank regulatory officials we contacted identified several steps that they have initiated to assess the effectiveness of their minority bank support efforts or to enhance such support efforts. They include the following actions:

- A Federal Reserve official told us that the agency has established a working group that is developing a pilot training program for minority banks and new banks. The official said that three training modules have been drafted for different phases of a bank's life, including starting a bank, operating a bank during its first 5 years of existence, and bank expansion. The official said that the program will be piloted throughout the U.S. beginning in early November 2007. Throughout the course of developing, drafting, and piloting the program, Federal Reserve officials said they have, and will continue to, consult with minority bankers to obtain feedback on the effort.
- An OCC official said that the agency recently sent a survey to minority banks on its education, outreach, and technical assistance efforts that should be completed by the end of October. OCC also plans to follow up this survey with a series of focus groups. In addition, the official said OCC just completed an internal survey of certain officials involved in supervising minority institutions, and

plans to review the results of the two surveys and focus groups to improve its minority bank support efforts.

- FDIC officials told us that the agency has developed a survey to obtain feedback on the agency's minority bank support efforts. They estimate that the survey will be sent out to all minority institutions (not just those minority banks FDIC supervises) in mid-December 2007.
- An OTS official told us that the agency will send out a survey to the minority banks the agency supervises on its efforts in the next couple weeks and that it has also conducted a series of roundtables with minority banks in the past year.

The federal banking agencies have also taken some steps to address other issues raised in our report. For example, Federal Reserve and FDIC officials told us that that the agencies will provide additional training on minority bank issues to their examiners. In addition, in July 2007 the federal banking agencies published a CRA Interagency Notice that requested comments on nine new "Questions and Answers" about community reinvestment.[19] One question covers how majority banks may engage in and receive positive CRA consideration for activities conducted with minority institutions. An OCC official said that the comments on the proposed "Q and As" are under review.

While the regulators' recent efforts to assess and enhance their minority bank support efforts and other activities are encouraging, it is too soon to assess their effectiveness. For example, the Federal Reserve's pilot training program for minority and new banks is not scheduled to begin until later this year. Further, the other regulators' efforts to survey minority banks on support efforts generally also are at an early stage. We encourage agency officials to ensure that they collect and analyze relevant data and take steps to enhance their minority bank support efforts as warranted.

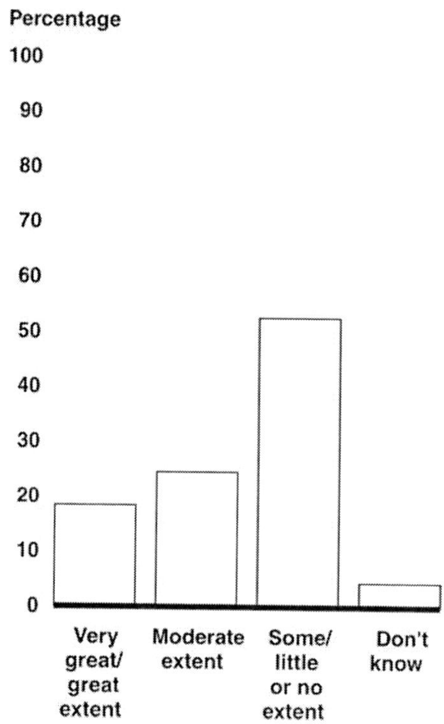

Source: GAO.

Figure 9. Minority Banks' Evaluation of the Extent to Which CRA Has Encouraged Partnerships with Other Institutions

Mr. Chairman, this concludes my prepared statement. I would be happy to address any questions that you or subcommittee members may have.

End Notes

[1] GAO, *Minority Banks: Regulators Need to Better Assess Effectiveness of Support Efforts*, GAO-07-6 (Washington, D.C.: Oct. 4, 2006). The term "minority banks" refers to all depository institutions—including thrifts—that are considered minority- or women-owned by the Department of the Treasury and the federal banking regulators—the Federal Deposit Insurance Corporation, the Board of Governors of the Federal Reserve System, the Office of the Comptroller of the Currency, and the Office of Thrift Supervision.

[2] FIRREA, Pub. L. No. 101-73, § 308, 103 Stat. 183, 353 (1989).

[3] While Treasury convened interagency panels on minority bank issues in the early 1990s, department officials said it no longer does so. According to Treasury officials, the FIRREA consulting requirement is open to some interpretation and the general view within the department was that ongoing consultations were not required. However, Treasury officials said that they do discuss minority bank issues with the regulators as the need arises.

[4] GAO, *Minority-Owned Financial Institutions: Status of Federal Efforts to Preserve Minority Ownership*, GAO/GGD-94-1 (Washington, D.C.: Nov. 3, 1993).

[5] Government Performance and Results Act of 1993, Pub. L. No. 103-62, §7, 107 Stat. 285, 292, (codified at 39 U.S.C. § 2801(1)).

[6] The FDIC definition for peer groups includes all institutions of a similar asset size, including minority and nonminority institutions.

[7] Examples of assets include loans and securities.

[8] Outcome-oriented performance measures assess the results of a program against its intended purposes.

[9] FDIC administers the fund, which provides deposit insurance for banks and thrifts.

[10] A weighted average is a variation on a simple average. Weighted averages take into account banks' asset size instead of counting each bank as an equal unit.

[11] In 2005, African-American banks did not occupy all asset size categories. The largest African-American banks had less than $1 billion in assets; thus, they did not populate in the two largest size categories: $1 billion to $10 billion and greater than $10 billion.

[12] While our review offers possible explanations for lower levels of profitability among some minority banks, it does not attempt to fully explain the differences among various minority groups or sizes of minority banks.

[13] The term "loan loss reserves" refers to the allowance each bank must maintain to absorb estimated credit losses associated with its loan and lease portfolio.

[14] Section 807 of the Community Reinvestment Act of 1977 requires the federal banking regulators in connection with their examination of each institution they supervise to assess the institution's record of meeting the credit needs of the entire community it serves, including moderate- and low-income neighborhoods. Pub. L. No. 95-128, § 807, 91 Stat. 1147 (codified as amended at 12 U.S.C. § 2906).

[15] Section 13(c) of the Federal Deposit Insurance Act (codified at 12 U.S.C. § 1823(c)), as amended in 1991, prohibits FDIC from engaging in the assisted resolution of any failed depository institution unless FDIC determines that the total amount of expenditures and obligations it would incur in doing so would represent the least costly alternative.

[16] The museum exhibition would have traced the history of minority banks in the United States. However, after conducting additional research on this proposal, FDIC decided not to pursue the project, in part because of limited interest from some minority banks.

[17] The survey did find that minority banks that FDIC and OTS regulated were more aware of the agencies' technical assistance outreach efforts than institutions that OCC and the Federal Reserve regulated. This finding is consistent with the fact that FDIC and OTS have formalized technical assistance outreach efforts, while the other regulators do not.

[18] The body of law commonly referred to as the Bank Secrecy Act (BSA) is codified at 31 U.S.C. §§ 5311-5322 and 12 U.S.C. §§ 1829b and 1951–1959.

[19] Community Reinvestment Act; Interagency Questions and Answers Regarding Community Investment, 72 Fed. Reg. 37922 (notice and request for comment Jul. 11, 2007).

In: Financial Institutions in Turmoil
Editor: Carl D. Aspelin
ISBN: 978-1-60692-044-2

Chapter 3

CREDIT DERIVATIVES: CONFIRMATION BACKLOGS INCREASED DEALERS' OPERATIONAL RISKS, BUT WERE SUCCESSFULLY ADDRESSED AFTER JOINT REGULATORY ACTION*

U. S. Government Accountability Office

WHY GAO DID THIS STUDY

Over-the-counter (OTC) credit derivatives are privately negotiated contracts that allow a party to transfer the risk of default on a bond or loan to another party without transferring ownership. After trading in these products grew dramatically in recent years, backlogs of thousands of trades developed for which dealers had yet to formally confirm the trade terms with end-users—such as hedge funds, pension funds, and insurance companies—and other dealers. Not confirming these trades raised the risk that losses could arise.

GAO was asked to review (1) what caused the trade confirmation backlogs and how they were being addressed and (2) how U.S. financial regulators were overseeing dealers' credit derivative operations, including the security and resiliency of the information technology systems used for these

* This is an edited, reformatted and augmented version of a U. S. Government Accountability Office publication dated June 2007.

products. GAO analyzed data on credit derivatives operations that dealers submitted to regulators, reviewed regulatory examination reports and work papers, and interviewed regulators, dealers, end-users, and industry organizations.

WHAT GAO FOUND

After trading volumes grew exponentially between 2002 and 2005, the 14 largest credit derivatives dealers—including U.S. and foreign banks and securities broker-dealers—accumulated backlogs of unconfirmed trades totaling over 150,000 in September 2005. These backlogs resulted from reliance on inefficient manual confirmation processes that failed to keep up with the rapidly growing volume and because of difficulties in confirming information for trades that end-users transferred to other parties without notifying the original dealer. Although these trades were being entered into the systems that dealers used to manage the risk of loss arising from price changes (market risk) and counterparty defaults (credit risk), the credit derivatives backlogs increased dealers' operational risk by potentially allowing errors that could lead to losses or other problems to go undetected. In response, a joint regulatory initiative involving U.S. and foreign regulators directed the 14 major dealers to work together to reduce the backlogs and address the underlying causes. By increasing automation and requiring end- users to obtain counterparty consent before assigning trades, the 14 dealers reduced their total confirmations outstanding more than 30 days by 94 percent to 5,500 trades by October 2006, as shown in the figure below.

Through ongoing supervision and examinations, U.S. banking and securities regulators became aware of the credit derivatives backlogs as early as late 2003 and had been monitoring efforts taken by each dealer to reduce its backlog. Under the joint regulatory initiative, regulators obtained aggregate data from the dealers that allowed regulators to better monitor how backlogs were being resolved. Recognizing the potential for similar problems to arise in other OTC derivatives markets, regulators began obtaining similar data for other OTC derivative products in November 2006.

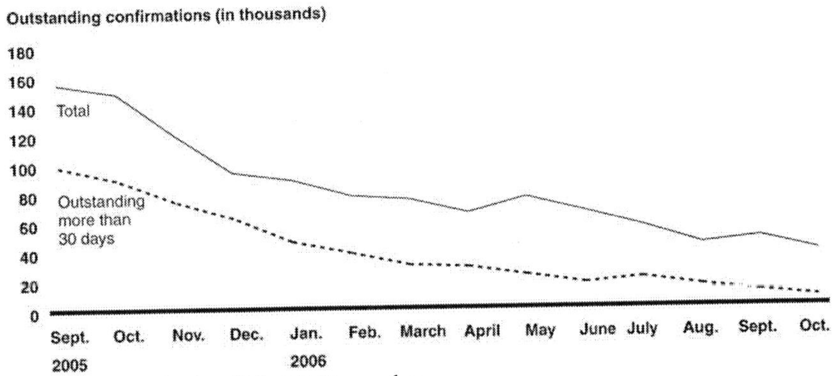

Source: GAO analysis of Markit Group data.

Outstanding Confirmations at 14 Major Dealers, September 2005 to October 2006

ABBREVIATIONS

BIS	Bank for International Settlements (Basel, Switzerland)
CSE	Consolidated Supervised Entity
FSA	Financial Services Authority (United Kingdom)
FRBNY	Federal Reserve Bank of New York
DTCC	Depository Trust and Clearing Corporation
ISDA	International Swaps and Derivatives Association
LIBOR	London Interbank Offered Rate
OCC	Office of the Comptroller of the Currency
OTC	over the counter
SEC	Securities and Exchange Commission

June 13, 2007
Congressional Requesters

Until late 2005, the growth in trading volume of over-the-counter (OTC) credit derivatives had greatly outpaced the processing capabilities of the financial firms offering these products—heightening the operational risk that such firms could incur losses from human errors or system failures. OTC credit derivatives are privately negotiated contracts that allow a party to transfer the risk of default on a bond or loan to another party without transferring ownership. In a credit default swap, for example, a bond investor agrees to pay a periodic premium to a financial firm in exchange for the firm's agreement to compensate the bond investor for any losses if the bond issuer defaults on the bonds. Like other OTC derivatives, credit derivatives are typically bought and sold through dealers, namely banks and securities broker-dealers, that stand ready to buy or sell credit derivatives to end-users, such as hedge funds, pension funds, and insurance companies. Although OTC trading in credit derivatives is not regulated in the United States, the dealers are subject to supervision by their respective regulators, including U.S. banking and securities regulators.[1]

Introduced in the early 1990s, credit derivatives surpassed a total notional amount of $34 trillion at year-end 2006.[2] As trading volume grew exponentially in recent years, major dealers developed backlogs of thousands of trades for which the trade terms had not been formally confirmed with their counterparties, which included end-users and other dealers. Having unconfirmed trades could allow errors to go undetected at dealers and later result in losses, a situation that an official from the United Kingdom's regulator of credit derivatives dealers characterized as "an accident waiting to happen."

Given the concerns about the inability of the credit derivatives market's infrastructure to keep up with the growth in trading volume, you asked us to review the causes of the confirmation backlogs and the steps U.S. financial regulators were taking to address the issue. This chapter discusses (1) what caused the backlogs and the steps being taken to address them and (2) U.S. financial regulators' oversight of the operational risk that dealers faced from the backlog in credit derivatives confirmations, including the security and resiliency of related information technology systems.[3]

To determine the causes of the backlogs and the steps that are being taken to address these issues, we analyzed the trading volume of credit derivatives, confirmation backlogs, and other transactional data provided by major dealers of credit derivatives to U.S. and foreign regulators through Markit Group, a provider of independent data, portfolio valuations, and trade processing for OTC derivatives. We examined the procedures that this firm employs to collect and analyze the data and determined that the data were sufficiently reliable for our purposes. We also reviewed and analyzed reports on the credit derivatives market by industry associations, international organizations, firms, and academics. We interviewed eight dealers of credit derivatives, a hedge fund, and various industry trade organizations, including organizations representing OTC derivatives dealers and derivatives end-users, including the

International Swaps and Derivatives Association (ISDA). To determine how dealers' exposures to operational risks associated with credit derivatives were being supervised, we interviewed staff from the Federal Reserve, including its examiners for two banks; the Office of the Comptroller of the Currency (OCC), including examiners for three banks; the Securities and Exchange Commission (SEC); and the United Kingdom's Financial Services Authority (FSA). We also reviewed and analyzed examinations conducted between 2004 and 2006 by the Federal Reserve and the OCC on the activities in credit derivatives of five banks and by the SEC covering the holding companies of five securities broker-dealers that engage in credit derivatives activities. We conducted our work in Charlotte, North Carolina; Chicago; New York; and Washington, D.C., from August 2006 to March 2007 in accordance with generally accepted government auditing standards. Appendix I provides a detailed description of our scope and methodology.

RESULTS IN BRIEF

Two factors largely led to the substantial backlogs of unconfirmed trades that dealers had amassed by 2005, though regulators, dealers, and others have since made considerable progress in reducing these backlogs. From 2002, trading volume in credit derivatives was expanding exponentially, with particularly rapid growth from 2004 to 2005, as the average number of trades done weekly at large dealers increased from 644 to 1,450. As a result, by the end of September 2005, 14 of the largest credit derivatives dealers had, in aggregate, over 150,000 unconfirmed trades, with nearly two-thirds of these remaining unconfirmed for more than 30 days. The delays in confirming trades largely resulted from (1) dealers and end-users relying on inefficient manual processes that could not adequately keep up with the rapidly growing volume and (2) the difficulty of confirming trade information after some end-users began frequently assigning their side of existing trades to new parties without notifying the original dealer. The backlog of unconfirmed trades created operational risk by potentially allowing trade errors to go undetected that could lead to losses and other problems. For example, undetected errors could result in legal disputes over contract terms and cause dealers to incorrectly measure and manage their market or credit risk.[4] To mitigate these risks, some dealers were informally verifying the key economic terms of trades with counterparties to ensure that trades were accurately recorded and risks were accurately measured, but the extent to which these practices were followed varied. According to regulators, the trade assignment practice posed a "collective action" problem because dealers could not individually stop the practice. As a result, in September 2005, U.S. and foreign financial regulators participated in a joint regulatory initiative organized by the Federal Reserve Bank of New York (FRBNY) and prompted the 14 major credit derivatives dealers to work together to reduce the number of unconfirmed trades and address the underlying causes of these backlogs. Using automated systems to confirm trades and adopting a protocol requiring end-users to obtain dealers' consent before assigning trades, the 14 dealers reduced the number of confirmations outstanding for more than 30 days by 94 percent (to around 5,500 trades) by the end of October 2006. Dealers and others are continuing to work to reduce operational risks, in part by further automating the market's infrastructure—for example, by developing a central depository to store virtually all trades and automate other processes.

U.S. bank and securities regulators had been overseeing the exposure of credit derivatives dealers to operational and other risks, but were better able to monitor the resolution of the backlog problem once they began receiving industrywide data under FRBNY's joint regulatory initiative. Through supervision and examinations, the pertinent U.S. federal bank regulators—the Federal Reserve and the OCC—became aware of the backlogs at U.S. banks engaged in credit derivatives activities as early as late 2003 and were monitoring banks' efforts to reduce their backlogs before the joint regulatory initiative. The securities regulator, SEC, was generally aware of the backlogs since late 2004, but SEC staff became more concerned about them through periodic discussions with broker- dealers subject to the SEC's Consolidated Supervised Entity (CSE) program during the summer of 2005. As part of their examinations, the bank and securities regulators have also been reviewing how these dealers maintained the security and resiliency of the information technology systems used for credit derivatives. Although U.S. and foreign regulators were aware of confirmation backlogs at individual dealers, none of the regulators oversaw all the dealers or had data on the size of the backlog industrywide. However, under the joint regulatory initiative begun in September 2005, the dealers have been providing the regulators with aggregate data on their backlogs and other operational measures, giving regulators an effective means for monitoring the industry's progress in reducing the backlogs. In recognition of the potential for similar operational problems to arise in other OTC derivatives markets, including OTC equity derivatives, U.S. and foreign regulators have begun to collect similar data for other OTC derivative products.

We provided a draft of this chapter to the Federal Reserve, OCC, and SEC for their review and comment. The Federal Reserve and SEC provided technical comments, which we incorporated as appropriate.

BACKGROUND

Introduced in the early 1990s, credit derivatives have been widely adopted as a tool for allowing market participants to take on or reduce their exposure to credit risk. First used primarily by banks to reduce credit exposures stemming from loans made to clients, credit derivatives have evolved to include an array of different products (table 1). According to regulators and others, credit derivatives have the potential to improve the overall efficiency and resiliency of the financial markets by spreading credit risk more widely across a large and diverse pool of investors. According to the British Bankers' Association, single-name credit default swaps remain the most common type of credit derivative, comprising about 33 percent of the market in 2006, though their share of the market has decreased since 2004. These swaps allow the buyer of protection to transfer the credit risk associated with default on debt issued by a single corporation or sovereign entity—called the reference entity.[5] With a standard credit default swap, the buyer of credit risk protection pays a quarterly premium payment to the seller of credit risk protection over the life of the contract, typically 5 or more years. Should a defined credit event occur, such as a default by the specified corporation on the referenced debt, the protection seller would assume the losses.[6] As table 1 shows, other commonly traded products include full index trades, synthetic collateralized debt obligations, and tranched index trades.

In the credit derivatives market, banks and securities broker-dealers generally serve as the product dealers, acting as the buyer or seller in credit derivative trades with end-users or other dealers. The top five dealers in 2005, ranked by total trading volumes as estimated by Fitch Ratings, were Morgan Stanley, Deutsche Bank, Goldman Sachs, JP Morgan Chase, and UBS. End-users of credit derivatives include hedge funds,[7] insurance companies, pension funds, and mutual funds.[8]

Table 1. Share of Market by Credit Derivative Product, 2006

Credit derivative product	Market share (percentage)	Product description
Single-name credit default swaps	33%	Credit derivatives based on bonds from a single issuer, such as a corporation or a sovereign entity.
Full Index trades	30	Credit derivatives referencing multiple corporations or sovereign entities that are gathered into a standardized portfolio and offered to investors as one unit. Indexes are usually categorized by characteristics such as industry, geographic region, or credit quality.
Synthetic collat-eralized debt obligations	16	Credit derivatives referencing multiple corporations or sovereign entities and gathered into a standardized portfolio—customized for investors—and separated into various risk categories (or tranches) that vary by the likelihood of incurring losses. Obligations from the tranches are then sold to investors according to the desired risk/return profile.
Tranched index trades	8	Index trades that are divided into various risk tranches, with investors selecting the risk and return profile they prefer among the various risk categories in the standardized index.
Others[a]	13	A variety of special-purpose products that collectively represent a relatively small share of the credit derivatives market.
Total	**100%**	

Source: Percentages from British Bankers' Association and definitions from GAO analysis of multiple sources.

[a] "Others" include products that each account for less than a 6 percent share of the market.

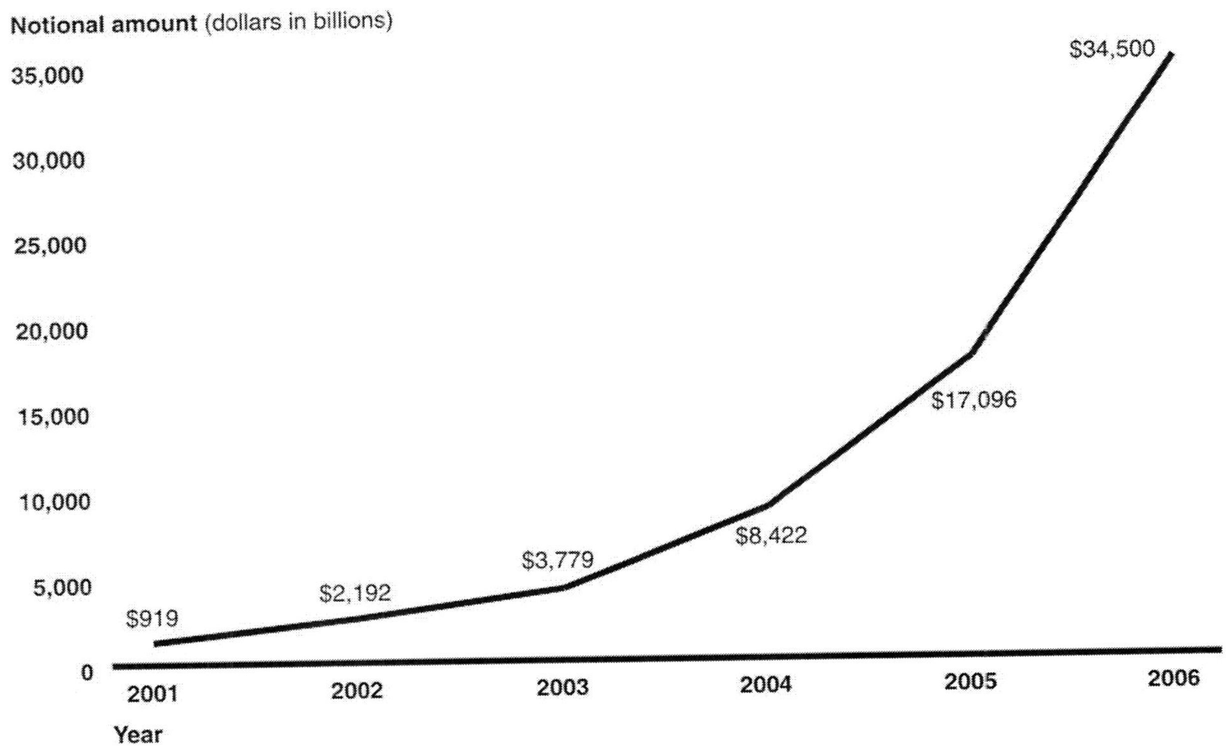

Source: ISDA.

Figure 1. Total Notional Amount of Credit Default Swaps Market, 2001 to 2006

According to ISDA, which conducts periodic surveys of market participants, the credit derivatives market has grown dramatically in recent years, increasing from an estimated total notional amount of nearly $1 trillion outstanding at year-end 2001 to over $34 trillion at year-end 2006 (see figure 1).[9] Part of this rapid growth has been attributed to product innovation and an increasing number of market participants, particularly hedge funds. Despite its expansion, the credit derivative market is still much smaller than the OTC interest rate derivatives market, which had a total notional amount outstanding of around $286 trillion at year-end 2006.[10]

Processing Credit Derivatives Trades

Traders and sales staff at dealers who interact with customers represent the dealer's "front office." The staff in the front office generally use electronic systems to capture the trade data and transmit it to the systems used to manage market and credit risk. Dealers also have "back offices," which include staff that record, verify, and confirm trades executed by the front office. As shown in figure 2, the steps for entering into and processing an OTC trade for credit derivatives include negotiation, capture, verification, and confirmation. These processes have been increasingly automated over time, but some remain manual. For example, a relatively small percentage of credit derivative products—generally those with more customized and complex terms—cannot be confirmed electronically. In addition, various post-trade processes occur during the life of a credit derivatives contract, including making or receiving premium payments, exchanging collateral, and settling contracts after a credit event occurs, such as a bond default.

Segregating these various duties into front and back office responsibilities serves to maintain operational integrity, such as by identifying data entry errors and to minimize fraud and other violations. Management responsibilities performed by the back office vary by institution, but they may include evaluating transactional exposure against established market and credit limits and risk management reporting. Some dealers have combined a number of the functions performed by the back office, such as risk management, into a middle office, and some use a separate risk management group.

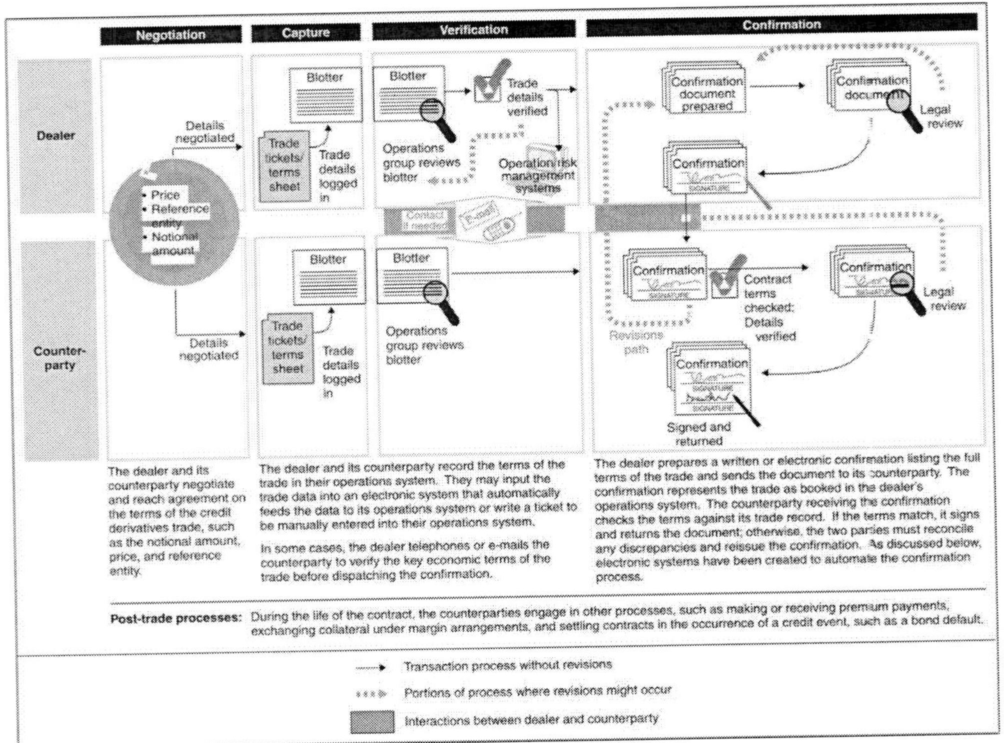

Source: GAO (based on material from Bearing Point, ISDA, and BIS).

Figure 2. Steps for Processing a Credit Derivative Trade

Regulation of OTC Credit Derivatives

Because OTC credit derivative transactions occur between private parties and are not traded on regulated exchanges, they are not subject to regulation in the United States, provided that the parties and other aspects of the transaction satisfy requirements of the Commodity Exchange Act.[11] For credit derivatives that would otherwise be securities, the transactions fall within the definition of "swap agreement" in the Gramm-Leach-Bliley Act.[12] The Commodity Exchange Act allows unregulated derivatives trading in certain types of commodities by eligible parties under limited circumstances.[13] Similarly, the Commodity Exchange Act and the Securities Act of 1933 allow unregulated derivatives trading by eligible parties under limited circumstances.[14] Although the OTC credit derivatives products themselves are not regulated, certain market participants are. If the dealer is a U.S. bank federally chartered as a national bank, it is supervised by OCC. If a bank is owned by a bank holding company, its holding company is regulated by the Federal Reserve.[15] These bank regulators oversee these entities to ensure the safety and soundness of the banking system and the stability of the financial markets. If the credit derivatives dealer is a securities broker-dealer, it is overseen by SEC. According to U.S. regulators, some of the U.S. banks and securities broker-dealers also conduct credit derivatives trades in foreign affiliates subject to foreign regulation. Similarly, other participants in the credit derivatives market include foreign banks that are supervised by foreign regulators and, in some cases, also by U.S. regulators if operating in the United States.

Manual Processes and Trade Assignments Led to Backlogs of Unconfirmed Trades at Dealers, but Industry Efforts Have Significantly Reduced the Backlogs

As the credit derivatives market grew, lack of automation and other factors led to large backlogs of unconfirmed trades at dealers. The eight dealers we interviewed told us that they began to experience a significant increase in their backlogs of unconfirmed trades ranging from the middle of 2003 to the first half of 2005. According to ISDA's survey data, trading volume in credit derivatives more than doubled around this period, with the average number of trades conducted at large firms increasing from 644 trades a week in 2004 to 1,450 trades a week in 2005. According to data provided to regulators by 14 of the largest credit derivatives dealers— which include U.S. and foreign banks and securities broker-dealers—these dealers collectively executed around 130,000 trades in September 2005, and dealers' backlogs of confirmations outstanding had risen to over 150,000 (table 2).[16] Of these, 63 percent had been outstanding for more than 30 days, and 41 percent had been outstanding for more than 90 days.

Two Factors Largely Caused the Confirmation Backlogs at Dealers

A major factor contributing to the backlogs was dealer and end-user reliance on largely manual processes for confirming credit derivative trades that could not keep up with the rapidly growing trade volume. Unlike highly automated processes for confirming trades in corporate stocks, the processes that dealers were generally using to confirm their credit derivative trades relied on inefficient manual procedures. For example, a dealer would manually prepare a confirmation and fax it to the counterparty; in turn, the counterparty would manually compare its trade record against the confirmation and, if the terms matched, fax the signed confirmation to the dealer. Such manual processes were resource intensive and generally lacked the scalability required to efficiently confirm the rapidly growing volume of trades.

Table 2. Number of Credit Derivatives Trade Confirmations Outstanding for 14 Major Dealers, September 2005

	Number of confirmations outstanding	**Percentage of the Total confirmations outstanding**
Confirmations outstanding 30	56,224	37%
Confirmations outstanding more than 30 days	97,650	63%
Confirmations outstanding more than 90 days	63,322	41%a
Total confirmations	**153,860**	**100%**

Source: GAO analysis of Markit Group data.

[a]The number of confirmations outstanding more than 90 days is included in the total of confirmations outstanding more than 30 days. As a result, the percentages do not add up to 100 percent.

Recognizing the need to improve the efficiency of the confirmation process for credit derivatives, dealers had been working with the Depository Trust and Clearing Corporation (DTCC) to increase the use of an automated confirmation system.[17] DTCC staff said that they started to work with several dealers in 2002 to create an automated system to electronically compare, match, and confirm credit derivative trades. The initial strategy was to have the system confirm only single-name credit default swaps and then to expand the system's capabilities to confirm other credit derivative products and provide other services. DTCC launched its automated system, Deriv/SERV, in late 2003, and 15 dealers and 7 end-users had signed up to use the system by around mid-2004. DTCC staff explained that obtaining wider use of Deriv/SERV took time, in part because of the need to publicize the system and because users needed to train their staff and revise their systems to use Deriv/SERV. According to staff at one hedge fund, many end-users did not initially use Deriv/ SERV because they lacked the necessary technology. Consequently, up to 85 percent of the credit derivative trades were being confirmed manually during 2004, according to market participants. However, DTCC has expanded Deriv/SERV's capabilities to confirm a broader range of credit default swaps and as much as 46 percent of trades were being confirmed electronically by September 2005, according to data provided to regulators by 14 major dealers.

The second major factor contributing to the backlogs was the increasing incidence of end-users transferring their positions to other counterparties. Although the length of the contract for the most popular credit derivatives typically spans 5 years, some end-users, particularly hedge funds, engaged in frequent "in and out" trading of these products or had other incentives to liquidate their positions earlier. To do so, the end-users assigned their sides of trades to third parties. Although the agreements accompanying the trades did not permit assignments without the dealer's prior consent, the dealers agreed to assignments after the fact because of competitive pressures and because the new counterparties (the assignees) tended to be other dealers. In effect, these assignments (also called novations) ultimately resulted in a new contract between the original dealer and the new counterparty, which would not be reflected on the dealer's records until the original dealer accepted the assignment. A hedge fund official told us that when his firm wanted to terminate trades early, it initially returned to the original dealers, but the dealers charged termination fees that made this method more costly than assigning the trades.[18] Assignments have provided greater market liquidity and price discovery,[19] but according to dealers and regulators, they complicated the confirmation process. Without prior knowledge of an assignment, the original dealer could not readily confirm the details of the new trade until the dealer became aware of the assignment. Some end-users said that they obtained consent from the original dealers but that the dealers were not communicating the information internally to the appropriate staff for the purpose of confirming the trade.

Although assigned trades were a small share of total trading volumes, they represented a disproportionately large share of unconfirmed trades because of the time required to identify the correct counterparty. According to data provided by the 14 major dealers to regulators, trade assignments accounted for 13 percent of dealers' trading volume in September 2005 but 40 percent of their total confirmations outstanding for more than 30 days at the end of September 2005. Dealers told us that they typically detected unilateral assignments through payment errors. For example, a dealer would receive a premium payment from a party other than the party with which it had entered into the trade. Importantly, market participants had agreed to settle premium payments due under credit default swaps on a quarterly basis in order to provide greater market liquidity. Bank examiners told us that because of this settlement cycle, it could take a dealer as many as 90 days or more to detect a unilateral assignment through a payment error.

Dealers we spoke with identified several other factors that hampered their efforts to confirm trades in a timely manner. First, some dealers told us that as the volume of trading in credit derivatives grew, they faced challenges hiring experienced back-office staff and that training new staff took months. Second, other dealers said that the lack of standardized documentation, particularly for new products, led to disputes over the trade terms or the need to negotiate them, further delaying confirmation.[20] Compounding matters, there was a shortage of derivatives attorneys available for such negotiations, according to a bank examiner. Finally, two dealers said that the industry lacked standardized reference data to identify the specific entities referenced in credit derivative contracts. One of the dealers told us that the lack of such data led to mistakes in recording trades and hampered electronic confirmations. Mistakes in documenting the correct reference entity prompted a group of dealers to develop a database of reference entities and obligations in 2003 that has become an industry standard.

Confirmation Backlogs and Unilateral Assignments Increased Dealers' Operational Risks

Although dealers were capturing their credit derivatives trades in their risk management systems to manage the associated market and credit risks, the substantial backlog of unconfirmed trades heightened dealers' operational risk, potentially hampering their ability to effectively manage other risks. As with any trading activity, dealers engaging in credit derivative trades are exposed to market, credit, and other risks that they must adequately measure, monitor, and control. According to dealers and their regulators, the major credit derivatives dealers generally were entering their credit derivatives trades promptly into their trade capture systems and, in turn, measuring, monitoring, and managing the credit and market risks associated with those trades.[21] Dealers, for example, measure and manage market risk by estimating the potential losses that a portfolio of positions may suffer and then impose limits that restrict the estimated losses to an acceptable level. Similarly, dealers manage counterparty credit risk—which can produce losses if the dealers fail to receive payments owed to them—generally by measuring the total credit exposure to, and creditworthiness of, individual counterparties, and not allowing these exposures to exceed pre-established limits.

Although the credit and market risks were being managed, the large backlogs of unconfirmed trades increased dealers' operational risks. Confirmations serve as an internal control to verify that both parties agree to the trade terms and have accurately recorded the trade in their systems. For this reason, trades should be confirmed as soon as possible. Having unconfirmed trades could allow errors to go undetected that might subsequently lead to losses and other problems. Errors could be made at any time—for example, counterparties could miscommunicate when making a trade or dealers could enter the wrong trade data into their systems. If such errors go undetected, a dealer could make an incorrect premium payment to a counterparty or inaccurately measure and manage risk exposures, notably market and counterparty credit risks. Similarly, errors could lead to legal disputes between a dealer and a counterparty if a credit event triggered a contract settlement.

Further, these operational risks have the potential to contribute to broader market problems. For example, in its July 2005 report on strengthening the stability of the global financial system, the Counterparty Risk Management Policy Group II, composed of representatives of dealers and end-users, noted that as the number of outstanding credit derivatives trades continues to grow, a credit event involving a popular reference entity could materially strain the ability of market participants to settle transactions in a timely and efficient manner.[22] However, these operational risks did not result in such broader market problems, in part because of favorable market conditions when the confirmation backlog arose and because only seven referenced entities in the United States have defaulted since 2005—with market participants able to effectively settle trades referencing these entities.

Although unconfirmed trade backlogs were growing, dealers had been taking steps to reduce the operational risks associated with these trades. To ensure that the trade data being captured and used to manage risks were accurate, dealers were informally contacting their counterparties before sending out confirmations to verify the key economic terms of the trades, but this practice varied among the nine dealers reviewed. Specifically, five dealers generally followed this practice for their credit derivative trades, according to their staff or examiners. In contrast, two dealers generally had been informally verifying trade terms for only those trades considered higher risk, according to their staff or examiners. Finally, staff at two other dealers said that they generally were not verifying trade terms before confirmation because their counterparties preferred not to do so.[23] The dealers also were monitoring their confirmation backlogs based on risk, such as by the number of days an unconfirmed trade was outstanding. Moreover, two dealers curtailed business with clients that had a large number of outstanding confirmations. In addition, the dealers had reviewed their confirmation processes and were improving them by, among other things, upgrading technology, reorganizing operations, and hiring staff. While dealers found some errors after confirming their trades, only two of the dealers interviewed told us that they had suffered a $1-million-or-more loss as a result of an error stemming from their confirmation backlog but characterized the losses as immaterial.

Like unconfirmed trades, unilateral assignments increased operational, credit, and legal risks. First, unilateral assignments led to operational risk by creating new trades that were not being confirmed promptly to detect errors. Second, to effectively manage credit risk, dealers must know, at a minimum, the correct identities of the counterparties to their credit derivative contracts. Unconfirmed trades arising from unilateral assignments meant that dealers did not always know the exact counterparty to which they were exposed. As a result, their ability to accurately measure their credit exposure and enforce their pre-established limits on it was hampered. Moreover, because dealers did not always know the correct counterparties for each of their trades, they often made premium payments to, or received payments from, the wrong entity.

Third, unconfirmed assigned trades also raised dealers' legal risk because of the potential for counterparties to later dispute the terms of the trade or the enforceability of the contract. For example, a court may deem an assigned trade as legally invalid if the original dealer did not provide its written consent. As the Counterparty Risk Management Policy Group II reported in 2005, some assignments occurred before the original trades were confirmed, increasing the risk of potential disputes over the status and the terms of the trade.

Several factors helped to mitigate the risks arising from unilateral assignments. According to dealers and regulators, the assignments did not increase market risk for dealers because dealers generally were capturing the key economic terms of the trades in their risk management systems accurately, and these terms remained the same when a trade was assigned. Further, although unilaterally assigned trades impaired the ability of dealers to measure and manage their counterparty credit risk, dealers and examiners told us that hedge funds and other end-users assigned nearly all of their trades to dealers, given their role as intermediaries to end-users. Because dealers were typically more creditworthy than the end-users assigning the trades, the original dealers ended up with more creditworthy counterparties after an assignment, according to dealers and examiners. Situations could arise, however, where this factor would not necessarily mitigate the original dealer's counterparty credit exposure.[24] In addition, dealers told us that they had collateral arrangements with their counterparties to manage their credit risk. For example, dealers required hedge funds to post a negotiated amount of initial collateral, such as cash or securities, for each trade they entered into with dealers.[25] As a risk management practice, two dealers told us that they would not release collateral to their counterparties until they verified that a trade was assigned. In addition, a provision of the standard contract that counterparties enter into as part of conducting derivatives transactions— known as the ISDA Master Agreement—required counterparties to obtain the written consent of their counterparty before assigning a trade.[26] Some dealers told us that they could have relied on this provision, if needed, to reject a unilateral assignment. Finally, none of the dealers said that their counterparties tried to nullify an assigned trade.

Under the Direction of FRBNY as well as Other Regulators, Dealers and Others Have Worked Collaboratively to Considerably Reduce the Backlog and Address Its Causes

The unilateral assignments and the increasing backlogs raised regulatory concerns that prompted U.S. and foreign regulators and the major credit derivative dealers to seek a collective solution. FSA, which oversees financial activities in the United Kingdom, took one of the first actions to address the backlogs by sending dealers a letter in February 2005.[27] The letter expressed FSA's concern about dealers' level of unsigned confirmations and asked them to consider the robustness of their operational processes and risk management frameworks in the rapidly evolving credit derivatives market. U.S. regulatory staff told us that they had been aware of the backlogs since at least 2004 through their oversight activities and discussions with other regulators. For example, in 2004, U.S. bank examiners began to identify the growing backlogs of unconfirmed trades at dealers, including how unilateral assignments were contributing to such backlogs. Although they began monitoring dealers' efforts to resolve these issues, the regulators recognized in spring of 2005 that individual dealer efforts to address the practice of unilateral assignments were proving unsuccessful and that greater automation was needed. Regulatory staff told us that these unilateral assignments posed a "collective action" problem, in that dealers could not individually stop the practice for fear of losing business to other dealers that did not require counterparties to notify them prior to assigning a trade. According to regulatory staff, the prevalence of unilateral assignments was especially troubling because dealers did not always know the counterparties to their trades, raising questions about dealers' ability to accurately manage the risks of these activities. In addition, regulatory staff said that the fact that dealers did not always know their counterparty's identity raised operational concerns about the ability of market participants to settle trades, should a large reference entity default. Finally, regulators noted that resolving the causes of the backlogs required multilateral regulatory involvement, because no single regulator oversaw all the dealers.

To address these problems with confirmation backlogs and unilateral trade assignments, FRBNY convened a meeting in September 2005 with the 14 major credit derivative dealers and their regulators—referred to as the joint regulatory initiative. Regulatory representatives from around the world—including OCC, SEC, FSA, the German Financial Supervisory Authority, and the Swiss Federal Banking Commission—attended the meeting as supervisors of at least one of the major dealers involved in the initiative. At this meeting, the U.S. and foreign regulators discussed how the dealers would improve assignment practices and resolve the confirmation backlogs. In October, the dealers sent FRBNY a letter that outlined the steps to be taken to improve the credit derivatives industry's practices and confirmation backlogs.[28] The plan included

- establishing target dates and levels by which to reduce the confirmation backlogs,
- increasing the use of electronic confirmations systems,
- supporting the implementation of a protocol to end unilateral assignments,
- improving the process for settling credit derivatives contracts after a credit event, and
- providing regulators with monthly data for measuring dealers' progress.

To enable the regulators to monitor the dealers' progress as part of the joint regulatory initiative, the 14 dealers agreed to collect data on their credit derivatives activities, including trading volume, unconfirmed trades, and trades confirmed using automated systems. Under the agreement, the dealers provide their individual data to Markit Group, a provider of independent data, portfolio valuations, and OTC derivatives trade processing. In turn, Markit Group aggregates the data across the dealers to protect the confidentiality of each dealer's data and then provides the regulators with aggregate data in a monthly report.

In February 2006, FRBNY hosted a follow-up meeting with the dealers and their regulators to discuss the progress and stated that it was encouraged by the progress that had been made. Following the meeting, the dealers sent FRBNY a letter committing to further improvements in market practices to "achieve a stronger steady state position for the industry."[29] Among the commitments the dealers made were (1) to ensure that all trades with standardized terms that were eligible for automated processing would be processed electronically, and (2) to work with DTCC to create a central depository to store electronically the details of all credit derivatives contract terms. In September 2006, FRBNY hosted a third follow-up meeting with the dealers and regulators to discuss the dealers' progress.

Since the initial meeting in September 2005, the 14 dealers have significantly reduced the number of outstanding confirmations. As shown in figure 3, the aggregated data that has been provided to regulators showed that the 14 dealers had reduced their total number of confirmations outstanding from 153,860 in September 2005 to 37,306, or by about 76 percent, by the end of October 2006.

Under the joint regulatory initiative organized by FRBNY, each dealer committed to incrementally reducing its number of confirmations outstanding more than 30 days by various amounts over the course of the following 9 months. The data that the dealers have been providing to regulators showed that they collectively exceeded each of the reduction goals they had agreed to meet and had reduced by 94 percent the total number of confirmations outstanding over 30 days from the September 2005 level to the October 2006 level (table 3). The dealers were able to achieve this reduction even though their monthly trading volume in credit derivatives generally increased during this period.

After October 2006, four additional foreign dealers have joined the original 14 dealers in providing monthly confirmation backlog and related data to Markit Group for aggregation and distribution to the regulators. As shown in table 4, with the inclusion of the additional dealer data, the total number of outstanding confirmations over 30 days has increased in comparison to the level at the end of October 2006, especially in March 2007. At the same time, table 4 shows that monthly trading volume has increased beginning in January 2007, and the number of confirmations outstanding more than 30 days as a share of the total number of outstanding confirmations has decreased slightly during this period. U.S. regulatory staff characterized the rise in the confirmation backlog as modest and attributed it generally to the increase in trading volume and noted that the automation of the confirmation process has helped dealers handle the increased volume.

Table 3. Outstanding Confirmation Reduction Goals and Totals for the 14 Credit Derivatives Dealers

As of date	Outstanding confirmation reduction goal	Trades unconfirmed for more than 30 days	Percent reduction
September 30, 2005		97,650	
January 31, 2006	30%	45,288	54%
April 30, 2006	50%	27,405	72%
June 30, 2006	70%	15,997	84%
October 31, 2006		5,558	94%

Source: GAO analysis of Markit Group data.

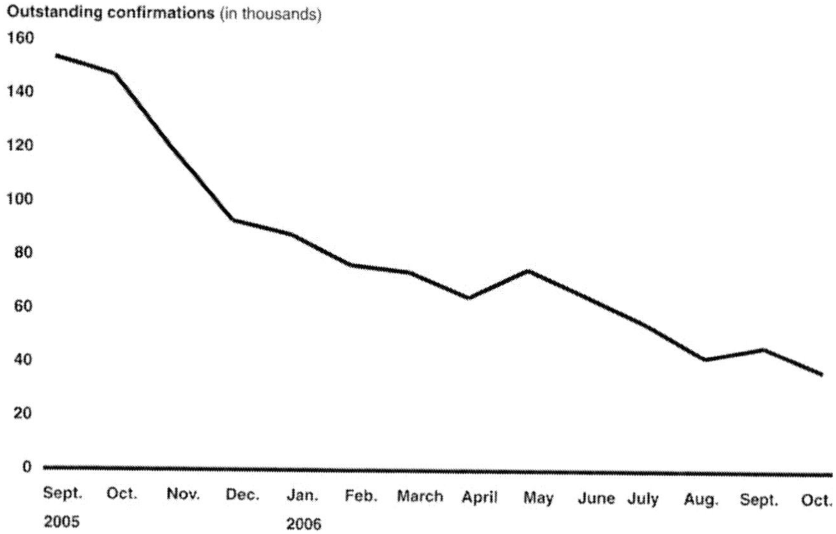

Source: GAO analysis of Markit Group data.

Figure 3. Total Outstanding Confirmations at 14 Major Dealers from September 2005 to October 2006

Table 4. Outstanding Confirmations and Related Data Provided by Dealers from October 2006 to March 2007

Time period	Number of dealers providing data	Total monthly trading volume	Total number of outstanding confirmations more than 30 days	Confirmations Outstanding more than 30 days as a share of total outst-anding confirmations
October 2006	14	190,849	5,558	15%
November 2006	16	185,352	5,802	16%
December 2006	17	139,649	8,282	25%
January 2007	18	216,850	6,784	16%
February 2007	18	234,155	7,380	13%
March 2007	18	347,061	11,940	14%

Source: GAO analysis of Markit Group data.

Dealers Reduced Backlogs through Various Steps

To achieve these reductions in their unconfirmed trade backlogs, dealers took various steps. For example, dealers engaged in events called "lock ins" with other dealers and, to a lesser extent, end-users. Under a lock in, operations staff from either two dealers or staff from one dealer and one of their key end-user customers convened in a room and compared the trades they had conducted together until all or almost all were reconciled and confirmed. Dealers and end-users also used "tear-up services" to reduce the total number of open trades and thus eliminate the number of trades that needed to be confirmed. In a tear-up process, an automated system matches up offsetting positions across many market participants, allowing those trades to be, in effect, terminated and thereby removing the need to confirm such trades.

To prevent new trades from adding to the backlog, the dealers also increased their use of automated confirmation systems and set deadlines for confirming trades. First, as part of the joint regulatory initiative, the 14 major dealers committed to use DTCC's automated system, Deriv/SERV, to confirm trades made with other dealers by the end of October 2005 and to require their active clients to use it or a comparable automated system, such as SwapsWire, by mid-January 2006.[30] As shown in figure 4, the share of the total monthly trades confirmed electronically increased from 46 percent to 85 percent between the end of September 2005 and the end of October 2006.[31] Moreover, at the end of October 2006, the dealers collectively had 3,900 active clients—of which 98 percent, on average, were using an automated confirmation system or were in the process of subscribing to one.

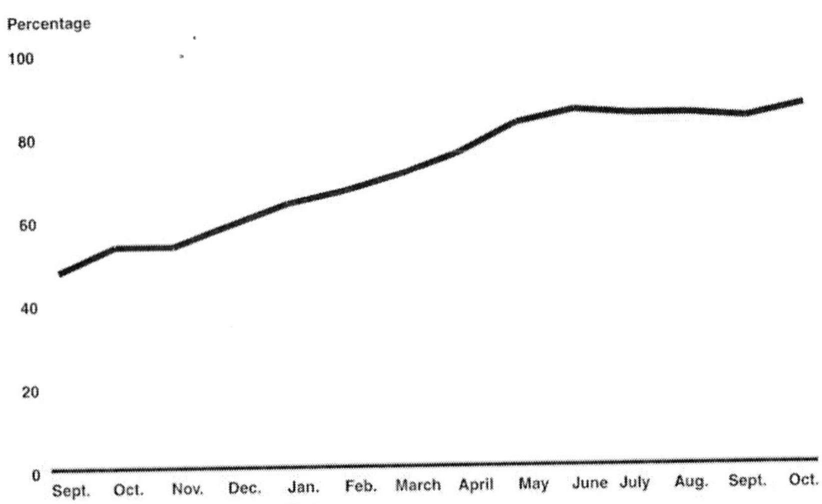

Source: GAO analysis of Markit Group data.

Figure 4. Share of Total Monthly Credit Derivatives Trades of the 14 Dealers Confirmed Electronically, September 2005 to October 2006

Second, the 14 dealers committed to electronically confirming all trades that could be confirmed electronically (i.e., contracts with standardized terms) within 5 business days of the trade date, by the end of October 2006. Deriv/SERV has continually expanded its capabilities to electronically confirm not only a wider range of products but also changes to existing contracts, including assignments. At the end of October 2006, about 90 percent of the total trades were eligible to be confirmed electronically, and about 94 percent of those eligible trades were electronically confirmed, according to the data provided by the 14 dealers. Of the trades confirmed electronically, 84 percent, on average, were confirmed within the stipulated 5 business days.[32] In addition, the industry has taken steps to help ensure that new products do not create backlogs. Officials at DTCC and ISDA said that they have formed industry working groups and revised certain procedures to reduce the time it takes to standardize the legal documentation for new credit derivatives, in turn enabling these products to be confirmed electronically by Deriv/SERV.

Market Participants Agreed to End Unilateral Assignments and Thereby Addressed a Key Factor Contributing to the Backlogs

An additional step taken to prevent further confirmation backlogs was to end the practice of unilateral assignments, which ISDA and market participants had been attempting to address since at least 2002. For example, ISDA published a novation agreement to document assignments in 2002, issued provisions governing credit derivatives assignments as part of its 2003 documentation standards for credit derivatives, and issued novation definitions and guidance on best practices for assignments in 2004. Despite such efforts, an ISDA working group found that market participants were using different practices to process assignments, increasing risks to counterparties and creating operational inefficiency and backlogs in processing trades.

ISDA officials told us that in early 2005 they had the working group start (1) to develop a protocol to streamline practices for dealers and end-users to follow to assign a trade and (2) to reach out to end-users as part of the effort. In the summer of 2005, the working group began circulating a draft protocol for comment. Shortly before the regulators initiated their joint action in September 2005, ISDA issued its voluntary Novation Protocol, and major dealers signed up for it. In their October 2005 letter to FRBNY, the dealers committed to finalizing a guide to support the protocol's implementation. By signing the protocol, a party seeking to assign a trade agrees to obtain the consent of its original counterparty through e-mail or other electronic means. Although the major dealers signed the protocol in September, some end-users were initially reluctant to sign, in part because they were concerned that dealers would not be able to consent to assignments promptly. In response, all the major dealers agreed to reply to assignment requests within 2 hours. By November 30, 2005, 2,000 market participants had signed the protocol.[33] Most of the major hedge funds have signed the protocol, according to officials from the Managed Funds Association, which represents the majority of the largest hedge funds.

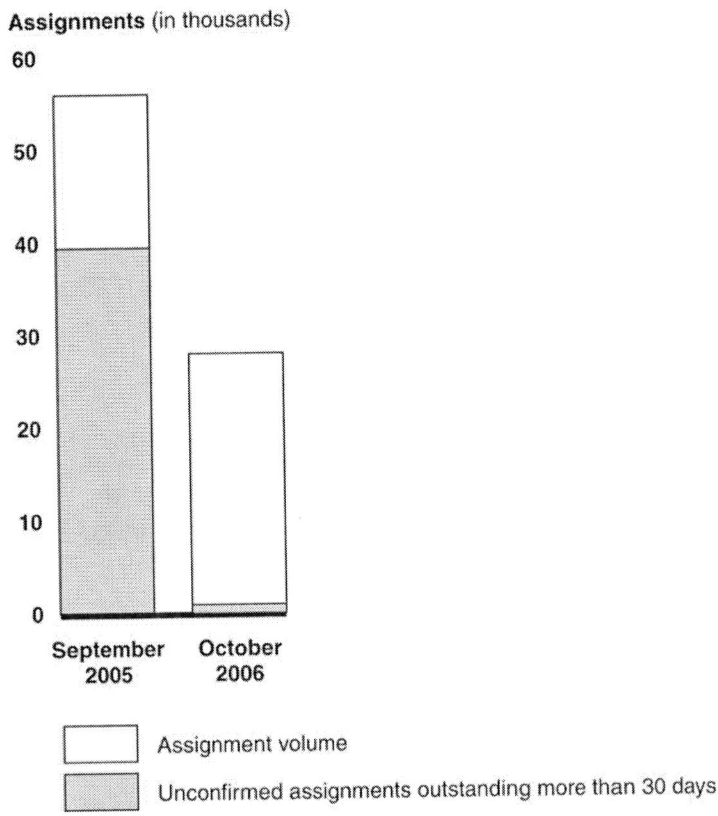

Sources: GAO analysis of Markit Group data.

Figure 5. Total Monthly Volume of Assigned Trades and Number of Unconfirmed Assignments Outstanding for More Than 30 Days for 14 Major Dealers, September 2005 and October 2006

According to some dealers and U.S. financial regulators, the widespread adoption of the ISDA Novation Protocol has effectively ended the practice of unilateral assignments, eliminating a key factor that had contributed to the backlogs. Because the vast majority of assignments become dealer-todealer trades, the protocol enables dealers to monitor each other to ensure that clients are complying with it. If a dealer were to allow its client to assign a trade without obtaining the original dealer's consent, the original dealer would discover the compliance failure when it discovered the assignment. To facilitate the confirmation of assignments, Deriv/SERV also expanded its system in mid-2005 to electronically confirm assignments. As a result of the ISDA protocol and automation of the assignment process, the number of unconfirmed assigned trades outstanding for more than 30 days declined from around 39,500 at the end of September 2005 to around 940 at the end of October 2006 (figure 5), even though the number of trades being assigned during this period generally increased.[34] From the end of September 2005 to the end of October 2006, the share of assignments confirmed electronically has increased from 24 percent to 82 percent.

Dealers Found Benefits in the Joint Regulatory Initiative

The dealers and other market participants we interviewed uniformly viewed the joint regulatory initiative as instrumental in reducing the backlog, automating the credit derivatives market's infrastructure, and bringing the industry together to address the confirmation backlog problem. The market participants noted that regulatory support was crucial in encouraging cooperation among dealers and end-users to address problems related to the confirmation backlog. Specifically, they said that regulators' involvement helped to persuade certain end-users to agree to adhere to ISDA's Novation Protocol. In addition, they told us that the joint regulatory initiative catalyzed industry efforts to move to automated confirmation matching services such as DTCC's Deriv/SERV— bringing about automation sooner than it otherwise would have occurred. Such intervention expedited the adoption of automated tools by end-users, enhancing dealers' efforts to implement such tools as Deriv/SERV. Additionally, the joint initiative led to the formation of a group composed of dealers that meets weekly to discuss, among other things, operational issues. Two dealers told us that this group has helped to resolve problems in processing confirmations and also allowed the dealers to hear the views of end-users.

Dealers and Other Market Participants Continue to Work to Reduce Backlogs, Diminish Operational Risks and Improve Market Infrastructure

While the dealers have made significant progress since 2005, they have continued their efforts to reduce backlogs and improve the infrastructure of the credit derivatives market. First, in addition to committing to confirm virtually all standardized trades electronically within 5 business days of the trade date, the dealers have committed to confirming all nonstandardized trades within 30 days after trade date. Because nonstandardized trades are complex and customized, such trades must be confirmed manually, according to ISDA officials. According to data provided by the dealers to regulators over the last 3 months, these trades have accounted for less than 10 percent of the total credit derivatives trading volume. According to regulators and dealers, these trades are generally complex and involve issues that require time to be legally negotiated before the trades can be confirmed. However, Federal Reserve and OCC staff have expressed concern that taking 30 days to confirm nonstandardized trades is too long and are continuing to work with dealers to reduce the confirmation time. The 14 dealers have made considerable progress in promptly confirming their nonstandardized trades, reducing the number of such trades remaining unconfirmed for more than 30 days from around 5,600 at the end of September 2005 to fewer than 440 by the end of October 2006. However, as the four additional dealers began providing their data after October 2006, the number of unconfirmed nonstandardized trades rose, reaching around 6,800 at the end of March 2007. To mitigate the risk of any unconfirmed nonstandardized trades, the dealers have committed to verifying the key economic terms of such trades informally within 3 business days of the trade date. As of the end of March 2007, dealers were meeting this commitment, on average, for around 54 percent of their nonstandardized trades.[35]

Second, under the joint regulatory initiative, the dealers have worked to reduce operational risks by committing to improvements in the settlement process for credit default swaps. For example, credit default swaps generally require that the purchaser of credit protection under a credit default swap deliver the bonds (or loans) referenced in the contract to the counterparty if the bond issuer goes bankrupt. In exchange, the counterparty pays the par, or face, value of the bonds to the protection purchaser. This settlement method avoids difficulties that could arise when the bonds are valued after a bankruptcy.[36] However, situations can arise in which the amount of bonds needing to be delivered exceeds the amount of outstanding securities.[37] For example, when the auto parts maker Delphi filed for bankruptcy in 2005, credit derivatives on its bonds and loans totaled an estimated $28 billion in notional amount, but Delphi had only $5.2 billion in bonds and loans outstanding. In addition to increasing the difficulty of meeting the delivery obligation under a credit derivatives contract, a temporary shortage of bonds also could cause the price of the needed securities to increase immediately following a default. To facilitate settlement in this type of situation, ISDA has developed protocols to allow contracts to be settled in cash rather than by delivery of the debt. Under this process, the bond's price is established through an auction, and the counterparties providing credit risk protection pay their counterparties in cash based on the difference between the bond's auction price and par value. Since 2005, ISDA has used its protocols to facilitate cash settlement in seven credit events involving U.S. firms. The protocols covering the first six credit events enabled cash settlement of only credit default swap indexes. In its most recent form, the protocol permits cash settlement in index, single-name, and certain other credit derivatives. ISDA plans to include the cash settlement mechanism in its revised documentation standards for credit derivatives in 2007.

Finally, DTCC is working with dealers and end-users to implement a central trade depository to automate trade processes other than confirmation and thus reduce operational risks. Under the joint regulatory initiative, the dealers committed to work with DTCC to create (1) a database to electronically store the official legal record of all credit derivative contracts eligible for automated confirmation, taking into account subsequent changes made to the contracts, such as assignments, and (2) a central infrastructure supporting the warehouse to standardize and automate post-trade processes over the life of each contract.[38] Specifically, the warehouse will support premium payment calculations and facilitate not only the bilateral payment settlement of electronically confirmed trades but also reconciliations for collateral management and credit event processing. DTCC launched the warehouse in November 2006, with all new trades electronically confirmed through Deriv/SERV automatically loaded into the warehouse. In addition, dealers are inputting their trade data for their existing credit derivatives contracts into the warehouse to create a complete database, and this effort is expected to continue through 2007. Two dealers told us that the trade input process is an extensive project, because around a million trades need to be inputted. DTCC also plans to expand the warehouse to support central payment calculation and settlement capability in 2007.

The Joint Regulatory Initiative Enhanced U.S. Regulators' Oversight of Dealers' Efforts to Reduce Their Backlogs

U.S. financial regulators were overseeing the operational and other risks at individual credit derivatives dealers through their continuous supervision and examinations. After the joint regulatory initiative, the industrywide data from the major dealers provided the regulators with more effective means of monitoring the resolution of the backlog and related problems.

Federal Bank Regulators Were Monitoring Efforts Taken by Banks to Address Confirmation Backlogs through Continuous Supervision and Examinations

The Federal Reserve and OCC were aware of the confirmation backlogs at banks and were monitoring efforts to address them before the joint regulatory initiative. Of the 14 dealers participating in the joint regulatory initiative, nine are U.S. or foreign banks. Five of the banks are chartered as national banks and individually supervised and examined by OCC through its teams of examiners. Each of these banks is a subsidiary of a bank holding company or financial holding company supervised by the Federal Reserve.[39] OCC staff told us that the five U.S. banks conduct around 90 percent of their credit derivatives activities within the bank, not in their holding companies or other subsidiaries. As a result, OCC bank examiners are primarily responsible for overseeing the banks' credit derivatives activities but coordinate their oversight with their Federal Reserve counterparts. Federal Reserve officials told us that their examiners also oversee the U.S. operations of the foreign banks that are major dealers participating in the joint initiative.

At the four national banks and one foreign bank we reviewed, management had become aware of the confirmation processing and backlog problems at their own banks primarily through internal audit reports or management information reports tracking outstanding confirmations. The timeframes in which the problems surfaced at the banks and were brought to management's attention varied, with one bank's management learning about the problems in late 2003 and another bank's management not until the summer of 2005. Nonetheless, according to examiners of these banks, as bank management became aware of these problems, they provided these audit or management reports or had discussions with the bank examiners supervising their institutions. Bank examiners told us that they continually supervise how the banks are identifying, monitoring, and managing their operational, credit, market, and other risks posed by credit derivatives and other products through reviews of internal audit and management reports, meetings with key bank officials, and examinations.

After learning of the backlog problems at the banks, the examiners said that they monitored each bank's efforts to address the processing problems and reduce the backlog, such as by periodically reviewing reports tracking the backlog, meeting with bank management and staff, or conducting examinations. Through their supervision, for example, the examiners reviewed the level of resources the banks were devoting to processing their credit derivatives trades. They also examined to varying degrees the credit derivatives confirmation process of four of the five banks between 2004 and 2006. For example, in 2004, examiners reviewed the progress that two banks were making in reducing their confirmation backlogs and in addressing the causes of the backlogs, including assignments of credit derivative trades. Based on examinations done in 2005, examiners directed two banks to develop plans to ensure that their infrastructures were capable of supporting the trading volume of credit derivatives, and the examiners said that the banks had developed such plans. In addition to focusing on the confirmation backlogs, examiners generally examined how well each of the five banks was managing its market, credit, and other risks associated with its credit derivatives activities. The examiners did not examine one bank's confirmation process because the bank was in the process of implementing a plan to address its backlog, but examiners monitored the bank's progress through informal reviews.

Bank regulators were also reviewing the banks' efforts to ensure the security and resiliency of their information technology systems. Managers at the four national banks we interviewed described taking various steps to ensure the security of their credit derivatives systems. For example, the systems used at these banks included restrictions on who could input or access data in the systems. Managers at these banks also were responsible for periodically reviewing and testing their staff's access rights to the systems to ensure that they were appropriate. According to bank staff, the security controls were reviewed or tested regularly by internal and external auditors—for example by conducting penetration tests in which auditors would attempt to obtain unauthorized access to the systems. In addition, the bank officials told us that they have taken steps to ensure the resiliency of their systems, including processing their credit derivatives in several different locations, creating off-site backup facilities, and developing disaster recovery plans. The examiners of these banks told us that they had tested or reviewed whether the banks were complying with controls designed to protect the security and resiliency of their information technology systems. For example, examiners told us that they reviewed managers' oversight of their staff's access rights to the systems and checked for testing of business continuity plans.

SEC Also Conducted Oversight of Credit Derivatives Confirmation Backlogs at Major Broker- Dealers

Unlike the bank regulators, SEC only recently began providing oversight of the credit derivatives activities of broker-dealers because such activities have generally been conducted in affiliates not subject to SEC regulation. According to SEC staff, the five U.S. broker-dealers that are active in the credit derivatives market generally book their trades in unregulated affiliates that are not subject to SEC supervision because they are not registered, nor required to be registered, with SEC.[40] However, in June 2004 SEC instituted its Consolidated Supervised Entity (CSE) program, under which large broker-dealers may qualify for alternative net capital rules in exchange for consenting to supervision on a consolidated basis by SEC.[41] The five U.S. broker-dealers engaged in credit derivatives trading applied for and were granted CSE status. Under the SEC's CSE program, SEC supervises the broker-dealers on a consolidated basis, with its prudential supervision extending beyond the broker-dealers to their unregulated affiliates and holding companies.[42] The five broker-dealers participating in the CSE program are also participating in the joint regulatory initiative.

Although aware that backlogs for OTC derivatives were an issue, SEC staff became aware of the extent of the credit derivatives backlogs at U.S. broker-dealers through continuous supervision and examinations conducted after these firms applied to the CSE program. SEC officials noted that although they were generally aware of the backlog in confirming credit derivatives through a study of the credit derivatives market conducted by the Joint Forum in 2004, they were surprised at the extent of the problem by the summer of 2005.[43] According to SEC staff, in 2005 risk managers and internal auditors at the CSE broker-dealers told SEC staff about the confirmations backlog and its potential impact on the credit derivatives market. Broker-dealer staff, during the summer of 2005, were periodically discussing with

SEC the resources they were devoting to reducing their backlogs and the associated risks. For example, one firm devoted about 30 full-time staff and 20 consultants to reducing its backlog, according to SEC staff. Supplementing this information about the confirmations backlog, examinations conducted as part of the CSE application process also assisted SEC in learning more about the nature of the backlog and related concerns. As part of the application process, SEC examined the firms' internal risk management systems and controls, issuing examination reports from November 2004 through January 2006. SEC targeted credit derivatives products within the scope of all but one of its five application examinations, choosing products that posed the greatest risks and represented the highest volume in the firms.[44] Examination findings related to the credit derivatives confirmation backlog included delays in issuing confirmations promptly after the trade date and discrepancies between confirmation documentation and output data from systems used to input trades. Broader examination findings included concerns that internal audits at some firms did not always document processes or sufficiently follow up on recommendations and that some firms did not accurately compute counterparty credit ratings, in some cases for hedge fund counterparties. The findings were shared with the firms, and SEC has monitored the firms' implementation of its recommendations.[45]

In addition to overseeing firms' credit derivatives backlogs, SEC staff told us that their CSE broker-dealer examinations conducted at the time of application also addressed the security and resiliency of these firms' information technology systems, including those that are used for credit derivatives activities. For example, at the broker-dealers, SEC staff reviewed reports by firms' internal audit departments on security and resiliency of information technology systems in general, as some of these systems handled credit derivatives transactions. In addition, SEC examinations included business continuity planning reviews based on draft interagency standards on protecting the resiliency of the U.S. financial system.

Through the Joint Regulatory Initiative, Regulators Are Obtaining Data to More Effectively Track Industrywide Progress on Reducing Confirmation Backlogs

Although both U.S. banking and securities regulators were individually overseeing aspects of U.S. dealers' credit derivatives activities, the joint regulatory initiative provided U.S. and foreign regulators with information that enabled them to better oversee the progress being made by the major dealers to address the backlog issue. While the individual regulators had data on the backlogs at the dealers under their supervision, no one regulator supervised all 14 major dealers and thus had data on the size of the problem across all dealers. Under the joint regulatory initiative, U.S. financial regulatory staff said that they told the 14 dealers what information they needed in order to track dealers' progress in addressing the backlog and related problems. Based on the capabilities of their management information systems, the dealers collectively developed a template to collect standardized metrics. The data include information on trading volume, trade assignments, trades confirmed electronically and manually, and confirmations outstanding based on length of time the trades remained unconfirmed. Under the arrangement, each dealer provides the standardized data to its primary regulator at the end of the month. For example, the U.S. broker-dealers provide their data to SEC, and the national banks provide their data to OCC. In addition, each dealer provides its data to Markit Group, which aggregates the data across all the dealers to preserve the confidentiality of each dealer's data and computes averages for the metrics, such as the average number of outstanding confirmations for the dealers. In turn, Markit Group provides the U.S. and foreign regulators and dealers participating in the joint regulatory initiative with a set of the aggregate data.

According to U.S. and foreign financial regulators, the aggregate and individual dealer data have provided regulators with an effective tool for tracking overall and individual dealer progress. According to U.S. regulators, using a template to standardize data collection has helped to ensure the comparability of the data across the dealers. The regulators also told us that the data are critical to the joint regulatory initiative, because the combined data provide transparency, enabling the regulators to track the progress of individual dealers under their supervision and helping each dealer to see how well it is doing relative to the average. Similarly, FSA officials told us that the aggregate data has provided regulators with a simple way to monitor the backlog level for the entire market and to compare individual dealers' backlog levels against the average. The officials also said that the common set of measures has helped to instill discipline among the dealers.

Under the joint regulatory initiative organized by FRBNY, the U.S. and foreign regulators are continuing to monitor the credit derivatives market and have expanded their efforts in September 2006 to address confirmation backlogs in the market for OTC derivatives based on equities.[46] According to dealers, it takes longer to confirm an OTC equity derivative trade than any other type of OTC derivative trade, because such trades are processed largely through manual rather than automated means because of the lack of standardized trade documentation. Based on data provided by the major dealers to the regulators, they had over 81,000 unconfirmed trades at the end of November 2006, with around 31,000, or 54 percent, of these trades remaining unconfirmed for over 30 days. In a November 2006 letter to FRBNY, 17 dealers committed to working with industry organizations to improve the efficiency of the equity derivatives market, in part through the greater adoption of automation.[47] Among other things, the dealers committed (1) to reduce by 25 percent the number of unconfirmed trades outstanding more than 30 days by the end of January 2007 based on dealers' highest level of outstanding confirmations from July to September 2006 and (2) to use at least one industry-accepted electronic confirmation service and one other such platform by the end of March 2007. U.S. regulatory staff told us that dealers met the first goal but that, as of April 2007, one dealer had not yet fully met the second goal. At the end of March 2007, the number of unconfirmed equity derivative trades outstanding more than 30 days rose to around 43,000 trades. U.S. regulatory staff said that the increase generally resulted from the inability of the manual processes used by dealers and end-users to confirm trades to keep pace with the increase in trading volume. The dealers also agreed to continue to provide the U.S. and foreign regulators with standardized data not only on credit derivatives but also on. OTC equities, interest rate, foreign exchange, and commodity derivatives.[48] U.S. regulators said that they wanted to track data across the major OTC derivatives products to ensure that work done in connection with equity derivatives does not hamper the ability of the dealers to process their other OTC derivative trades in a timely manner. Such data will assist regulators in monitoring the operational and other risks raised by OTC derivative products.

Given that individual efforts could not fully resolve the backlog problem, U.S. and foreign regulators we interviewed said that the joint regulatory initiative proved instrumental in ensuring that the problem was addressed. According to representatives of FSA, bringing together the various financial regulators from throughout the world was an approach that worked very well to ensure collaboration among regulatory bodies. Similarly, U.S. bank examiners told us that the joint regulatory initiative served an important role in getting the dealers to work collectively and by providing a level regulatory playing field. U.S. and foreign regulators and dealers are already applying this model to address similar issues in the OTC equity derivatives market.

AGENCY COMMENTS

We provided a draft of this chapter to the Federal Reserve, OCC, and SEC for their review and comment. The Federal Reserve and SEC provided technical comments, which we incorporated as appropriate.

Yvonne Jones
Director, Financial Markets and Community Investment

Congressional Requesters
The Honorable John D. Dingell, Chairman
The Honorable Joe Barton, Ranking Member
Committee on Energy and Commerce
House of Representatives

The Honorable Edward J. Markey, Chairman
The Honorable Fred Upton, Ranking Member
Subcommittee on Telecommunications and the Internet
Committee on Energy and Commerce
House of Representatives

The Honorable Bobby L. Rush, Chairman
The Honorable Cliff Stearns, Ranking Member
Subcommittee on Commerce, Trade, and Consumer Protection
Committee on Energy and Commerce
House of Representatives

The Honorable Jan Schakowsky
House of Representatives

APPENDIX I: SCOPE AND METHODOLOGY

To identify what caused the credit derivatives dealers' trade confirmation backlogs and how the backlogs are being addressed, we analyzed credit derivatives trading volume, confirmation backlog, and other transaction data provided by the major dealers to Markit Group, a provider of independent data, portfolio valuations, and over-the-counter derivatives trade processing. We also analyzed operations and other data that dealers provided to the International Swaps and Derivatives Association (ISDA), a global over-the-counter derivatives trade association. We conducted data reliability assessments for the Markit Group and ISDA data and determined that the data were sufficiently reliable for our purposes. We also reviewed reports and relevant publications from industry associations, industry working groups, international organizations, companies, and academics on the credit derivatives market. Of the 14 dealers participating in the joint regulatory initiative, we interviewed operations and other staff from three U.S. banks, one foreign bank, and four U.S. securities broker-dealers.[49] We selected these dealers to ensure that we included a range of characteristics, based on type of regulator (bank or broker-dealer), trading volume (high or low), and headquarters location (United States or foreign). We also interviewed staff from the Federal Reserve, including its examiners for two banks; the Office of the Comptroller of the Currency (OCC), including its examiners for three banks; the Securities and Exchange Commission (SEC); and the U.K.'s Financial Services Authority (FSA). We reviewed examinations conducted between 2004 and 2006 and other supervisory materials covering the eight dealers we interviewed and two other dealers that also participated in the joint regulatory initiative. In addition, we interviewed representatives from industry associations, including ISDA, the Managed Funds Association (representing hedge funds) and the Securities Industry and Financial Markets Association (representing securities firms, banks, and asset managers).[50] Finally, we interviewed officials from the Depository Trust and Clearing Corporation about its automated services for processing credit derivative trades and an official from a hedge fund.

To determine how U.S. financial regulators were overseeing the dealers' operational risk, including related information technology systems associated with credit derivatives activities, we reviewed examination manuals and other supervisory or regulatory guidance prepared by the Federal Reserve, the OCC, and the SEC. We also reviewed and analyzed supervisory strategies prepared and examinations conducted between 2004 and 2006 by the Federal Reserve and the OCC on the credit derivatives activities of five banks participating in the joint regulatory initiative. In addition, we reviewed and analyzed examinations conducted between 2004 and 2006 by SEC covering the holding companies of the five securities broker-dealers participating in the joint regulatory initiative. Also, we interviewed staff at the Federal Reserve, OCC, and SEC participating in the joint regulatory initiative. We also interviewed Federal Reserve or OCC examiners assigned to supervise and examine five of the banks participating in the joint regulatory initiative and SEC staff who examined the holding companies of the five securities broker-dealers participating in the joint regulatory initiative. Finally, we interviewed FSA officials to understand their efforts in identifying the confirmation backlogs and in participating in the joint regulatory initiative.

We conducted our work in Charlotte, North Carolina; Chicago; New York; and Washington, D.C., from August 2006 to March 2007 in accordance with generally accepted government auditing standards.

End Notes

[1] The Securities and Exchange Commission has antifraud authority over credit derivatives that are "security-based swap agreements," as defined in Section 206B of the GrammLeach-Bliley Act (15 U.S.C. 78c note). See, e.g., Section 10(b) of the Securities Exchange Act of 1934 (15 U.S.C. 78j(b)).

[2] The notional amount is the amount upon which payments between counterparties to certain types of derivatives contracts are based. For credit derivatives, the notional amount serves as the basis for determining the periodic premium payment made by one party to another in return for compensation in the event of loss from a default. In this regard, the credit derivatives market's notional amount is an indicator of the market's volume but does not necessarily represent the credit and market risks to which counterparties are exposed from their credit derivatives contracts.

[3] While organized futures exchanges recently announced their plans to offer credit derivatives, our report discusses only credit derivatives traded in the OTC derivatives market. In addition, although concerns have been raised about the potential for credit derivatives to raise systemic risk and be used to trade on insider information, our report addresses only the operational risks raised by credit derivatives.

[4] Market risk is the potential for loss because of a decrease in value of a credit derivative contract resulting from a change in market conditions. Credit risk is the potential for loss from the failure of the counterparty to perform on its credit derivative contract.

[5] Market participants can buy or sell credit derivatives for the purposes of speculating, arbitraging, or hedging, even if they do not have a direct exposure to the referenced entity.

[6] Credit events include, for example, failure to pay, restructuring, and bankruptcy.

[7] Hedge funds are generally considered private investment funds that are not required to register with SEC because of the limited number or sophisticated nature of their investors. Hedge funds commonly seek to achieve a positive, absolute return and invest in a wide variety of financial instruments, such as equity and fixed income securities, currencies, over-the-counter derivatives, and futures contracts.

[8] The top five end-users of credit derivatives are banks and broker-dealers (44 percent), hedge funds (32 percent), insurers (17 percent), pension funds (4 percent), and mutual funds (3 percent). Ross Barrett and John Ewan, *BBA Credit Derivatives Report 2006* (London: British Bankers' Association, September 2006).

[9] ISDA is a global trade association representing market participants in privately negotiated derivative transactions, which are commonly called OTC derivatives. Since 2000, ISDA has conducted an annual operations benchmarking survey of its members to collect performance data on operations processing of OTC derivatives.

[10] The market for OTC interest-rate derivatives includes interest-rate swaps and options as well as cross-currency interest rate swaps. For example, an interest-rate swap is a transaction in which one party pays periodic amounts based on a specified fixed rate and the other party pays periodic amounts based on a specified floating rate that is reset periodically, such as the London Interbank Offered Rate, or LIBOR (the interest rate paid on interbank deposits in the international money markets).

[11] 7 U.S.C. §§ 1 – 25, as amended.

[12] 15 U.S.C. 78c note.

[13] Under the Commodity Exchange Act, credit derivatives transactions generally are not subject to regulation if the transactions are between "eligible contract participants" (as defined in the act) and either do not take place on a "trading facility" or occur only on an electronic trading facility and are conducted on a principal-to-principal basis or are subject to individual negotiation by the parties. See 7 U.S.C. §§ 1a(12), 1a(13), 2(d), 2(g).

[14] The Securities Exchange Act of 1934 and the Securities Act of 1933 each exclude from the definition of security both "security-based swap agreements" and "non-security-based swap agreements," as defined in Sections 206B & C of the Gramm-Leach-Bliley Act (15 U.S.C. 78c note). See [15] U.S.C. 78c-1 and 15 U.S.C. 77b-1. However, SEC has antifraud authority over credit derivatives that are security-based swap agreements. See note 1.

[15] For a more detailed description of the regulation of banks and securities broker-dealers, see GAO, *Financial Regulation: Industry Changes Prompt Need to Reconsider U.S. Regulatory Structure,* GAO-05-61, (Washington, D.C.: October 2004).

[16] As identified in an attachment to the Federal Reserve Bank of New York's September 15, 2005, press release, the 14 dealers are Bank of America; Barclays Capital; Bear, Stearns & Co.; Citigroup; Credit Suisse; Deutsche Bank; Goldman Sachs Group; HSBC; JP Morgan Chase; Lehman Brothers; Merrill Lynch & Co.; Morgan Stanley; UBS; and Wachovia Bank.

[17] Through subsidiaries, DTCC provides clearance, settlement, and information services for equities, corporate and municipal bonds, government and mortgage-backed securities, and OTC credit derivatives.

[18] To economically terminate a trade, an end-user could enter into an equal but opposite trade that offsets the original trade. This approach has the disadvantage of building up large netted positions between market participants. Hedge funds prefer to avoid this outcome because it creates additional operational costs.

[19] Liquidity is the extent to which market participants can buy and sell contracts in a timely manner without changing the market price, and price discovery is the process of determining price on the basis of supply and demand factors.

[20] ISDA issued a standard confirmation form for credit derivatives in 1998, a set of definitions for credit derivatives in 1999, and a set of revised definitions in 2003 to reflect industry changes.

[21] Dealers also told us that their trade capture systems automatically feed the data on credit derivatives trades to their accounting systems. Thus, the dealers captured their trades in their books and records, which are used to prepare their financial statements.

[22] See, Counterparty Risk Management Policy Group II, *Toward Greater Financial Stability: A Private Sector Perspective* (July 27, 2005).

[23] In March 2006, the 14 dealers committed to verify the key economic terms of (1) standardized trades whose terms remained unmatched and thus unconfirmed for 5 or more business days after trade date and (2) nonstandardized trades within 3 business days after trade date.

[24] The original dealer would not necessarily benefit from the trade being assigned to a more creditworthy dealer. As an example, if a hedge fund unilaterally assigned a contract to a new dealer to realize a gain from the contract, the new dealer would now be exposed to credit risk relative to the original dealer. However, the original dealer's credit risk exposure to the hedge fund could increase after the assignment if the trade had been offsetting other trades that the dealer had with the hedge fund.

[25] The dealers also required hedge funds and other counterparties to periodically post additional collateral to cover their credit risk exposure resulting from changes in the value of the contracts.

[26] The ISDA Master Agreement sets forth standardized terms regulating general obligations of the parties, events of default, netting, early termination, transfer, currency provisions, and definitions. The Master Agreement and its related documentation are designed, among other things, to allow parties to establish under a single agreement all the "non-economic" terms—such as representations and warranties, events of default, and termination events—that will govern each individual derivative transaction between the parties. The specific "economic" terms of the individual derivatives contracts—such as the rate or price, notional amount, maturity, and collateral—are then negotiated and documented on a transaction-by-transaction basis. The Master Agreement contained a provision requiring the written consent of the other party prior to a party's assignment of its rights and obligations under the transaction to a third party. The Master Agreement, together with any amendments by the parties, is given effect in confirmations.

[27] Gay Huey Evans, Director, Markets Division, Capital Markets Sector Leader, Financial Services Authority, to Chief Executive Officers (regarding operations and risk management in the credit derivatives market), February 2005, http://www.fsa.gov.uk/pages/library/communication/pr/2005/022.shtml (accessed May 2007).

[28] Senior management of Bank of America; Barclays Capital; Bear, Stearns & Co.; Citigroup; Credit Suisse First Boston; Deutsche Bank AG; Goldman, Sachs & Co.; HSBC Group; JP Morgan Chase; Lehman Brothers; Merrill Lynch & Co.; Morgan Stanley; UBS AG; and Wachovia Bank; letter to Mr. Timothy Geithner, President, Federal Reserve Bank of New York, October 4, 2005, http://www.newyorkfed.org/newsevents/news/markets/2005/an051005.html (accessed May 2007).

[29] Senior management of Bank of America; Barclays Capital; Bear, Stearns & Co.; Citigroup; Credit Suisse; Deutsche Bank AG; Goldman, Sachs & Co.; HSBC Group; JP Morgan Chase; Lehman Brothers; Merrill Lynch & Co.; Morgan Stanley; UBS AG; and Wachovia Bank; letter to Mr. Timothy Geithner, President, Federal Reserve Bank of New York, March 10, 2006, http://www.newyorkfed.org/newsevents/news/markets/2006/an060313.html (accessed May 2007).

[30] The term "active client" was initially defined as a client that executed five or more Deriv/SERV-eligible trades a week, on average, for the past 3 months with an individual dealer. The standards were changed at the end of March 2006 to mean a client that executed one Deriv/SERV-eligible trade or more a week, on average, for the past 3 months with an individual dealer.

[31] At the end of March 2007, 86 percent of the total credit derivatives trades were confirmed electronically, based on data provided by 18 dealers to Markit Group.

[32] At the end of March 2007, about 92 percent of the total trades were eligible to be confirmed electronically, and about 93 percent of these eligible trades were confirmed electronically based on data provided by 18 dealers to Markit Group. Of the trades confirmed electronically, about 86 percent on average were confirmed within 5 business days after the trade date.

[33] ISDA subsequently issued the Novation Protocol II to allow new participants to the credit derivatives market to obtain the benefits of the original protocol. As of May 9, 2007, 268 market participants have adhered to the new protocol.

[34] After October 2006, Markit Group stopped providing data on outstanding confirmations for assigned trades.

[35] Although 18 dealers provided data to Markit Group on the number of their nonstandardized trades not confirmed within 30 days, only 12 of these dealers provided data on the extent to which they were verifying the economic terms of such trades within 3 business days after the trade.

[36] Since 1998, ISDA documentation for credit derivatives has provided counterparties with the option of settling their contracts in cash rather than by physical delivery. Under the cash-settlement option, price quotations are obtained for the referenced debt and used to determine the amount of the settlement payment. Most market participants have preferred the physical delivery option because of concerns about being able to obtain accurate quotations after a credit event.

[37] Because counterparties need not own the debt referenced in a credit derivative, they can enter into an essentially unlimited number of credit derivative contracts referencing such debt. In comparison, the amount of outstanding debt issued by a firm is fixed at any particular time.

[38] The potential expansion to other OTC derivative products will depend on market demand and input from the senior group working with DTCC.

[39] The Bank Holding Company Act of 1956, as amended, generally requires that holding companies with bank subsidiaries register with the Federal Reserve as bank holding companies. Among other things, the act restricts the activities of the bank holding companies to those the Federal Reserve determined, as of November 11, 1999, to be closely related to banking. Under amendments to the act made by the Gramm-Leach-Bliley Act, a bank holding company can qualify as a financial holding company and may engage in a broad range of additional financial activities, such as securities and insurance underwriting.

[40] Affiliates of broker-dealers that do not engage in the securities business within the United States are not required to register with SEC as broker-dealers.

[41] 69 Fed. Reg., 34428 (June 21, 2004). The rule release states that the rule amendments respond, in part, to international developments. Affiliates of certain U.S. broker-dealers that conduct business in the European Union (EU) have stated that they must demonstrate that they are subject to consolidated supervision at the ultimate holding company level that is "equivalent" to EU consolidated supervision. SEC supervision incorporated into these rule amendments is intended to meet this standard.

[42] According to the SEC, under this program, SEC staff conduct various supervisory activities with respect to firms subject to the program, including reviewing monthly, quarterly, and annual filings; holding monthly meetings with senior management at the holding company; and conducting examinations of the holding company, the broker-dealer, and material affiliates not subject to supervision by a principal regulator.

[43] The Joint Forum—comprising a group of international bank, broker-dealer, and insurance company supervisors that includes SEC—issued a 2004 study of the credit derivatives market. The study reviews financial stability issues associated with credit derivatives and recommends, among other things, that confirmations be promptly executed after completing a transaction and that the industry issue clear guidance on the time required to issue and receive confirmations.

[44] According to an SEC examination official, credit derivatives were not covered for one firm for a number of reasons. First, the selection of products to review for this particular examination came before the widespread concern about the backlog in credit derivative confirmations was known. Second, other products were also high volume and high risk at the firm. Third, most of the credit derivative trades were booked in this firm's London subsidiary and therefore regulated by FSA. The goal of the examinations was to capture

information about unregulated affiliates of the firm that had not previously been subject to review by any regulator.

[45] While the SEC examinations did not initially focus on the confirmation backlog specifically, this was included as part of the examination process when SEC became aware that the backlog in credit derivatives was an industrywide concern.

[46] OTC equity derivatives are financial contracts whose value is derived from an underlying equity or equity index. For example, an equity or equity index swap is a transaction in which one party pays periodic amounts based on a fixed price or rate and the other party pays periodic amounts based on the performance of an individual equity or equity index, such as the Standard and Poor's 500 Index.

[47] As identified in an attachment to the Federal Reserve Bank of New York's November 21, 2006, press release, the 17 dealers are Bank of America, N.A.; Barclays Capital; Bear, Stearns & Co.; BNP Paribas; Citigroup; Credit Suisse; Deutsche Bank AG; Dresdner Kleinwort; Goldman, Sachs & Co.; HSBC Group; JP Morgan Chase; Lehman Brothers; Merrill Lynch & Co.; Morgan Stanley; Société Générale; UBS AG; and Wachovia Bank, N.A.

[48] The dealers are providing standardized data on their OTC credit, equity, and interest rate derivative trades to regulators through Markit Group. A foreign exchange committee sponsored by the Federal Reserve Bank of New York is separately monitoring the foreign exchange derivatives market. Interest rate, foreign exchange, and commodity derivatives are financial contracts whose value is respectively derived from an underlying (1) interest rate, such as the London Interbank Offered Rate (the interest rate paid on interbank deposits in the international money markets); (2) currencies, such as the U.S. dollar and Canadian dollar; and (3) commodities, such as natural gas or gold.

[49] As identified in an attachment to the Federal Reserve Bank of New York's September 15, 2005, press release, the 14 dealers are Bank of America; Barclays Capital; Bear, Stearns & Co.; Citigroup; Credit Suisse First Boston; Deutsche Bank; Goldman Sachs Group; HSBC; JP Morgan Chase; Lehman Brothers; Merrill Lynch & Co.; Morgan Stanley; UBS; and Wachovia Bank.

[50] The Securities Industry and Financial Markets Association is the result of a merger between the Securities Industry Association and the Bond Market Association.

In: Financial Institutions in Turmoil
Editor: Carl D. Aspelin

ISBN: 978-1-60692-044-2

Chapter 4

COMMODITY FUTURES TRADING COMMISSION: TRENDS IN ENERGY DERIVATIVES MARKETS RAISE QUESTIONS ABOUT CFTC'S OVERSIGHT*

U. S. Government Accountability Office

WHY GAO DID THIS STUDY

Energy prices for crude oil, heating oil, unleaded gasoline, and natural gas have risen substantially since 2002, generating questions about the role derivatives markets have played and the scope of the Commodity Futures Trading Commission's (CFTC) authority. This testimony focuses on (1) trends and patterns in the futures and physical energy markets and their effects on energy prices, (2) the scope of CFTC's regulatory authority, and (3) the effectiveness of CFTC's monitoring and detection of abuses in energy markets. The testimony is based on the GAO report, *Commodity Futures Trading Commission: Trends in Energy Derivatives Markets Raise Questions about CFTC's Oversight* (GAO-08-25, October 19, 2007). For this work, GAO analyzed futures and large trader data and interviewed market participants, experts, and officials at six federal agencies.

---

* This is an edited, reformatted and augmented version of a U. S. Government Accountability Office publication dated October 2007.

WHAT GAO RECOMMENDS

As part of CFTC's reauthorization process, GAO recommended that Congress consider exploring the scope of the agency's authority over energy derivatives trading, in particular for trading in exempt commercial markets. In addition, GAO recommends that CFTC improve the usefulness of the information provided to the public, better document its monitoring activities, and develop more outcome-oriented performance measures for its enforcement program. CFTC generally agreed with GAO's recommendations.

To view the full product, including the scope and methodology, click on GAO-08-174T. For more information, contact Orice Williams at (202) 512-8678 or williamso@gao.gov.

WHAT GAO FOUND

Various trends in both the physical and futures markets have affected energy prices. Specifically, tight supply and rising demand in the physical markets contributed to higher prices as global demand for oil has risen rapidly while spare production capacity has fallen since 2002. Moreover, increased political instability in some of the major oil-producing countries has threatened the supply of oil. During this period, increasing numbers of noncommercial participants became active in the futures markets (including hedge funds) and the volume of energy futures contracts traded also increased. Simultaneously, the volume of energy derivatives traded outside of traditional futures exchanges increased significantly. Because these developments took place concurrently, the effect of any individual trend or factor on energy prices is unclear.

Under the authority granted by the Commodity Exchange Act (CEA), CFTC focuses its oversight primarily on the operations of traditional futures exchanges, such as the New York Mercantile Exchange, Inc. (NYMEX), where energy futures are traded. Increasing amounts of energy derivatives trading also occur on markets that are largely exempt from CFTC oversight. For example, exempt commercial markets conduct trading on electronic facilities between large, sophisticated participants. In addition, considerable trading occurs in over-the-counter (OTC) markets in which eligible parties enter into contracts directly, without using an exchange. While CFTC can act to enforce the CEA's antimanipulation and antifraud provisions for activities that occur in exempt commercial and OTC markets, some market observers question whether CFTC needs broader authority to more routinely oversee these markets. CFTC is currently examining the effects of trading in the regulated and exempt energy markets on price discovery and the scope of its authority over these markets—an issue that will warrant further examination as part of the CFTC reauthorization process.

CFTC conducts daily surveillance of trading on NYMEX that is designed to detect and deter fraudulent or abusive trading practices involving energy futures contracts. To detect abusive practices, such as potential manipulation, CFTC uses various information sources and relies heavily on trading activity data for large market participants. Using this information, CFTC staff may pursue alleged abuse or manipulation. However, because the agency does not maintain complete records of all such allegations, determining the usefulness and extent of these activities is difficult. In addition, CFTC's performance measures for its enforcement program do not fully reflect the program's goals and purposes, which could be addressed by developing additional outcome-based performance measures that more fully reflect progress in meeting the program's overall goals. Because of changes and innovations in the market, the reports that CFTC receives on market activities may no longer be accurate because they use categories that do not adequately separate trading being done for different reasons by various market participants.

Mr. Chairman and Members of the Subcommittee:

I am pleased to be here today to discuss our recent report on the trading of derivatives for energy commodities, including crude oil and natural gas, and the Commodity Futures Trading Commission's (CFTC) oversight of these markets.[1] The expansion of derivatives trading in energy markets, particularly by participants such as hedge funds, and rapid growth in trading off regulated exchanges have raised questions about the quality and quantity of reporting on and oversight of these trading activities.[2]

Specifically, I will discuss (1) trends in the physical and energy derivatives markets and their effect on energy prices, (2) the scope of CFTC's authority for protecting market users in the trading of energy derivatives, and (3) CFTC's monitoring and detection of market abuses in energy futures markets. I should point out that our review was intended to identify trends in both the physical and derivatives energy markets and to provide information on the current regulatory structure for energy derivatives trading, including analyzing the various perspectives of market participants on these issues.

While our report frames issues that need to be addressed, we do not offer specific policy solutions.

During the course of our review, we obtained and analyzed energy futures prices and trading volumes from the New York Mercantile Exchange, Inc. (NYMEX). Specifically, we collected data for crude oil, heating oil, natural gas, and unleaded gas from January 2002 through December 2006. We also analyzed data obtained from CFTC on market participants and the outstanding trading positions of different categories of traders. We reviewed publicly available information, including academic studies and reports and market data. Finally, we interviewed a broad range of market participants and observers, representatives of energy trading markets, and government regulators and agencies involved with the energy markets. This work was done in accordance with generally accepted government auditing standards.

SUMMARY

Physical and derivatives markets for crude oil, unleaded gasoline, heating oil, and natural gas have experienced substantial changes in recent years. Within the physical market, tight supply and rising global demand, ongoing political instability in oil-producing regions, limited refining capacity, and other supply disruptions all contributed to higher prices. While these changes were occurring in the physical markets, in the derivatives markets volatility of energy prices generally remained above historic averages for most of the period but declined during 2006 to levels at or near the historical average. Moreover, trading volumes for futures increased, at least in part because a growing number of managed-money traders (including hedge funds) began to see energy futures as attractive investment alternatives. Another change occurring during this time was the increased trading of energy derivatives outside the organized exchanges. Trading in these markets—specifically electronic commercial markets and over-the-counter (OTC) markets—is much less transparent than trading on futures exchanges, and comprehensive data are not available because these energy markets are not regulated. Given that the developments in the physical and derivatives markets were occurring simultaneously, determining their effect on energy prices is difficult. Continued monitoring of the various factors that affect market prices, and how those factors are changing, will be important in protecting the public and ensuring market integrity.

Energy derivatives are traded on futures exchanges and off-exchange in exempt commercial and OTC markets.[3] Exempt commercial markets are electronic trading facilities that trade exempt commodities, including energy commodities, on a principal-to-principal basis solely between commercial entities meeting certain eligibility requirements. In the OTC markets, parties meeting certain requirements can enter into bilateral energy derivatives transactions. Unlike the futures exchanges, which are subject to comprehensive oversight by CFTC, exempt commercial markets and OTC markets are not subject to general CFTC oversight, although CFTC can enforce the CEA's antimanipulation provisions and, where applicable, the antifraud provisions. To provide transparency about trading on the futures exchanges, CFTC routinely publicly reports aggregate information on trading by large commercial (such as oil companies, refineries, and other hedge traders) and noncommercial (such as hedge funds) participants that occurs on the exchanges. However, in the way the data are currently categorized, no distinction is made between commercial traders who use the exchanges to hedge their positions in the physical markets and those commercial traders, such as investment banks, who trade futures to hedge their trading in off-exchange derivatives. Given the developments and growth in the energy trading markets, questions have been raised over whether CFTC needs broader authority over the off- exchange derivative markets, particularly those involving exempt commodities and exempt commercial markets.

At an operational level, we also reported that while CFTC conducts reporting, surveillance, and enforcement activities in the energy markets to help provide transparency to the public, detect fraudulent or manipulative trading practices, and deter abuses, the effectiveness of these efforts is unclear. For example:

- Although CFTC monitors exchange trading activity through its surveillance program and gathers additional information from NYMEX officials, traders, or other sources to determine if further action is warranted, staff did not routinely document the results of these inquiries. Instead, they kept formal records of their findings only in cases in which improper trading was identified. As a result, CFTC may be limiting its opportunities to identify trends and its ability to measure the extent and usefulness of its monitoring activities.
- We also found that CFTC has successfully pursued energy-related cases, but we were not able to determine how effectively CFTC's enforcement activities were in identifying violations and deterring

misconduct because the agency lacked meaningful outcome-based measures.

Our report includes a matter for congressional consideration and three recommendations to CFTC. In light of recent developments and the uncertainty over the adequacy of CFTC's oversight, we recommend that Congress, as part of the CFTC reauthorization process, further explore whether the current regulatory structure for energy derivatives, in particular for those traded in exempt commercial markets, adequately provides for fair trading and accurate pricing of energy commodities. To improve the transparency of market activities and the functioning of CFTC's oversight, we recommend that CFTC reconsider how information it publishes in trading reports for energy products could be improved and CFTC has agreed to reexamine the classifications used in these reports. CFTC also agreed with our recommendations aimed at better documenting its surveillance activities and developing more outcome-based performance measures and has taken steps to implement them.

BACKGROUND

Energy commodities are bought and sold on both the physical and financial markets. The physical market includes the spot market where products such as crude oil or gasoline are bought and sold for immediate or near-term delivery by producers, wholesalers, and retailers. Spot transactions take place between commercial participants for a particular energy product for immediate delivery at a specific location. For example, the U.S. spot market for West Texas Intermediate crude oil is the pipeline hub near Cushing, Oklahoma, while a major spot market for natural gas operates at the Henry Hub near Erath, Louisiana. The prices set in the specific spot markets provide a reference point that buyers and sellers use to set the price for other types of the commodity traded at other locations.

In addition to the spot markets, derivatives based on energy commodities are traded in financial markets. The value of the derivative contract depends on the performance of the underlying asset—for example, crude oil or natural gas. Derivatives include futures, options, and swaps. Energy futures include standardized exchange-traded contracts for future delivery of a specific crude oil, heating oil, natural gas, or gasoline product at a particular spot market location. An exchange designated by CFTC as a contract market standardizes the contracts. The owner of an energy futures contract is obligated to buy or sell the commodity at a specified price and future date. However, the contractual obligation may be removed at any time before the contract expiration date if the owner sells or purchases other contracts with terms that offset the original contract. In practice, most futures contracts on NYMEX are liquidated via offset, so that physical delivery of the underlying commodity is relatively rare.

Market participants use futures markets to offset the risk caused by changes in prices, to discover commodity prices, and to speculate on price changes. Some buyers and sellers of energy commodities in the physical markets trade in futures contracts to offset or "hedge" the risks they face from price changes in the physical market. Exempt commercial markets and OTC derivatives are also used to hedge this risk. The ability to reduce their price risk is an important concern for buyers and sellers of energy commodities, because wide fluctuations in cash market prices introduce uncertainty for producers, distributors, and consumers of commodities and make investment planning, budgeting, and forecasting more difficult. To manage price risk, market participants may shift it to others more willing to assume the risk or to those having different risk situations. For example, if a petroleum refiner wants to lower its risk of losing money because of price volatility, it could lock in a price by selling futures contracts to deliver the gasoline in 6 months at a guaranteed price. Without futures contracts to manage risk, producers, refiners, and others would likely face greater uncertainty.

By establishing prices for future delivery, the futures market also helps buyers and sellers determine or "discover" the price of commodities in the physical markets, thus linking the two markets together. Markets are best able to perform price discovery when (1) participants have current information about the fundamental market forces of supply and demand, (2) large numbers of participants are active in the market, and (3) the market is transparent. Market participants monitor and analyze a myriad of information on the factors that currently affect and that they expect to affect the supply of and demand for energy commodities. With that information, participants buy or sell an energy commodity contract at the price they believe the commodity will sell for on the delivery date. The futures market, in effect, distills the diverse views of market participants into a single price. In turn, buyers and sellers of physical commodities may consider those predictions about future prices, among other factors, when setting prices on the spot and retail markets.

Other participants, such as investment banks and hedge funds, which do not have a commercial interest in the underlying commodities, generally use the futures market for profit. These speculators provide liquidity to the market but also take on risks that other participants, such as hedgers, seek to avoid. In addition, arbitrageurs attempt to make a profit by simultaneously entering into several transactions in multiple markets in an effort to benefit from price discrepancies across these markets.

SEVERAL FACTORS HAVE CAUSED CHANGES IN THE ENERGY MARKETS, POTENTIALLY AFFECTING ENERGY PRICES

The physical markets for energy commodities underwent change and turmoil from 2002 through 2006, which affected prices in the spot and futures markets. We reported that numerous changes in both the physical and futures markets may have affected energy prices. However, because these changes occurred simultaneously, identifying the specific effect of any one of these changes on energy prices is difficult.

Various Changes in the Physical Market Contributed to Rising Prices

The physical energy markets have undergone substantial change and turmoil during this period, which can affect spot and futures markets. Like many others, we found that a number of fundamental supply and demand conditions can affect prices. According to the Energy Information Administration (EIA), world oil demand has grown since 1983 from a low of about 59 million barrels per day in 1983 to more than 85 million barrels per day in 2006 (figure 1). While the United States accounts for about a quarter of this demand, rapid economic growth in Asia also has stimulated a strong demand for energy commodities. For example, EIA data show that during this time frame, China's average daily demand for crude oil increased almost fourfold.

The growth in demand does not, by itself, lead to higher prices for crude oil or any other energy commodity. For example, if the growth in demand were exceeded by a growth in supply, prices would fall, other things remaining constant. However, according to EIA, the growth in demand outpaced the growth in supply, even with spare production capacity included in supply.

Spare production capacity is surplus oil that can be produced and brought to the market relatively quickly to rebalance the market if there is a supply disruption anywhere in the world oil market. As shown in figure 2, EIA estimates that global spare production capacity in 2006 was about 1.3 million barrels per day, compared with spare capability of about 10 million barrels per day in the mid-1980s and about 5.6 million barrels a day as recently as 2002.

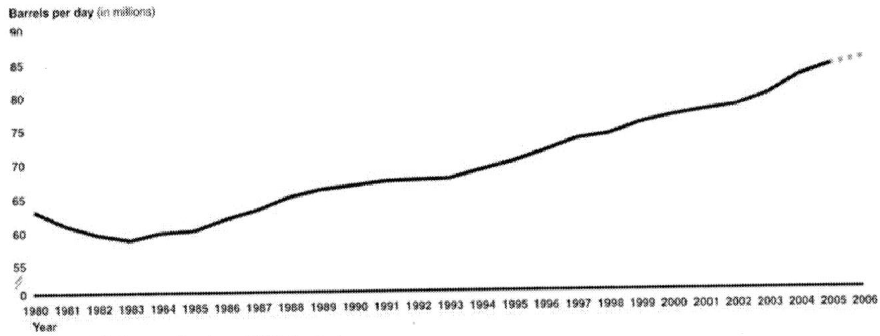

Source: GAO analysis of EIA data.

Note: The world oil demand data for 2006 represent a preliminary estimate.

Figure 1. Increase in World Demand for Crude Oil (Actual and Estimated), 1980–2006

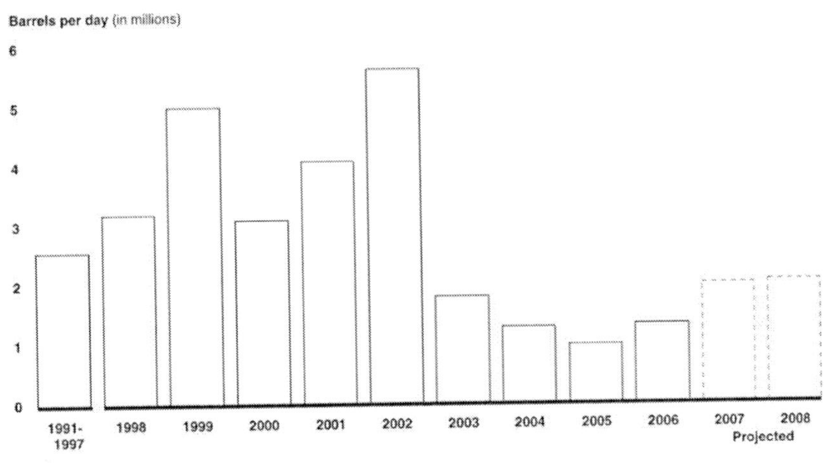

Source: GAO analysis of EIA data.

Figure 2. Estimates of World Oil Spare Production Capacity, 1991 –2008

Major weather and political events also can lead to supply disruptions and higher prices. In its analysis, EIA has cited the following examples:

- Hurricanes Katrina and Rita removed about 450,000 barrels per day from the world oil market from June 2005 to June 2006.
- Instability in major oil-producing countries of the Organization of Petroleum Exporting Countries (OPEC), such as Iran, Iraq, and Nigeria, have lowered production in some cases and increased the risk of future production shortfalls in others.
- Oil production in Russia, a major driver of non-OPEC supply growth during the early 2000s, was adversely affected by a worsened investment climate as the government raised export and extraction taxes.

The supply of crude oil affects the supply of gasoline and heating oil, and just as production capacity affects the supply of crude oil, refining capacity affects the supply of those products distilled from crude oil. As we have reported, refining capacity in the United States has not expanded at the same pace as the demand for gasoline.[4] Inventory, another factor affecting supplies and therefore prices, is particularly crucial to the supply and demand balance, because it can provide a cushion against price spikes if, for example, production is temporarily disrupted by a refinery outage or other event. Trends toward lower levels of inventory may reduce the costs of producing gasoline, but such trends also may cause prices to be more volatile. That is, when a supply disruption occurs or there is an increase in demand, there are fewer stocks of readily available gasoline to draw on, putting upward pressure on prices.

Another consideration is that the value of the U.S. dollar on open currency markets could affect crude oil prices. For example, because crude oil is typically denominated in U.S. dollars, the payments that oil-producing countries receive for their oil also are denominated in U.S. dollars. As a result, a weak U.S. dollar decreases the value of the oil sold at a given price, and oil-producing countries may wish to increase prices for their crude oil in order to maintain the purchasing power in the face of a weakening U.S. dollar to the extent they can.

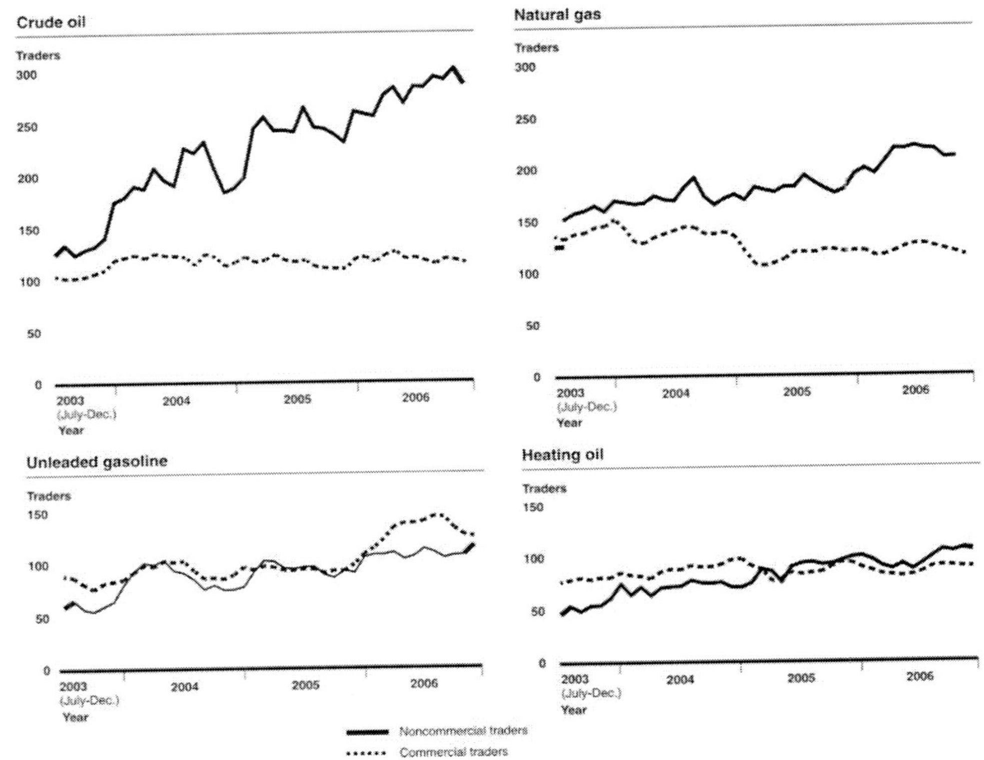

Source: GAO analysis of CFTC data.

Figure 3. Average Daily Number of Large Commercial and Noncommercial Traders per Month, July 2003–December 2006

The Effect on Prices of Relatively High but Falling Volatility and a Growing Volume of Trading in Derivatives Is Unclear

As you can see, conditions in the physical markets have undergone changes that can help explain at least some of the increases in both physical and derivatives commodity prices. As we have previously reported, futures prices typically reflect the effects of world events on the price of the underlying commodity such as crude oil.[5] For example, political instability and terrorist acts in countries that supply oil create uncertainties about future supplies, which are reflected in futures prices. Conversely, news about a new oil discovery that would increase world oil supply could result in lower futures prices. In other words, changes in the physical markets influence futures prices.

At the same time that physical markets were undergoing changes, we found that financial markets also were amidst change and evolution. For example, the annual historical volatilities between 2000 and 2006— measured using the relative change in daily prices of energy futures—generally were above or near their long-term averages, although crude oil and heating oil declined below the average and gasoline declined slightly at the end of that period. We also found that the annual volatility of natural gas fluctuated more widely than that of the other three commodities and increased in 2006 even though prices largely declined from the levels reached in 2005. Although higher volatility is often equated with higher prices, this pattern illustrates that an increase in volatility does not necessarily mean that price levels will increase. In other words, price volatility measures the variability of prices rather than the direction of the price changes.

Elsewhere in the futures market, we found an increase in the number of noncommercial traders such as managed money traders.[6] Attracted in part by the trends in prices and volatility, a growing number of traders sought opportunities to hedge against those changes or profit from them. Using CFTC's large trader data, we found that from July 2003 to December 2006, crude oil futures and options contracts experienced the most dramatic increase, with the average number of noncommercial traders more than doubling from about 125 to about 286. As shown in figure 3, while the growth was less dramatic in the other commodities, the average number of noncommercial traders also showed an upward trend for unleaded gasoline, heating oil, and natural gas.

Not surprisingly, our work also revealed that as the number of traders increased, so did the trading volume on NYMEX for all energy futures contracts, particularly crude oil and natural gas. Average daily contract volume for crude oil increased by 90 percent from 2001 through 2006, and natural gas increased by just over 90 percent. Unleaded gasoline and heating oil experienced less dramatic growth in their trading volumes over this period.

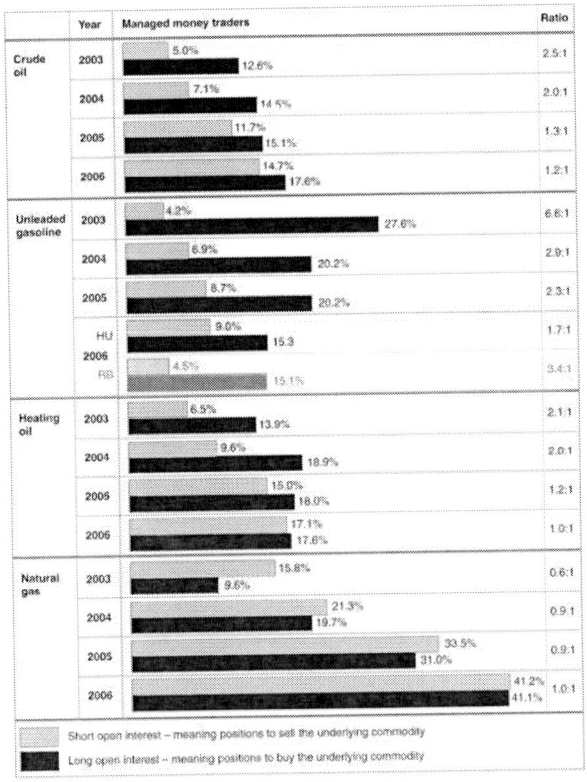

Source: GAO analysis of CFTC data.

Note: Data for 2003 were for July through December. The percentages indicate what portion of long and short open interest was held by managed money traders. For example, in 2004, managed money traders held 14.5 percent of the total long open interest for crude oil and 7.1 percent of the total short open interest. Because data are not included for all categories of traders, the percentages for these three categories within a particular period do not total 100. These data should be viewed as a general overview of managed money traders' positions. They do not provide insights into how traders' individual positions changed over time. Our data for 2006 include contract trading data for NYMEX reformulated gasoline blendstock (RB) and for the NYMEX gasoline contract (HU) that began to replace RB.

Figure 4. Percentage of Long and Short Open Interest in Futures and Options for Managed Money Traders, July 2003–December 2006

While much harder to quantify, another notable trend was the significant increase in the amount of energy derivatives traded outside exchanges. Trading in these markets is much less transparent, and comprehensive data are not available because these energy markets are not regulated. However, using the Bank for International Settlements data as a rough proxy for trends in the trading volume of OTC energy derivatives, the face value or notional amounts outstanding of OTC commodity derivatives excluding precious metals, such as gold, grew from December 2001 to December 2005 by more than 850 percent to over $3.2 trillion. [7]

Further, while some market observers believe that managed money traders were exerting upward pressure on prices by predominantly buying futures contracts, CFTC data we analyzed revealed that from the middle of 2003 through the end of 2006, the trading activity of managed money participants became increasingly balanced between buying (those that expect prices to go up) and selling (those that expect prices to go down). Using CFTC large trader reporting data, we found that from July 2003 through December 2006, managed money traders' ratio of buying (long) to selling (short) open interest positions was 2.5:1 indicating that on the whole, this category of participants was 2.5 times as likely to expect prices to rise as opposed to fall throughout that period, which they did. However, as figure 4 illustrates, by 2006, this ratio fell to 1.2:1, suggesting that managed money traders as a whole were more evenly divided in their expectations about future prices. As you can see, managed money trading in unleaded gasoline, heating oil, and natural gas showed similar trends.

Overall, we found that views were mixed about whether these trends put any upward pressure on prices. Some market participants and observers have concluded that large purchases of oil futures contracts by speculators could have created an additional demand for oil that could lead to higher prices. Conversely, some federal agencies and other market observers took the position that speculative trading activity did not have a significant impact on prices. For example, an April 2005 CFTC study of the markets concluded that increased trading by speculative traders, including hedge funds, did not lead to higher energy prices or volatility. This study also argued that hedge funds provided increased liquidity to the market and dampened volatility. Still others told us that while speculative trading in the futures market could contribute to short-term price movements in the physical markets, they did not believe it was possible to sustain a speculative "bubble" over time, because the two markets were linked and both responded to information about changes in supply and demand caused by such factors as the weather or geographical events. In the view of these observers and market participants, speculation could not lead to artificially high or low prices over a long period.

CFTC Oversees Exchanges and Has Limited Authority over Other Derivatives Markets

Under CEA, CFTC's authority for protecting market users from fraudulent, manipulative, and abusive practices in energy derivatives trading is primarily focused on the operations of traditional futures exchanges, such as NYMEX, where energy futures are traded. Off exchange markets, which are available only to eligible traders of certain commodities under specified conditions, are not regulated, although CFTC may enforce antimanipulation and antfraud provisions of the CEA with respect to trading in those markets. The growth in trading off exchange has raised questions about the sufficiency of CFTC's limited authority over these markets. These changes and innovations also have brought into question the methods CFTC uses to categorize published data about futures trading by participants in the off exchange markets and whether information about their activities in off exchange markets would be useful to the public. CFTC is taking steps to better understand these issues. Most importantly, it is currently examining the relationship between trading in the regulated and exempt energy markets and the role this trading plays in the price discovery process. It is also examining the sufficiency of the scope of its authority over these markets—an issue that will warrant further examination as part of the CFTC reauthorization process.

CFTC Has General Oversight Authority over Futures Exchanges, but Information on These Exchanges Reported to the Public Has Not Kept Pace With Changing Market Conditions

To help provide transparency in the markets, CFTC provides the public information on open interest in exchange-traded futures and options by commercial and noncommercial traders for various commodities in its weekly Commitment of Traders (COT) reports.[8] As we reported, CFTC observed that the exchange-traded derivatives markets, as well as trading patterns and practices, have evolved. In 2006, CFTC initiated a comprehensive review of the COT reporting program out of concern that the reports in their present form might not accurately reflect the commercial or noncommercial nature of positions held by nontraditional hedgers, such as swaps dealers.[9] A disconnect between the classifications and evolving trading activity could distort the accuracy and relevance of reported information to users and the public, thereby limiting its usefulness for both.

In December 2006, CFTC announced a 2-year pilot program for publishing a supplemental COT report that includes positions of commodity index traders in a separate category. However, the pilot does not include any energy commodities. Although commodity index traders are active in energy markets, according to CFTC officials, currently available data would not permit an accurate breakout of index trading in these markets. For example, some traders, such as commodity index pools, use the futures markets to hedge commodity index positions they hold in the OTC market. However, these traders also may have positions in the physical markets, which means the reports that CTFC receives on market activities, which do not include such off-exchange transactions, may not present an accurate picture of all positions in the market place for the commodity. In response to our recommendation to reexamine the COT classifications for energy markets, CFTC agreed to explore whether the classifications should be refined to improve their accuracy and relevance.

CFTC Authority over Exempt Commercial Markets and OTC Markets Is Limited, and Views Vary about the Sufficiency of Its Regulatory Authority with Respect to Off-Exchange Energy Derivatives

Now let me address some of the larger policy issues associated with CFTC's oversight of these markets. Under CEA, CFTC's authority for protecting market users from fraudulent, manipulative, and abusive practices in energy derivatives trading is primarily focused on the operations of traditional futures exchanges, such as NYMEX, where energy futures are traded. Currently, CFTC receives limited information on derivatives trading on exempt commercial markets—for example, records of allegations or complaints of suspected fraud or manipulation, and price, quantity, and other data on contracts that average five or more trades a day. The agency may receive limited information, such as trading records, from OTC participants to help CFTC enforce the CEA's antifraud or antimanipulation provisions. The scope of CFTC's oversight authority has raised concerns among some members of Congress and others that activities on these markets are largely unregulated, and that additional CFTC oversight is needed.

While some observers have called for more oversight of OTC derivatives, most notably for CFTC to be given greater oversight authority of this market, others oppose any such action. Supporters of more CFTC oversight authority believe that regulation of OTC derivatives markets is necessary to protect the regulated markets and consumers from potential abuse and possible manipulation. One of their concerns is that, due to the lack of complete information on the size of this market or the terms of the contracts, CFTC may not be assured that trading on the OTC market is not adversely affecting the regulated markets and, ultimately, consumers. However others, including the President's Working Group, have concluded that OTC derivatives generally are not subject to manipulation because contracts are settled in cash on the basis of a rate or price determined in a separate, highly liquid market that does not serve a significant price discovery function.[10] The Working Group also noted that if electronic markets were to develop and serve a price discovery function, then consideration should be given to enacting a limited regulatory regime aimed at enhancing market transparency and efficiency through CFTC, as the regulator of exchange-traded derivatives.

However, the lack of reported data about this market makes addressing concerns about its function and effect on regulated markets and entities challenging. In a June 2007 *Federal Register* release clarifying its large trader reporting authority, CFTC noted that having data about the off-exchange positions of traders with large positions on regulated futures exchanges could enhance the commission's ability to deter and prevent price manipulation or other disruptions to the integrity of the regulated futures markets.[11] According to CFTC officials, the commission has proposed amendments to clarify its authority under the CEA to collect information and bring fraud actions in principal-to-principal transactions in these markets, enhancing CFTC's ability to enforce antifraud provisions of the CEA.[12]

Also, in September 2007, CFTC conducted a hearing to begin examining trading on regulated exchanges and exempt commercial markets more closely. The hearing focused on a number of issues, including

- the current tiered regulatory approach established by the Commodity Futures Modernization Act, which amended the CEA, and whether this model is beneficial;

- the similarities and differences between exempt commercial markets and regulated exchanges, and the associated regulatory risks of each market; and
- the types of regulatory or legislative changes that might be appropriate to address any identified risks.

Given ongoing questions about the similarity of products traded on the markets and how and whether exempt markets play a role in the price discovery process and whether existing reporting requirements are sufficient, we recommend that Congress take up this issue during the CFTC reauthorization process to begin to answer some of these questions and the implications for the current regulatory structure in light of the changes that have occurred in this market.

CFTC Engages in Large Trader Reporting, Surveillance, and Enforcement Activities, but the Effectiveness of the Activities Is Largely Uncertain

CFTC provides oversight for commodity futures markets by analyzing large trader reporting data, conducting routine surveillance, and investigating and taking enforcement actions against market participants and others. The commission uses information gathered from surveillance activities to identify unusual trading activity and possible market abuse. In particular, CFTC's large trader reporting system (LTRS) provides essential information on the majority of all trading activity on futures exchanges. CFTC staff said they routinely investigate traders with large open positions, but do not routinely maintain information about such inquiries, thereby making it difficult to determine the usefulness and extent of these activities. According to recent data provided by CFTC, about 10 percent of the enforcement actions involved energy-related commodities. However, as with programs operating in regulatory environments where performance is not easily measurable, evaluating the effectiveness of CFTC's enforcement activities is challenging because it lacks effective outcome-based performance measures.

CFTC Oversight Includes Surveillance of Energy Futures Trading, but the Full Extent of Follow-up Activities Is Uncertain

CFTC conducts regular market surveillance and oversight of energy trading on NYMEX and other futures exchanges, focusing on detecting and preventing disruptive practices before they occur and keeping the CFTC commissioners informed of possible manipulation or abuse. According to CFTC staff, when a potential market problem has been identified, surveillance staff generally contact the exchange or traders for more information. To confirm positions and determine intent, staff may question exchange employees, brokers, or traders. According to the staff, CFTC's Division of Market Oversight may issue a warning letter or make a referral to the Division of Enforcement to conduct a nonpublic investigation into the trading activity. Markets where surveillance problems have not been resolved may be included in reports presented to the commission at weekly surveillance meetings.

According to CFTC staff, they routinely make inquiries about traders with large open positions approaching expiration, but formal records of their findings are only kept in cases with evidence of improper trading. If LTRS data revealed that a trader had a large open market position that could disrupt markets if it were not closed before expiration, CFTC staff would contact the trader to determine why the trader had the position and what plans the trader had to close the position before expiration or ensure that the trader was able to take delivery. If the trader provided a reasonable explanation for the position and a reasonable delivery or liquidation strategy, staff said no further action would be required. CFTC staff said they would document such contacts on the basis of their importance in either informal notes, e-mails to supervisors, or informal memorandums. According to one CFTC official, no formal record would be made unless some signal indicated improper trading activity. However, without such data, CFTC's measures of the effectiveness of its actions to combat fraud and manipulation in the markets would not reflect all surveillance activity, and CFTC management might miss opportunities to identify trends in activities or markets and better target its limited resources. In response to our recommendation, CFTC agreed to improve its documentation of its surveillance activities.

CFTC Energy-Related Enforcement Actions Generally Involved Allegations of False Reporting and Attempted Manipulation, but Its Program Received a Mixed Rating and Lacks Effective Outcome-Based Performance Measures

CFTC's Division of Enforcement is charged with enforcing the antimanipulation sections of the CEA.[13] The enforcement actions CFTC has taken in its energy-related cases generally have involved false public reporting as a method of attempting to manipulate prices on both the NYMEX futures market and the off-exchange markets. CFTC officials said that from October 2000 to September 2005, the agency initiated 287 enforcement cases and more than 30 of these cases involved energy trading. In the past several months, CFTC has taken a series of actions involving energy commodities, including allegations of false reporting, attempted manipulation of NYMEX natural gas futures prices, and attempted manipulation of physical natural gas prices.

Although CFTC has undertaken enforcement actions and levied fines, measuring the effectiveness of these activities is an ongoing challenge. For example, the Office of Management and Budget's most recent 2004 Program Assessment Rating Tool (PART) assessment of the CFTC enforcement program identified a number of limitations of CFTC's performance measures.[14] As is the case with most enforcement programs, identifying outcome-oriented performance measures can be particularly challenging.[15] However, as we point out in the report, there are a number of other ways to evaluate program effectiveness, such as using expert panel reviews, customer service surveys, and process and outcome evaluations. We have found with other programs that the form of the evaluations reflects differences in program structure and anticipated outcomes, and that the evaluations are designed around the programs and what they aim to achieve.[16] Without utilizing these or other methods to evaluate program effectiveness, CFTC is unable to demonstrate whether its enforcement program is meeting its overall objectives. CFTC has agreed that this is a matter that should be examined and has included development of measures to evaluate its effectiveness in its strategic plan and has requested funding to study the feasibility of developing more meaningful measures.

In closing, I would like to reemphasize the difficulty in attributing increased energy prices to any one of the numerous changes in the physical or derivatives markets. As I have mentioned, our research shows that the physical and derivatives markets have both undergone substantial change and evolution, and market participant and regulatory views were mixed about the extent to which these developments exerted upward pressure on prices. Because of the importance of understanding the potential effects of such developments in these markets, ongoing review and analysis are warranted. As the scope of CFTC's authority is debated, additional information is needed to understand what may need to be done to best protect investors from fraudulent, manipulative, and abusive practices. Such information includes

- how different or similar are the characteristics and uses of exchange and off-exchange products being traded and do these continue to justify different regulatory treatment;
- to what extent does trading in off-exchange financial derivatives affect price discovery and what are the regulatory and policy implications;
- how large of an effect are nontraditional market participants, such as commodity index funds, having in these markets; and
- are the changes in the energy markets unique or are such concerns also worth reviewing for other commodity markets.

By answering questions such as these, CFTC and the Congress will be better positioned to determine what changes, if any, may be needed to oversee these markets.

Mr. Chairman, this concludes my prepared statement. I would be happy to respond to any questions that you or other members of the subcommittee might have.

End Notes

[1] GAO, *Commodity Futures Trading Commission: Trends in Energy Derivatives Markets Raise Questions about CFTC's Oversight*, GAO-08-25 (Washington, D.C.: Oct. 19, 2007).

[2] Our analysis of energy prices and energy financial markets is generally limited to the time period from January 2002 through December 2006.

[3] Energy swap transactions also may be conducted off-exchange if they satisfy the requirements for excluded swap transactions contained in section 2(g) of the Commodity Exchange Act.

[4] GAO, *Motor Fuels: Understanding the Factors That Influence the Retail Price of Gasoline*, GAO-05-525SP (Washington, D.C.: May 2005).

[5] GAO-05-525SP.

[6] CFTC collects data on traders holding positions at or above specific reporting levels set by the Commission. This information is collected as part of CFTC's large trader reporting system.

[7] The Bank for International Settlements is an international organization that fosters international monetary and financial cooperation and serves as a bank for central banks.

[8] These reports include the number of traders, changes since the last report, and open positions.

[9] 71 Fed. Reg. 35627, 35630-31 (June 21, 2006).

[10] President's Working Group on Financial Markets, *Over-the-Counter Derivatives Markets and the Commodity Exchange Act* (Nov. 9, 1999). Members of group are the Chairman of CFTC, the Secretary of the Treasury, the Chairman of the Board of Governors of the Federal Reserve, and the Chairman of the Securities and Exchange Commission.

[11] As stated by CFTC, the purpose of the proposed regulation is to make it explicit that persons holding or controlling reportable positions on a reporting market must retain books and records and make available to the commission upon request any pertinent information with respect to all other positions and transactions in the commodity in which the trader has a reportable position, including positions held or controlled or transactions executed over-the-counter or pursuant to sections 2(d), 2(g) or 2(h)(1)–(2) of the CEA or part 35 of the commission's regulations, on exempt commercial markets operating pursuant to sections 2(h)(3)–(5) of the CEA, on exempt boards of trade operating pursuant to Section 5d of the CEA, and on foreign boards of trade (hereinafter referred to collectively as non-reporting transactions); and to make the regulation clearer and more complete with respect to hedging activity. The purpose of the amendments is to clarify CFTC's regulatory reporting requirements for such traders. 72 Fed. Reg. 34413..

[12] Section 4b of the CEA is CFTC's main antifraud authority. In a November 2000 decision, the 7th Circuit Court of Appeals ruled that CFTC only could use section 4b in intermediated transactions—those involving a broker. *Commodity Trend Service, Inc. v. CFTC*, 233 F.3d 981, 991-992 (7th Cir. 2000). As amended by the Commodity Futures Modernization Act of 2000, the CEA permits off-exchange futures and options transactions that are done on a principal-to-principal basis, such as energy transactions pursuant to CEA sections 2(h)(1) and 2(h)(3). According to CFTC, House and Senate CFTC reauthorization bills introduced during the 109th Congress (H.R. 4473 and S. 1566) would have amended section 4b to clarify that Congress intends for CFTC to enforce section 4b in connection with off-exchange principal-to-principal futures transactions, including exempt commodity transactions in energy under section 2(h) as well as all transactions conducted on derivatives transaction execution facilities.

[13] Section 9(a)(2) of the CEA prohibits "(a)ny person to manipulate or attempt to manipulate the price of any commodity in interstate commerce, or for future delivery on or subject to the rules of any registered entity, or to corner or attempt to corner any such commodity or knowingly to deliver or cause to be delivered for transmission through the mails or interstate commerce by telegraph, telephone, wireless, or other means of communication false or misleading or knowingly inaccurate reports concerning crop or market information or conditions that affect or tend to affect the price of any commodity interstate commerce...."

[14] The assessment includes a series of questions meant to serve as a diagnostic performance tool, drawing on available program performance and evaluation information to form conclusions about program benefits and recommend adjustments that may improve results.

[15] GAO, *Results Oriented Government: GPRA Has Established a Solid Foundation for Achieving Greater Results*, GAO-04-594T (Washington, D.C.: Mar. 31, 2004).

[16] GAO, *Program Evaluation: OMB's PART Reviews Increased Agencies' Attention to Improving Evidence of Program Results*, GAO-06-67 (Washington, D.C.: Oct. 28, 2005).

In: Financial Institutions in Turmoil
Editor: Carl D. Aspelin
ISBN: 978-1-60692-044-2

Chapter 5

INTERNAL CONTROL: IMPROVEMENTS NEEDED IN SEC'S ACCOUNTING AND FINANCIAL REPORTING PROCESS*

U. S. Government Accountability Office

April 1, 2008
The Honorable Christopher Cox
Chairman
U.S. Securities and Exchange Commission

Subject: *Internal Control: Improvements Needed in SEC's Accounting and Financial Reporting Process*

Dear Mr. Cox:

On November 16, 2007, we issued our report[1] on the U.S. Securities and Exchange Commission's (SEC) fiscal years 2007 and 2006 financial statements and on SEC's internal control as of September 30, 2007. We also reported on the results of our tests of SEC's compliance with selected provisions of laws and regulations during fiscal year 2007.

The purpose of this chapter is to present areas of SEC's internal controls identified during our fiscal year 2007 audit that could be improved.[2] This

* This is an edited, reformatted and augmented version of a U. S. Government Accountability Office publication dated April 2008.

chapter contains 14 recommendations to SEC to improve these internal controls and procedures. These recommendations are in addition to those we already provided to SEC as a result of our prior audits of SEC's financial statements.[3]

RESULTS IN BRIEF

Our November 16, 2007, report concluded that SEC had a material weakness[4] in internal control over its financial reporting process, and therefore did not maintain effective internal control over financial reporting as of September 30, 2007. This weakness is comprised of four significant deficiencies,[5] which taken collectively result in more than a remote likelihood that a material misstatement of the financial statements will not be prevented or detected. These significant deficiencies concern (1) the period-end financial reporting process, (2) disgorgements and penalties accounts receivable, (3) accounting for transaction fee revenue, and (4) preparing financial statement disclosures.

In addition to the material weakness discussed above, we identified three significant deficiencies in internal control, which although not material weaknesses, represent significant deficiencies in the design or operation of internal control. These significant deficiencies concern (1) information security controls, (2) property and equipment, and (3) accounting for budgetary resources.

As of January 2008, SEC had taken actions to fully address 3 of the 23 recommendations that remained open as of January 2007 from our audits of the agency's 2004, 2005, and 2006 financial statements.

We also identified one other internal control weakness that although not considered to be a material weakness or significant deficiency, we believe warrants SEC management's consideration as to whether additional actions are warranted. This issue concerns certification of employees' time cards, documentation of monitoring of time card certification, and approval of personnel actions.

Tables 1, 2, and 3 of enclosure I provide summary information on the status of recommendations from our 2004, 2005, and 2006 audits of SEC's financial statements, respectively.[6] Our 14 new recommendations follow the sections in which the corresponding issues are discussed.

In providing written comments on a draft of this chapter, the SEC Chairman expressed his commitment to remediate the control deficiencies this fiscal year and summarized SEC's corrective action plans to address GAO's recommendations.

SCOPE AND METHODOLOGY

As part of our audit of SEC's fiscal years 2007 and 2006 financial statements, we evaluated SEC's internal controls and tested its compliance with selected provisions of laws and regulations. We designed our audit procedures to test relevant controls over financial reporting, including those designed to provide reasonable assurance that transactions are properly recorded, processed, and summarized to permit the preparation of the financial statements in conformity with U.S. generally accepted accounting principles, and that assets are safeguarded against loss from unauthorized acquisition, use, or disposition. This chapter is based on the work performed during our audit of SEC's fiscal years 2007 and 2006 financial statements. We requested comments on a draft of this chapter from the Chairman of SEC. SEC's written comments are reprinted in enclosure II. We conducted our audit in accordance with U.S. generally accepted government auditing standards. Further details on our scope and methodology are included in our report on the results of our audit of SEC's fiscal years 2007 and 2006 financial statements[7] and are briefly summarized in enclosure III.

PERIOD-END FINANCIAL REPORTING PROCESS

SEC's financial management system does not conform to the systems requirements of Office of Management and Budget (OMB) Circular No. A-127, *Financial Management Systems*. Specifically, Circular No. A-127 requires that financial management systems be designed to provide for effective and efficient interrelationships between software, hardware, personnel, procedures, controls, and data contained within the systems. Circular No. A-127 further states that financial systems must have common data elements, common transaction processing, consistent internal controls, and efficient transaction entry, and that reports produced by the systems shall provide financial data that can be traced directly to the general ledger accounts.

SEC's period-end financial reporting process for recording transactions, maintaining account balances, and preparing financial statements and disclosures is supported to varying degrees by a collection of automated systems that are not integrated or compatible with its general ledger system. These automated systems' lack of integration and compatibility require that extensive compensating manual and labor-intensive accounting procedures, involving large spreadsheets and numerous posting and routine correcting journal entries, dominate SEC's period-end financial reporting process. Some of SEC's subsidiary systems, such as those for property and equipment and for disgorgements and penalties, do not share common data elements and common transaction processing with the general ledger system. Therefore, intermediary information processing steps, including extensive use of spreadsheets, manipulation of data, and manual journal entries, are needed to process the information in SEC's general ledger. For example, at period end, SEC personnel must extract the period's transactions from each subsidiary system and forward these data, in various formats, to accountants in the Financial Statements Preparation Branch, who use them to develop the journal vouchers (JV) necessary to include these transactions in period-end balances. These JVs are uploaded in batches to the core financial management system and posted to the general ledger. Once the general ledger is thus updated, a trial balance is created from which the accountants prepare the financial statements.

While the accounting staff make extensive use of desktop applications and workstations to perform calculations and to store the data used to prepare JVs and financial statements, little of the data processing that takes place during SEC's financial reporting cycle is fully automated. The information security controls necessary to prevent or recover from any inadvertent data corruption or to permit independent verification of the processing that has taken place have not been established for period-end accounting and reporting. SEC has developed a standard voucher template and a standardized review form for JVs, which were used to prepare the final fiscal 2007 financial statements. However, SEC's current period- end closing process taken as a whole complicates review of the transactions and greatly increases the risk that the transactions are not recorded completely, properly, or consistently, ultimately affecting the reliability of the data presented in the financial statements. Our identification this year of errors in SEC's calculation of disgorgement and penalty accounts receivable, discussed below, illustrates this risk.

The risk to data reliability is further increased because basic controls over electronic data, such as worksheet and password protection, change history, and controls over data verification, such as control totals and record counts, were not consistently used during the data processing between the source systems and the general ledger. In addition, currently, SEC's general ledger has several unconventional posting models and other limitations that prevent proper recording of certain transactions. As a result, SEC's year-end reporting process requires extensive routine correcting journal entries to correct errors created by incorrectly posted transactions in its general ledger. We also noted that SEC's documentation used to crosswalk individual accounts to the financial statement line items contained an incorrect routing to a line item on SEC's Statement of Budgetary Resources for SEC's yearend financial statement preparation process, which caused a material error in SEC's draft financial statements for 2007.

Also, SEC did not have detailed written documentation of its methodologies and processes for preparing financial statements and disclosures, increasing the risk of inconsistent and improper reporting and the risk that disruptions and error may arise when staff turnover occurs. Specifically, SEC did not have current written policies and procedures for over 15 areas, including investments, property and equipment, accounts receivable, other liabilities, and for the preparation of JV uploads into SEC's financial management system.

Recommendations

We recommend that SEC take the following actions to improve its period-end financial reporting process controls:

1. Integrate subsystems that process significant accounting data with the general ledger.
2. Until subsystems are fully integrated, develop and implement documented data reliability checks for data extracted from nonintegrated subsidiary systems, including spreadsheets. These data reliability checks should include supervisory review.
3. Prepare written procedures which describe explicitly the steps required to accomplish and document each significant activity in the general ledger closing process and in the generation of the financial statements, including related disclosures.

DISGORGEMENTS AND PENALTIES ACCOUNTS RECEIVABLE

As part of its enforcement responsibilities, SEC issues orders and administers judgments ordering, among other things, disgorgements, civil monetary penalties, and interest against violators of federal securities laws.[8] SEC recognizes a receivable when SEC is designated in an order or a final judgment to collect the assessed disgorgements, penalties, and interest. At September 30, 2007, the gross amount of disgorgements and penalties accounts receivable was $330 million, with a corresponding allowance of $266 million resulting in a net receivable of $64 million.

SEC's Phoenix system, which maintains financial data pertaining to disgorgements and penalties, is not integrated with SEC's general ledger system. To determine disgorgement and penalty receivable amounts, SEC downloads the data from Phoenix into a spreadsheet, manipulates selected data, and uses cell formulas to determine balance totals. This manual process for determining disgorgement and penalty balances presents high inherent risk in SEC's financial reporting process and demands effective compensating controls to ensure the accuracy and proper recording of related financial statement amounts, including effective supervisory review.

In our reviews of the interim June 30, 2007, and year-end September 30, 2007, balances of accounts receivable for disgorgements and penalties, we found errors in SEC's spreadsheet formulas resulting in overstatements of these receivable balances for both periods. Specifically, for the interim balance as of June 30, 2007, the spreadsheet formula did not reduce the disgorgement receivable for offset amounts that had already been paid by debtors to a non-SEC entity. SEC subsequently detected and corrected the June 30 errors, but then made different spreadsheet calculation errors in the year-end balances as of September 30, 2007, which we detected as part of our audit and which SEC corrected prior to the issuance of the financial statements. For example, SEC incorrectly included in its disgorgement receivable balance at September 30, 2007, amounts that had been terminated.

The main cause of these errors was the breakdown this year in the manual controls that were intended to compensate for the lack of an integrated accounting system for disgorgements and penalties, as discussed above.

Although SEC reviewed the journal entries posting the amounts to the general ledger, this review did not extend to the preparation of the spreadsheet SEC used to document the accounts receivable calculation at June 30 and

September 30, 2007, and therefore, was not sufficient to detect significant spreadsheet formula errors. For example, the review did not include (1) reviewing the detailed manual process of downloading data from Phoenix, (2) determining which Phoenix data elements to use and the rationale used in selecting those data elements, (3) reviewing the manipulation of selected data, and (4) reviewing the accuracy of the spreadsheet cell formulas used in calculating the accounts receivable balance.

Recommendations

We recommend that SEC take the following action to improve its disgorgement and penalties accounts receivable controls:

4. Develop and implement controls over the calculation of disgorgement and penalties accounts receivable, including the reliability of data downloaded from Phoenix and the accuracy of spreadsheet cell formulas and related methodologies.

ACCOUNTING FOR TRANSACTION FEE REVENUE

As one of its sources of revenue, SEC collects securities transaction fees paid by self- regulatory organizations (SRO) to SEC for stock transactions. SRO transaction fees are payable to SEC twice a year – in March for the previous months September through December, and in September for the previous months January through August. SEC calculates the fees due and bills the SROs based on actual transaction volume reported on a monthly basis by the SROs to SEC. Since the SROs are not required to report the actual volume of transactions until 10 business days after the end of each month, SEC estimates and records an amount receivable for fees payable by the SROs to SEC for activity during the month of September. At September 30, 2007, SEC estimated this receivable amount at $100.6 million based on previous months' transaction volume. Based on information SEC received from the SROs in mid-October concerning the actual volume of transactions, the amount of claims receivable at September 30, 2007, for activity during the month of September should have been $74.4 million. In addition, also in mid-October, one of the SROs submitted amended transaction volume to SEC for the months March, April, May, and June 2007, reflecting an additional receivable amount of approximately $75,000. In previous years, SEC made adjustments to reflect the actual volume of transactions; however, SEC does not have written procedures to help ensure that these adjustments are made as a routine part of its year-end financial reporting process. We proposed, and SEC posted, the necessary audit adjustments to correct the amount of transaction fee revenue and related receivable for fiscal year 2007.

Statement on Auditing Standards No.1, *Codification of Auditing Standards and Procedures*, which explains the accounting requirements for subsequent events, requires that events or transactions that existed at the date of the balance sheet and affect the estimates inherent in the process of preparing financial statements should be considered for adjustment to or disclosure in the financial statements through the date that the financial statements are issued. In addition, the concept of consistency in financial reporting provides that accounting methods, including those for determining estimates, once adopted, should be used consistently from period to period unless there is good cause to change.

Recommendations

We recommend that SEC take the following action to improve its accounting for transaction fee revenue controls:

5. Establish and implement detailed written procedures for recording transaction fee revenue and the related receivable, including procedures for recognizing data received after the balance sheet date but prior to issuance of the financial statements.

PREPARING FINANCIAL STATEMENT DISCLOSURES

In our review of SEC's year-end draft financial statement disclosures, we noted numerous errors including misstated amounts, improper breakout of line items, and amounts from fiscal year-end 2006 incorrectly brought forward as beginning balances for fiscal year 2007. For example, in its disclosure for *Custodial Revenues and Liabilities*, SEC improperly excluded approximately $320 million in collections. In another example, for its disclosure on Fund Balance with Treasury, SEC misclassified approximately $90 million into incorrect line items. Also, in its disclosure for Fiduciary Assets and Liabilities,

SEC's beginning balances for *Fund Balance with Treasury* and for *Liability for Fiduciary Activity* were each misstated by $8.9 million due to errors in carrying forward ending balances from September 30, 2006. We also noted numerous instances in which amounts reported in the footnote disclosures were not consistent with amounts presented in the financial statements or Management's Discussion and Analysis. SEC revised the financial statement disclosures to correct the errors that we noted in its final year-end financial statements for fiscal year 2007. However, correction of these errors required multiple revisions before all errors were properly corrected.

We believe that these and numerous other errors in the disclosures were due mainly to the lack of a documented timeline and process for completing the fiscal year 2007 financial statements and disclosures, including review of the disclosures. In addition, the cumbersome and complicated nature of SEC's financial reporting process discussed above did not allow SEC finance staff sufficient time to carry out thorough and complete reviews of the disclosures in light of the November 15 reporting deadline.[9]

Recommendations

We recommend that SEC take the following action to improve its financial statement disclosure preparation controls:

6. Establish and implement detailed written procedures for the preparation and review of the financial statement disclosures, including the comparison of financial statement disclosure amounts to related information presented in the current and previous year financial statements and Management's Discussion and Analysis.

Property and Equipment

SEC's property and equipment consists of general-purpose equipment used by the agency; capital improvements made to buildings leased by SEC for office space; and internal-use software development costs for projects in development and production. SEC acquired approximately $27 million dollars in property and equipment during fiscal year 2007. Similar to our last year's audit, during the course of testing fiscal year 2007 additions, we noted numerous instances of inaccuracies in recorded acquisition dates and costs for property and equipment purchases, as well as unrecorded property and equipment purchases. We also identified an internal control deficiency related to SEC's property receipt function and errors in amounts capitalized and amortized for internal-use software projects.

In 21 of the 53 unique personal property, leasehold improvement, and software items we reviewed, SEC recorded items in subsidiary ledgers or systems with incorrect acquisition dates which affected depreciation calculations. In 12 instances, the incorrect acquisition dates were related to software items SEC recorded on a quarterly basis, rather than in the month of acquisition. SEC has since changed from quarterly to monthly recording of software items. In the remaining 9 instances, SEC recorded items using the incorrect acquisition dates due to administrative errors. In addition to the 21 errors we identified, there were 5 instances for which SEC lacked reliable documentation of receipt date.

Also during our testing, we noted eight instances in which SEC incorrectly recorded property costs. SEC incorrectly recorded costs based on contracts or purchase orders rather than invoices. We also identified approximately $200,000 in unrecorded additions to SEC's telephone system. This omission from SEC's property ledger is in addition to approximately $2.5 million in telephone equipment which we identified in our previous audit and SEC failed to record during fiscal year 2006 or to correct during fiscal year 2007.

Contributing to the cause of these errors is that SEC does not have a formalized, documented process for comparing quantity and type of item received against the corresponding order for property purchases. Seven of the 23 personal property items we reviewed did not have sufficient evidence of this comparison. SEC's draft Property Management Manual, scheduled for implementation during calendar year 2008, calls for the Assistant Property Management Officer to "ensure that receipts are matched against Purchase Orders as a condition of acceptance and payment." However, SEC's guidance does not prescribe a standardized form to document this review. A lack of standardized, documented review procedures increases the risk that SEC will accept, pay for, and record property not yet received.

SEC's property subsidiary system is not integrated with the general ledger. SEC uses a spreadsheet to calculate depreciation and amortization related to additions to existing property items. We found formula errors in these calculations, which we communicated to SEC in September 2007. SEC subsequently corrected these systemic errors, but this situation highlights the risks associated with the lack of an integrated financial management system and the need for additional compensating control procedures.

Overall, these systemic errors did not materially affect the balances reported for property and equipment or the corresponding depreciation and amortization expense amounts in SEC's financial statements for fiscal year 2007. However, these conditions evidence a significant deficiency in control over the recording of property and equipment that affects the reliability of its recorded balances for property and equipment. Further, SEC's lack of an integrated financial management system for accounting for property and equipment, as discussed above, requires compensating procedures, which were not effective, to ensure that manual calculations, such as those for depreciation and amortization, are accurate. Until it has a systemic process that incorporates effective controls over receiving, recording, capitalizing, and amortizing property and equipment purchases, SEC will not have sufficient assurance over the accuracy and completeness of its reported balances for property and equipment.

Recommendations

We recommend that SEC, in addition to our previous recommendations in this area which are included in enclosure I, take the following actions to improve its property and equipment controls:

7. Establish and implement controls over invoiced property costs and dates to ensure that property and equipment acquisitions are accurately recorded in the relevant subsidiary ledgers for personal property, leasehold improvement, and software.
8. Establish and implement controls to ensure proper calculation of depreciation and amortization of additions to existing items over the remaining useful lives of the associated items.

Accounting for Budgetary Resources

For fiscal year 2007, SEC incurred $877 million in obligations, which represents legal liabilities against funds available to SEC to pay for goods and services ordered. At September 30, 2007, SEC reported that the amount of budgetary resources obligated for undelivered orders was $255 million, which reflects obligations for goods or services that had not been delivered or received as of that date. In our testing of undelivered order transactions for this year's audit, we identified several concerns over SEC's accounting for obligations and undelivered orders. Specifically, we found numerous instances in which SEC (1) recorded obligations prior to having documentary evidence of a binding agreement for the goods or services, (2) recorded invalid undelivered order transactions due to an incorrect posting configuration in SEC's general ledger, and (3) made errors in recording new obligations and deobligations due to the use of incorrect accounts and by posting incorrect amounts in the general ledger.

During our interim and year-end testing of obligation activity we identified 12 instances in which SEC recorded obligations prior to the signing execution of a written contract. We also found one instance where funds were obligated with the expectation that a contract would be ratified, but the ratification request was later denied. SEC does not have policies or internal controls to prevent recording of obligations that are not valid. Recording obligations prior to having documentary evidence of a binding agreement for the goods and services is a violation of the recording statute,[10] and may result in funds being reserved unnecessarily and therefore made unavailable for other uses should the agreement not materialize. Early recording of obligations also may result in charging incorrect fiscal year funds for an agreement executed in a later fiscal year.

We noted approximately $76 million in general ledger posting errors, including both upward and downward adjustments to prior-year undelivered orders. Due to a system error, deobligations of funds in 1-year Treasury Account Fund Symbols (TAFS) did not process correctly, materially overstating both the upward and downward adjustment accounts. This process results in the need to routinely correct entries. Extensive reviews of the adjusting journal entries are needed to compensate for the system limitations. This process unnecessarily complicated transaction processing and caused SEC to misstate various line items on the Statement of Budgetary Resources. While SEC identified and manually corrected this error for fiscal year 2007, there is a risk that, if the error is not corrected in the financial management system, SEC could materially misstate its Statement of Budgetary Resources in future periods.

In addition to the systemic posting errors, we noted several additional errors impacting SEC's budgetary accounting. SEC incorrectly recorded new obligations by posting incorrect amounts in the general ledger. For example, in 8 of the 147 items we tested, SEC recorded obligations at incorrect amounts, due to either recording obligations early using the requisition amounts instead of the final contract amounts or making administrative errors. In addition, SEC made errors in recording deobligations due to administrative errors in posting amounts to the incorrect accounts. We identified approximately $1 million in net errors in which SEC's financial management system did not properly process downward adjustments of prior-year funds in no-year TAFS. SEC's financial management system improperly treats all budget years maintained in this fund as current-year funds, thereby understating downward adjustments for those years.

Overall, the majority of exceptions related to these issues were corrected by SEC through adjusting journal entries. While the remaining uncorrected amounts did not materially affect the balances on the Statement of Budgetary Resources at September 30, 2007, ineffective processes that caused these errors constitute a significant deficiency in SEC's internal control over recording and reporting of obligations, and put SEC at risk that the amounts recorded in the general ledger and reported on SEC's Statement of Budgetary Resources are misstated.

Recommendations

We recommend that SEC take the following actions to improve its budgetary accounting controls:

9. Correct general ledger system configurations to properly account for upward and downward adjustments of prior-years' undelivered orders in accordance with the U.S. Standard General Ledger.
10. Establish and implement controls over obligation-related entries (including original obligations, corrections, and deobligations) to ensure the use of correct *U.S. Standard General Ledger* accounts and the recording of correct amounts.
11. Clarify administrative control of funds guidance and document the responsibilities of the staff performing obligation-related activities with regard to recording obligations in accordance with the recording statute.
12. Establish and implement controls to ensure that SEC staff adheres to existing policies and procedures to prevent violations of the recording statute.

Other Issues

Although not considered to be a significant deficiency, the following weaknesses warrant management's consideration.

Certification of Employees' Time Cards, Documentation of Monitoring of Time Card Certification, and Approval of Personnel Actions

We identified three internal control issues with regard to payroll transactions. Specifically, these issues concern the certification of employees' time cards, the documentation of monitoring procedures over time card certification, and the approval of personnel actions.

During our fiscal year 2007 audit, we noted nine instances in which time cards were improperly certified by lower-level employees. We previously noted concerns with administrative officers approving time cards for higher-level employees on a regular basis during fiscal year 2006.

SEC time and attendance (T&A) policies instruct that each organization designate timekeepers who are responsible for initiating time cards and designate supervisors or managers as certifiers who have responsibility for reviewing the accuracy of time cards. The T&A instructions state that administrative officers may certify time cards for higher-level officials for emergency situations only.

As noted above, during our fiscal year 2006 audit, we found cases in which administrative officers improperly certified time cards of higher-level employees on a regular basis. We communicated this finding to SEC officials in August 2006. In response to our finding, SEC's Office of Human Resources (OHR) began to actively monitor the level of employees certifying time cards to determine compliance with its current stated policy. During our fiscal year 2007 audit, we observed SEC's monitoring of time card certifications for a particular pay period. However, SEC did not document when, or what, they were monitoring or the results of what they found. Lack of documentation of these control procedures may delay or prevent SEC management from becoming aware that monitoring of time card certifications has ceased or that there are instances of employees certifying higher-level officials' time cards on an other than emergency basis.

Consistent with GAO's *Standards for Internal Control in the Federal Government*,[11] internal control should be clearly documented, and the documentation readily available for examination. According to SEC's OUR, development of this documentation will be undertaken after determining how best to document its monitoring of time card certifications.

Also, during our interim testing of payroll, we compared selected personnel actions on the employee roster against Standard Form-50 ("Notification of Personnel Action") documentation and identified one employee who approved a valid personnel action for an increase in his own salary without evidence of additional review from another level of management. According to GAO's *Standards for Internal Control in the Federal Government,* "key duties and responsibilities need to be divided or segregated among different people to reduce the risk of error, waste, or fraud." In addition, "no one individual should control all key aspects of a transaction or event." Because one individual performed incompatible duties regarding his own personnel actions, there is a risk of fraud.

Recommendations

We recommend that SEC, in addition to our previous recommendations in this area which are included in enclosure I, take the following actions to improve its payroll controls:

13. Establish and implement procedures for documenting evidence of monitoring of time card certifications and include procedures to document any identified exceptions.
14. Segregate key responsibilities over the approval of personnel actions so that no one individual approves his own personnel action.

AGENCY COMMENTS

In providing written comments on a draft of this chapter, the SEC Chairman stated his commitment to remediate the control deficiencies this fiscal year. The SEC Chairman reported several actions SEC has already taken to address financial reporting processes, documentation, and controls, and summarized SEC's Corrective Action Plan (CAP) to address GAO's recommendations. The Chairman cited developing a fully integrated financial management system as the keystone of SEC's CAP to remediate the deficiencies relative to system integration, noncompliance with *U.S. Standard*

General Ledger (SGL) at the transaction level, and compensating controls. The Chairman noted that remediation strategies are presented in the CAP in terms of both short-term solutions that are expected to be achieved this fiscal year and long-term solutions that will achieve greater efficiency, effectiveness, and risk mitigation by minimizing reliance on detective controls. Specifically, the short-term strategies are to develop or improve process documentation; overlay manual processes with additional compensating controls as needed; implement SGL-compliant posting models; and implement process improvements to enhance efficiencies and effectiveness of internal controls and monitor performance. The long-term strategies are to automate integration of financial management systems and to comply with the SGL at the transaction level. We will evaluate SEC's actions and initiatives during our fiscal year 2008 audit.

SEC's written comments are reprinted in enclosure II of this chapter.

This chapter contains recommendations to you. The head of a federal agency is required by 31 U.S.C. § 720 to submit a written statement on actions taken on the recommendations to the Senate Committee on Homeland Security and Governmental Affairs and the House Committee on Oversight and Government Reform not later than 60 days from the date of this chapter. A written statement also must be sent to the House and Senate Committees on Appropriations with agency's first request for appropriations made more than 60 days after the date of this chapter.

Sincerely yours,

Jeanette M. Franzel
Director
Financial Management and Assurance
Enclosures – 3

ENCLOSURE I

Table 1. Recommendations from 2004 Audit Reported as Open at Conclusion of 2006 Audit

Audit area/recommendation	Status of recommendation	
	Closed	Open
Disgorgements and penalties		
1. Implement a system that is integrated with the accounting system or that provides the necessary input to the accounting system to facilitate timely, accurate, and efficient recording and reporting of disgorgement and penalty activity.		X
2. Implement controls so that the ongoing activities involving disgorgements and penalties are properly, accurately, and timely recorded in the accounting system.		X
3. Develop and implement written policies covering the procedures, doc-umentation, systems, and responsible personnel involved in recording and reporting disgorgement and penalty financial information. The written procedures should also address quality control and managerial review responsibilities and documentation of such a review.		X
Financial statement preparation and reporting		
4. Consider a "formal closing" of all accounts at an interim date(s), which will reduce the level of accounting activity and analysis required at year end. The formal closing entails ensuring that all transactions are recorded in the proper period through month's end.	X	
5. Develop or acquire an integrated financial management system to prov-ide timely and accurate recording of financial data for financial reporti-ng and management decision making.		X
Property and equipment leases		
6. Review all existing leases for property and equipment to determine if they should be capitalized or expensed and make any necessary adjusttments to the related general ledger balances.		X
7. Develop policies and procedures to properly account for future property and equipment leases on an ongoing basis.		X
Closing recommendation to address Federal Managers' Financial Integrity Act weaknesses		
8. Require documented support and review of SEC's corrective actions to provide evidence that actions taken in response to audit recommenddations fully correct identified deficiencies prior to closing out the audit issues in the tracking system.		X

Source: GAO.

Note: Recommendations made in GAO-05-691R and GAO-05-693R.

Table 2. Recommendations from 2005 Audit Reported as Open at Conclusion of 2006 Audit

Audit area/recommendation	Status of recommendation	
	Closed	Open
Financial statement preparation and reporting		
1. Determine cutoff dates for significant account balances that are both appropriate and practical to facilitate interim financial reporting and meeting year-end financial reporting deadlines.	X	
Disgorgements and penalties		
Develop, document in writing, and implement comprehen-sive policies, procedures, and controls over disgorgement and penalty transactions that include the following (see items 2-5):		
2.. An accounting policy for disgorgements and penalties that will provide SEC management with reasonable assurance that the subsidiary ledger for disgorgement/penalty receivables is accurate and complete.		X
3. The type of documentation and procedures needed to record the termination or waiver of a debt and the proper notification and communication for approved terminations and waivers, such that management has assurance that only valid and approved terminations are recorded.		X
4. The recording of activity by case for fiduciary balances, including monthly reconciliations and management review, to ensure that balances by case are accurate.		X
5. The initiation, recording, and monitoring of investments, including the monthly reconciliation of investment activity, to provide assurance that these fiduciary amounts are accurate and complete.		X
Responsibilities of contracting officer's technical representative (COTR)		
6. Clarify guidance regarding policies and procedures (as described in SECR 10-8 and SECR 10-15) for the COTR's responsibilities and take actions to help ensure existing policies and procedures are being followed consistently.		X
Internal review of filing fee calculations		
7. Take action to help ensure that its policy on recalculating fee-bearing filing amounts is consistently followed.		X
8. Take action to help ensure that the recalculation of the required filing fees is clearly documented.		X
Compliance with Prompt Payment Act		
9. Take action to help ensure that the policy requiring the timely return of improper invoices to the vendor to allow for timely payment is followed.	X	

Source: GAO.

Note: Recommendations from GAO-06-459R.

Table 3. Recommendations from 2006 Audit

Audit area/recommendation	Status of recommendation	
	Closed	**Open**
Property and equipment		
1. Include, in its updated property management policies, deta-iled procedures for recording proper acquisition costs and dates in its asset-tracking system, and take steps to ensure that these procedures are being consi-stently implemented.		X
2. Implement procedures requiring periodic comparisons of related details in disbursement and property/equipment subsidiary records to identify any unrecorded purchases that satisfy established capitalization criteria.		X
3. Implement procedures to ensure that internal use soft-ware project managers have a complete and consistent understand-ding of the requirements that should govern compilation of cost data submitted for capitalization, including considera-tion of joint Office of Information Technology and Office of Financial Management (OFM) training to software project managers on the requirements of applicable generally accepted account-ting principles.		X
4. Implement procedures whereby OFM staff routinely review capitalized amounts for software projects aga-inst supporting documentation to provide additional assurance that the recor-ded amounts are accurate and complete.		X
Payroll system access, approval of time and attendance records, and process documentation		
5. Evaluate the overall effectiveness of its actions taken in response to our findings regarding payroll and personnel action processing, when fully implemented, to determine whether any modifications, additional acti-ons, or both are needed.		X
Comparison of furniture and equipment received and ordered		
6. Retain, in its updated property management policy, a procedure to document comparison of quantity and type of item received with the corresponding purchase order, and take actions to ensure that the comparisons are being consistently documented.		X

Source: GAO.

Note: Recommendations made in GAO-07-482R.

ENCLOSURE II

Comments from the Securities and Exchange Commission

CHRISTOPHER COX
CHAIRMAN

HEADQUARTERS
100 F STREET, NE
WASHINGTON, DC 20549

REGIONAL OFFICES
ATLANTA, BOSTON, CHICAGO,
DENVER, FORT WORTH,
LOS ANGELES, MIAMI, NEW YORK,
PHILADELPHIA, SALT LAKE CITY,
SAN FRANCISCO

UNITED STATES
SECURITIES AND EXCHANGE COMMISSION

March 21, 2008

Ms. Jeanette M. Franzel
Director
Financial Management and Assurance
Government Accountability Office
441 G Street N.W.
Washington, DC 20548

Dear Ms. Franzel:

Thank you for the opportunity to review and comment on the draft report of the Government Accountability Office (GAO) entitled *Internal Control: Improvements Needed in SEC's Accounting and Financial Reporting Process*, GAO-08-461R. The report presents recommendations for improvements to internal control as identified in the GAO's financial statement audit of the Securities and Exchange Commission (SEC) for fiscal years 2007 and 2006.

I am pleased that the GAO's FY 2007 audit found that the SEC's financial statements and notes were presented fairly, in all material respects, in conformity with U.S. generally accepted accounting principles. However, the GAO found that the SEC did not maintain effective internal control over financial reporting as of September 30, 2007. Because no material weakness is acceptable, we are committed to remediating the control deficiencies this fiscal year.

The SEC takes its responsibility for financial reporting very seriously. As the GAO found in the FY 2007 audit report, the SEC improved its controls over the accuracy, timeliness, and completeness of the disgorgement and penalty data and used a much improved database for the initial recording and tracking of these data. The GAO also noted that the SEC continued to make progress in resolving deficiencies in information security. In 2007, the SEC took the opportunity afforded by significant turnover in senior financial positions to fully review and evaluate existing financial reporting policies and procedures. During fiscal year 2007, the SEC committed extensive resources to improving financial reporting processes, documentation and controls. The SEC began the evaluation of manual processes and controls used to integrate subsidiary data sources with the General Ledger and initiated systematic improvements to these processes and controls. This review of policies and procedures and completion of related documentation will continue in fiscal year 2008.

In order to fully remediate the control deficiencies this fiscal year, we have prepared a comprehensive Corrective Action Plan (CAP) which builds on the efforts initiated in fiscal year 2007. On February 7, 2008, the SEC provided your office with the draft *FY 2008 Corrective Action Plan for Remediation of Internal Control Deficiencies*. Work has already begun on several fronts. The plan specifically addresses the recommendations made by GAO. We welcome your feedback regarding any aspect of this plan and its completeness in addressing the concerns outlined by GAO.

Developing a fully integrated financial management system is the keystone of the SEC's Corrective Action Plan to remediate the deficiencies identified by the GAO. Fully integrated financial management systems and compliance with the U.S. Standard General Ledger (SGL) at the transaction level are fundamental requirements for federal financial management systems. The SEC's lack of automated system integration is the underlying cause of the system non-conformance reported. Currently, data is manually entered at a summary level; however, compliance with SGL is required at the transaction, or detail, level. The deficiencies in internal control over financial reporting are attributable to ineffective compensating controls over the manual processes and spreadsheets supporting financial statement balances that, in the desired state, will be replaced by fully automated integration.

We have developed remediation strategies to address the deficiencies found relative to system integration, non-compliance with SGL at the transaction level, and compensating controls. The strategies are presented in the Corrective Action Plan in terms of both long-term and short-term solutions. The short-term strategies represent improvements that are expected to be achieved this fiscal year. We are confident that these additional compensating controls will be successful in mitigating the risk associated with manual processes. The long-term solution will achieve greater efficiency, effectiveness and risk mitigation by minimizing reliance on detective controls.

The short-term strategies are to develop or improve process documentation; overlay manual processes with additional compensating controls as needed; implement SGL compliant posting models; and implement process improvements to enhance efficiencies and effectiveness of internal controls and monitor performance. In FY 2008, the SEC will continue to take a risk-based approach to ensure that process and procedural documentation is in place, as discussed above. The documentation will be comprehensive enough that management and auditors can clearly ascertain who is performing the control activities, the frequency of the control activities and how they are performed and evidenced. The SEC's first quarter 2008 financial statements were prepared using the newly documented methodologies.

In addition, the SEC is eliminating manual data handling and the use of multiple labor-intensive spreadsheets by automating the generation of financial statements. The implementation of a central data repository for financial statement preparation and analysis will mitigate the risk and the internal control deficiencies identified by the GAO. The automated tool has been run in parallel with the existing process for preparation of the monthly statements since December. The SEC will fully implement the tool beginning with the second quarter statements.

The long-term strategies are to automate integration of financial management systems to eliminate manual processes and comply with SGL at the transaction level. System integration will eliminate the need for the bulk of the manual data manipulation and entry currently required, resulting in enhanced timeliness, accuracy and reliability of the data, while reducing the need to maintain redundant schedules. The ability to fully comply with the SGL at the transaction level is dependent on SEC's ability to integrate or interface all transactional activity with Momentum, which is currently being upgraded to accommodate the necessary integration. Nonetheless, substantial compliance may be demonstrated in the short-term through eliminating use of unconventional posting models and other limitations that prevent proper recordation as discussed above.

As Chairman, I take the SEC's responsibility over financial reporting very seriously. I remain committed to improving the SEC's financial integrity and operational efficiencies so that the agency can lead by example when it comes to establishing and maintaining effective internal control over financial reporting. I appreciate your support of these efforts and look forward to continuing our productive dialogue during the course of this year's audit.

Thank you again for the opportunity to comment on this report. If you have any questions relating to our response, please contact our Chief Financial Officer, Kristine Chadwick, at 202-551-7840.

Sincerely,

Christopher Cox
Chairman

cc: Diego Ruiz
Kristine Chadwick

ENCLOSURE III

Summary of Audit Scope and Methodology

To fulfill our responsibilities as auditor of the financial statements of the Securities and Exchange Commission (SEC), we did the following[12]:

- Examined, on a test basis, evidence supporting the amounts and disclosures in the financial statements.
- Assessed the accounting principles used and significant estimates made by SEC management.
- Evaluated the overall presentation of the financial statements.
- Obtained an understanding of SEC and its operations, including its internal control related to financial reporting and compliance with laws and regulations.
- Obtained an understanding of the recording, processing, and summarizing of performance measures as reported in Management's Discussion and Analysis.
- Tested relevant internal controls over financial reporting and compliance with applicable laws and regulations, and evaluated the design and operating effectiveness of internal control.
- Considered SEC's process for evaluating and reporting on internal control and financial management systems under the Federal Managers' Financial Integrity Act of 1982.
- Tested compliance with selected provisions of the following laws and their related regulations: the Securities Exchange Act of 1934, as amended; the Securities Act of 1933, as amended; the Antideficiency Act; laws governing the pay and allowance system for SEC employees; the Prompt Payment Act; and the Federal Employees' Retirement System Act of 1986.

We requested comments on a draft of this chapter from the Chairman of SEC. We received written comments from SEC and summarized the comments in our report. We conducted our audit in accordance with U.S. generally accepted government auditing standards.

End Notes

[1] GAO, *Financial Audit: Securities and Exchange Commission's Financial Statements for Fiscal Years 2007 and 2006*, GAO-08-167 (Washington, D.C.: Nov. 16, 2007).

[2] The internal control issues concerning information security are discussed in a separate report: GAO, *Information Security: Securities and Exchange Commission Needs to Continue to Improve Its Program*, GAO- 08-280 (Washington, D.C.: Feb. 29, 2008).

[3] We made recommendations in our internal control reports issued as part of our fiscal years 2004, 2005, and 2006 SEC financial statement audits: GAO, *Material Internal Control Issues Reported in SEC's Fiscal Year 2004 Financial Statement Audit Report*, GAO-05-691R (Washington, D.C.: July 27, 2005); *Management Report: Opportunities for Improvements in SEC's Internal Controls and Accounting Procedures*, GAO-05- 693R (Washington, D.C.: Aug. 12, 2005); *Internal Control: Improvements Needed in SEC's Accounting and Financial Reporting Procedures*, GAO-06-459R (Washington, D.C.: Apr. 21, 2006); and GAO, *Internal Control: Improvements Needed in SEC's Accounting and Operational Procedures*, GAO-07-482R (Washington, D.C.: Apr. 3, 2007).

[4] A material weakness is a significant deficiency or combination of significant deficiencies that results in more than a remote likelihood that a material misstatement of the financial statements will not be prevented or detected.

[5] A significant deficiency is a control deficiency, or combination of deficiencies, that adversely affects the entity's ability to initiate, authorize, record, process, or report financial data reliably in accordance with generally accepted accounting principles such that there is more than a remote likelihood that a misstatement of the entity's financial statements that is more than inconsequential will not be prevented or detected.

[6] GAO-05-691R, GAO-05-693R, GAO-06-459R, and GAO-07-482R.

[7] GAO-08-167.

[8] A disgorgement is the repayment of illegally gained profits (or avoided losses) for distribution to harmed investors whenever feasible. A penalty is a monetary payment from a violator of securities law that SEC obtains pursuant to statutory authority. A penalty is fundamentally a punitive measure, although penalties occasionally can be used to compensate harmed investors.

[9] OMB directs executive branch agencies to issue their audited financial statements by November 15 for the preceding fiscal year ending on September 30. OMB Circular No. A-136, *Financial Reporting Requirements*, § I.5 (rev. June 27, 2007).

[10] An amount shall be recorded as an obligation of the U.S. Government only when supported by documentary evidence of a binding agreement between an agency and another person (including an agency) that is in writing and executed before the end of the period of availability for obligation of the appropriation. 31 U.S.C. § 1501(a)(1). Under the plain terms of the statute, an oral agreement may not be recorded as an obligation. *See* GAO, *Principles of Federal Appropriations Law*, vol. 2, 3rd ed., GAO-06-382SP (Washington, D.C.: February 2006), page 7-15.

[11] GAO, *Standards for Internal Control in the Federal Government*, GAO/AIMD-00-21 .3.1 (Washington, D.C.: November 1999).

[12] For further, more detailed, explanation of our audit scope and methodology, see the discussion in our related financial audit report (GAO-08-167).

In: Financial Institutions in Turmoil
Editor: Carl D. Aspelin
ISBN: 978-1-60692-044-2

Chapter 6

MANAGEMENT REPORT: OPPORTUNITIES FOR IMPROVEMENTS IN FDIC'S INTERNAL CONTROLS AND ACCOUNTING PROCEDURES*

U. S. Government Accountability Office

June 27, 2007

Mr. Steven O. App

Deputy to the Chairman and Chief Financial Officer Federal Deposit Insurance Corporation

Subject: *Management Report: Opportunities for Improvements in FDIC's Internal Controls and Accounting Procedures*

Dear Mr. App:

In February 2007, we issued our opinions on the calendar year 2006 financial statements of the Deposit Insurance Fund (DIF) and the FSLIC Resolution Fund (FRF).[1] We also issued our opinion on the effectiveness of the Federal Deposit Insurance Corporation's (FDIC) internal control over financial reporting (including safeguarding assets) and compliance as of December 31, 2006, and our evaluation of FDIC's compliance with significant provisions of selected laws and regulations for the two funds for the year ended December 31, 2006.[2]

The purpose of this chapter is to present issues identified during our audits of the 2006 financial statements regarding internal controls and accounting procedures and to recommend actions to address these issues. Although these issues were not material in relation to the financial statements, we believe they warrant management's attention. We are making seven recommendations for strengthening FDIC's internal controls and accounting procedures. We conducted our audits in accordance with U.S. generally accepted government auditing standards.

RESULTS IN BRIEF

During our audits of the 2006 financial statements, we identified several internal control issues that affected FDIC's accounting for the funds it administers. Although we do not consider them to be material weaknesses[3] or significant deficiencies,[4] we believe they warrant management's consideration. Specifically, we found the following:

- FDIC had inadequate or incomplete written procedures for key segments of its general ledger monthly closing process and other financial operations. The absence of adequate written procedures increases the risk that (1) all necessary steps in the monthly general ledger closing process and other processes may not be completely, correctly, and consistently performed and (2) disruptions and errors may arise when staff changes occur. This, in turn, could affect the reliability of data presented in FDIC's financial statements.
- FDIC lacked adequate supervisory reviews of key tasks in the monthly general ledger closing process and other financial operations, increasing the risk that errors in preparing financial statements might not be timely detected and corrected.
- FDIC incorrectly excluded certain receivership data used in the calculation of loss rates from bank failures, resulting in an error in these loss rates that could have affected the accuracy/reliability of the contingent liability presented in the financial statements.

* This is an edited, reformatted and augmented version of a U. S. Government Accountability Office publication dated June 2007.

- FDIC lacked appropriate control to safeguard checks received in its Dallas mailroom and did not provide proper oversight of contractor lockbox operations, increasing the risk of theft, loss, or misappropriation of assets.

We are making seven recommendations to improve FDIC's internal controls and accounting procedures. Implementation of these recommendations would strengthen FDIC's conformance with the internal control standards that federal agencies are required to follow[5] and minimize the risk of future misstatements in the two funds' financial statements.

In its comments, FDIC agreed with our recommendations and described actions it has taken or plans to take to address the control weaknesses described in this chapter. At the end of our discussion of each of the issues in this chapter, we have summarized FDIC's related comments and our evaluation.

Scope and Methodology

As part of our audits of the 2006 and 2005 financial statements of the two funds administered by FDIC, we evaluated FDIC's internal controls and its compliance with selected provisions of laws and regulations. We designed our audit procedures to test relevant controls, including those intended to ensure proper authorization, execution, accounting, and reporting of transactions.

We requested comments on a draft of this chapter from the FDIC Deputy to the Chairman and Chief Financial Officer. We received written comments and have reprinted the comments in enclosure I. Further details on our scope and methodology are included in our report on the results of our audits of the 2006 and 2005 financial statements, and are reproduced in enclosure II.

General Ledger Closing and Other Financial Processing Procedures

During our observations of FDIC's monthly general ledger closing process and other financial operations related to the preparation of DIF's and FRF's financial statements, we identified several critical steps in the processes in which the documentation of procedures was either inadequate or incomplete and could be improved. These critical steps involved activities that were performed outside the automated processes of the PeopleSoft application within FDIC's financial environment. GAO's *Standards for Internal Control in the Federal Government* requires that internal control procedures be clearly documented in management directives, policies, or operating manuals. Further, all documentation should be properly managed and maintained.

Specifically, we observed that there were inadequate written procedures covering the (1) preparation of the DIF and FRF financial statements, (2) closing out of terminated receiverships, (3) review of the vendor maintenance log, and (4) number and types of oversight reports and audit logs that are used to monitor financial processes, including documentation of the periodic review of these reports and audit logs.

We also identified the following activities in the monthly general ledger closing process where the extent of written procedures could be improved:

- Preparation and entering spreadsheet adjustments to the general ledger for (1) estimated legal contingent liabilities, (2) loan loss reserve, and (3) accounts payable accruals.
- Preparation and recording entries to the general ledger for the payroll liability accruals.
- Preparation of final accounts payable accrual analysis reports.

Additionally, we found that there was incomplete detailed documentation (run sheets) for automated transactions used to accomplish the monthly closing process.

According to FDIC officials, the lack of adequate written procedures was caused by the fact that management attention and resources have been devoted to higher priorities in ensuring the successful implementation of the new financial management system. Nonetheless, inadequate or incomplete written procedures reduce the assurance that critical processes and operating activities have been completely, correctly, and consistently performed; increase the risk of disruption and errors when staff changes occur; and could affect the reliability of data presented in FDIC's financial statements.

Recommendation

We recommend that FDIC improve its written procedures by describing more explicitly the steps required to accomplish and document each significant activity in the monthly general ledger closing process and other financial operations related to financial statement preparation in order to help ensure that such steps are completely, consistently, and accurately performed.

FDIC Comments and Our Evaluation

FDIC agreed with our recommendation. In response to our finding, FDIC stated that existing procedures and process documentation will be enhanced to more explicitly capture the key steps and activities required to support the monthly general ledger closing process and other related financial operation areas. FDIC further stated that this procedures work is scheduled to be completed in phases, starting with the most critical areas by June 30, 2007, and the other processes completed by December 31, 2007. We will evaluate the effectiveness of FDIC's actions during our 2007 financial audit.

Supervisory Review of General Ledger Closing and Other Financial Operations

During our observations of the monthly general ledger closing process and related activities, we identified several instances in which there was inadequate supervisory review of key tasks or activities outside the automated financial processes. Supervisory review of key activities is important to ensure that errors in the data or processes leading to preparation of the annual financial statements are timely detected and corrected. GAO's *Standards for Internal Control in the Federal Government* requires agencies to implement internal control procedures to ensure the accurate and timely recording of transactions and events. In addition, these standards require that qualified and continuous supervision be provided to ensure that internal control objectives are achieved.

Specifically, we identified the following activities in the monthly general ledger closing and related processes where there was inadequate supervisory review:

- Manual compilation of spreadsheets containing expense accrual data used to update monthly balances prior to the system upload.

- Manual compilation of final expense accrual analysis reports prior to distribution.
- Preparation of reports relating to fiscal year comparisons and the corporate closing trial balance prior to the fiscal year end system close.
- Changes to business rules that specify how certain financial transactions are to be processed.
- Override of accounts payable match exception transactions.

According to FDIC officials, the lack of adequate supervisory review was caused by management's attention being devoted to higher priorities in ensuring the successful implementation of new financial management processes and the administrative challenges posed by the merger of the Bank Insurance Fund and the Savings Association Insurance Fund. Nonetheless, inadequate supervisory review of the activities noted above increases the risk to FDIC that errors might not be detected and corrected in a timely manner. This, in turn, increases the risk of misstatements in the DIF's and FRF's financial statements.

Recommendation

We recommend that FDIC emphasize to its staff the importance of completing required supervisory review of key transactions and procedures in the monthly general ledger closing process and other financial operations to ensure that they are properly executed and that these reviews are documented.

FDIC Comments and Our Evaluation

FDIC agreed with our recommendation. FDIC stated that it has and will continue to emphasize to staff the importance of documented supervisory review of key tasks and activities. We will evaluate the effectiveness of FDIC's actions during our 2007 financial audit.

Calculation of Loss Rates for Anticipated Bank Failures

During our testing of contingencies related to the anticipated failures of insured institutions, we identified an error in one of the statistical analysis programs FDIC uses to estimate expected loss rates for various categories of assets. Specifically, FDIC incorrectly excluded certain asset data for an individual receivership from this statistical program. GAO's *Standards for Internal Control in the Federal Government* requires agencies to implement internal control procedures to ensure the accurate and timely recording of transactions and events. In addition, these standards require that qualified and continuous supervision be provided to ensure that internal control objectives are achieved.

FDIC records a contingent liability and loss provision for DIF-insured institutions that are likely to fail within 1 year of the financial statement reporting date, absent some favorable event such as obtaining additional capital or merging, when the liability becomes probable and reasonably estimable. The contingent liability is derived by applying expected failure and loss rates to institutions based on supervisory ratings, balance sheet characteristics, and projected capital levels.

To derive expected loss rates, FDIC uses historical information from receiverships to compute actual losses on six categories of assets that constitute total bank assets: installment loans, commercial loans, securities, mortgages, other real estate owned, and all other assets. These actual losses are converted to expected loss rates for each asset category. These expected loss rates are then applied to the book value of each asset category of the institution deemed likely to fail to determine the total loss anticipated from the likely institution failure.

To perform the analysis necessary to derive the expected loss rates and the contingent liability, FDIC uses statistical programs. However, during our audit, we found an error in the program used to estimate loss rates on the six categories of assets. Specifically, FDIC incorrectly included loss rates on securities of a receivership it intended to exclude, while mistakenly excluding loss rates of securities of another receivership. FDIC did not identify this error because it resulted from a transposition error that was not detected in FDIC's routine review of its statistical program.

After we brought this error to FDIC's attention, FDIC corrected the error and recalculated the loss rates for 2006. While this revised calculation showed that the error had an immaterial effect on the loss rate computation in this instance, such an error, if undetected and uncorrected, could have had a significant effect on the calculation of loss rates and thus on the contingent liability presented in the financial statements.

Recommendation

We recommend that FDIC emphasize to its staff the importance of thoroughly verifying the accuracy of all data elements included in the calculation of loss rates used in estimating the contingent liability for anticipated failures.

FDIC Comments and Our Evaluation

FDIC agreed with our recommendation. FDIC stated that at the time of the review existing audit procedures required the review of all statistical programs but focused primarily on program logic. After GAO identified the error, FDIC modified the review process to also check any hard-coded data for errors. Additionally, FDIC stated that its staff was apprised of the new procedures, which became effective January 31, 2007. We will evaluate the effectiveness of FDIC's actions during our 2007 financial audit.

Receivership Receipts (Mailroom and Cashier Controls)

During our testing of FDIC's internal controls in the mailroom and cashier operations of its Dallas field office, we identified deficiencies in controls over checks received that increased the risk of theft, loss, or misappropriation of receipts. GAO's *Standards for Internal Control in the Federal Government* requires agencies to establish physical control to secure and safeguard vulnerable assets. Examples include security for, and limited access to, assets such as cash, securities, inventories, and equipment that might be vulnerable to risk of loss or unauthorized use.

The mailroom of the Dallas field office is responsible for opening mail, including monetary receipts for receivership activities. These receipts are in the form of checks that generally consist of loan repayments from debtors of failed financial institutions. For those checks not received in the Dallas mailroom, FDIC uses a lockbox administered by JPMorgan Chase Bank, N.A. (JPMorgan). The lockbox is emptied several times a day and the checks are deposited in an FDIC account at JPMorgan. Each day, JPMorgan forwards to FDIC online image copies of the checks deposited that day and all supporting documentation received with the checks. For calendar year 2006, the mailroom of the Dallas field office directly processed 1,870 checks totaling approximately $31.9 million, while the lockbox operation processed 1,758 checks totaling approximately $5.2 million. Whether checks are received in the mailroom or lockbox, the Cashiers Unit is responsible for accounting for all receivership receipts.

In our tests of controls of FDIC's Dallas field office mailroom and Cashiers Unit operations, we found the following control deficiencies:

- The mailroom contractor staff did not adequately account for checks upon receipt and prior to storing the checks in a safe. Specifically, we found that the check log prepared upon extraction of receipts from the envelopes was not reconciled to the total number of checks and the total dollar value of checks received. Additionally, the check log was not initialed and dated by the preparer, and a tape recording agreement of checks to the check log was not prepared. Finally, we observed that the checks were not locked in a secured bag.
- The file cabinet used by the Cashiers Unit to store checks overnight requires only one person to open it. We observed that four individuals had keys and unlimited access to the file cabinet.

In addition, we found that FDIC's policies and procedures do not require the examination of any internal audit reviews of internal controls at JPMorgan's lockbox operation to ensure that these controls are effective and operating as intended. We were informed that JPMorgan's internal audit department conducts periodic reviews of lockbox operations using a risk-based approach. This approach includes an assessment of the key risks and processes within lockbox operations and an evaluation of associated controls, as well as an examination of policies and procedures to determine their overall effectiveness.

JPMorgan's internal audit department completed its most recent review of lockbox operations in August 2006. However, its reviews are not required to be obtained and evaluated by FDIC.

Safeguarding controls are critical in preventing the theft of cash or checks. The lack of effective safeguarding controls increases the risk of theft, loss, or misappropriation of assets.

Recommendations

To improve physical security in the Dallas field office mailroom and cashier operations, we recommend that FDIC instruct

- mailroom contractor employees to reconcile checks received to the check log, initial and date the log, and prepare a tape recording agreement of the checks to the check log;
- mailroom contractor employees to lock the checks in a secured bag immediately upon receipt and prior to storing the checks in a safe; and
- Cashiers Unit employees to store checks overnight in a locked file cabinet that requires two individuals to open it.

In addition, we recommend that FDIC modify its policies and procedures to require regular review and take appropriate actions to address the results of examinations of internal controls at the contractor's lockbox operation to ensure that controls are effective and operating as intended.

FDIC Comments and Our Evaluation

FDIC agreed with the intent of our recommendations. In response to our findings related to FDIC's Dallas field office mailroom and Cashiers Unit, FDIC cited corrective actions completed by January 31, 2007, that address the issues we identified and are consistent with the intent of our recommendations. As to FDIC's policies and procedures related to the internal audit reviews of internal controls at JPMorgan's lockbox operation, FDIC stated that its policies and procedures will be modified by June 30, 2007, to request annual audit reports from JPMorgan and for FDIC to review those reports for possible internal control weaknesses and proposed corrective actions. We will evaluate the effectiveness of FDIC's actions during our 2007 financial audit.

Sincerely yours,

Steven J. Sebastian
Director
Financial Management and Assurance
Enclosures - 3

ENCLOSURE I

Comments from the Federal Deposit Insurance Corporation

FDIC

Federal Deposit Insurance Corporation
550 17th Street NW, Washington, D.C. 20429-9990

Deputy to the Chairman and CFO

June 15, 2007

Mr. Steven J. Sebastian, Director
Financial Management and Assurance
U.S. Government Accountability Office
441 G Street, NW
Washington, DC 20548

Dear Mr. Sebastian: Steve

Thank you for the opportunity to respond to the draft report entitled, *Management Report: Opportunities for Improvement in FDIC's Internal Controls and Accounting Procedures, GAO-07-942R*. The report discusses matters that were identified during the 2006 financial statements audit regarding internal controls and accounting procedures that could be improved, and recommendations to address them. Although the Government Accountability Office (GAO) believes that these matters warrant management's attention, we are pleased that GAO acknowledged that they were not material in relation to the financial statements and does not consider them to be material weaknesses or significant deficiencies.

We welcome your recommendations to improve our internal controls and recognize the benefit of implementing them. The FDIC has already completed actions to address some of the recommendations and we look forward to completing the corrective actions on the remaining ones. Our detailed management responses to the recommendations are provided in Attachment I.

We appreciate your diligent work on these matters. If you have any questions relating to the responses, please contact James H. Angel, Jr., Director, Office of Enterprise Risk Management, at 703-562-6456.

Sincerely,

Steven O. App

Steven O. App
Deputy to the Chairman
and Chief Financial Officer

Attachment

cc: John F. Bovenzi
Bret D. Edwards
Arthur J. Murton
Arleas Upton Kea
Mitchell Glassman
James H. Angel, Jr.
Alice C. Goodman

Attachment 1

General Ledger Closing and Other Financial Processing Procedures

GAO found that FDIC had inadequate or incomplete written procedures for key segments of its general ledger monthly closing process and other financial operations. The absence of adequate written procedures increases the risk that 1) all necessary steps in the closing process may not be completely, correctly, and consistently performed and 2) disruptions and errors may arise when staff changes occur. This could impact the reliability of data presented in FDIC's financial statements.

Recommendation 1:
GAO recommended that FDIC improve its written procedures by describing more explicitly the steps required to accomplish and document each significant activity in the monthly general ledger closing process and other financial operations related to financial statement preparation in order to help ensure that such steps are completely, consistently, and accurately performed.

Management Response:
We concur with the recommendation and agree that existing procedures and process documentation can be enhanced to more explicitly capture the key steps and activities required to support the monthly general ledger closing process and other financial operation related areas. This procedures work is scheduled to be completed in phases, starting with the most critical areas by June 30, 2007, and other processes completed by December 31, 2007.

Supervisory Review of General Ledger Closing and Other Financial Operations

GAO found that FDIC lacked adequate supervisory reviews of key tasks in the closing process and other financial operations, increasing the risk that errors in preparing financial statements might not be timely detected and corrected.

Recommendation 2:
GAO recommended that FDIC emphasize to its staff the importance of completing required supervisory review of key transactions and procedures in the monthly general ledger closing process and other financial operations to ensure that they are properly executed and that these reviews be documented.

Management Response:
We concur with the recommendation and have and will continue to emphasize to staff the importance of documented supervisory review of key tasks and activities. Additionally, we believe the enhanced procedures referred to in the previous response will more explicitly detail the supervisory review steps and required documentation.

Calculation of Loss Rates for Anticipated Bank Failures

GAO found that FDIC incorrectly excluded certain receivership data used in the calculation of loss rates from bank failures, resulting in an error in these loss rates which could have impacted the accuracy/reliability of the contingent liability presented in the financial statements.

Recommendation 3:
GAO recommended that FDIC emphasize to its staff the importance of thoroughly verifying the accuracy of all data elements included in the calculation of loss rates used in estimating the contingent liability for anticipated failures.

Management Response:
We concur with the recommendation. At the time of the review, existing audit procedures required the review of all statistical programs, which focused primarily on program logic. After the identification of the error, which GAO acknowledges had no material effect on the loss rate computation, the review process was immediately modified also to check any hard-coded data as part of the audit of program files. The staff was apprised of the new procedures, which became effective January 31, 2007.

Receivership Receipts (Mailroom and Cashier Controls)

GAO found FDIC did not maintain adequate control to safeguard checks received in its Dallas mailroom and did not provide proper oversight of contractor lock box operations, increasing the risk of theft, loss, or misappropriation of assets.

Recommendation 4:
To improve its physical security over the Dallas field office mailroom operations, GAO recommended that FDIC instruct mailroom contractor employees to reconcile checks received to the check log, initial and date the log, and prepare a tape recording agreement of the checks to the check log.

Management Response:
We concur with the recommendation. To improve the security over these checks, the mailroom check processing procedures were revised in January 2007. As has been the mailroom's practice, all checks received must be promptly recorded. The revised procedures instruct the mailroom staff to run a tape of the checks as they are received, initial and date the tape, and attach the tape to the checks. Additionally, as part of the revised process, the mailroom staff must place the checks and tapes in a sealed envelope, place that envelope into a wall mounted safe depository drop box, and contact the Division of Resolutions and Receiverships (DRR) Cashier Unit for pickup. The Cashier Unit maintains the key to the safe depository and retrieves the checks upon notification by the mailroom staff. Under this new process, the Cashier sends an email confirmation of the pick-up indicating the number of checks, total amount, and receipt date. The email is then reconciled to the check log. We have attached the revised Mailroom Check Processing procedures as well as a description of the secure drop box used for check depository. The corrective actions were completed January 31, 2007.

Recommendation 5:
To improve its physical security over the Dallas field office mailroom operations, GAO recommended that FDIC instruct mailroom contractor employees to lock the checks in a secured bag immediately upon receipt and prior to storing the checks in a safe.

Management Response:
This recommendation is not applicable since the Division of Administration (DOA) no longer uses a secured bag to lock and store checks. As stated in our response to Recommendation 4, the DOA mailroom staff puts checks into a sealed envelope immediately upon receipt and places the envelope into a wall mounted locked safe depository drop box for pickup by the Cashier Unit. This process replaced the use of a secured bag and safe. The drop box can only be opened by the Cashier Unit. This process satisfies the intent of the recommendation.

Recommendation 6:
To improve its physical security over the Dallas field office cashier operations, GAO recommended that the Cashiers Unit employees store checks overnight in a locked file cabinet that requires two individuals to open.

Management Response:
We concur with the recommendation. The corrective activity for this recommendation was implemented during the audit. The file cabinet used by the Cashier Unit is a locking fire proof cabinet within a secure room. A combination lock was added to the file cabinet with access given to DRR accounting personnel who do not have a key to the file cabinet lock or knowledge of the cipher lock combination to the room. All monetary items in the possession of the Cashier Unit are secured in the file cabinet requiring two individuals to unlock the cabinet. This corrective activity was coordinated with DOA in conjunction with changes to the DOA mailroom procedures. A second lock was installed on the cashiers file on or about January 12, 2007.

Recommendation 7:
GAO recommended that FDIC modify its policies and procedures to require regular review and take appropriate actions to address the results of examinations of internal controls at the contractor's lock box operation to ensure that controls are effective and operating as intended.

Management Response:
We concur with the recommendation. DRR will modify its procedures and policies by June 30, 2007, to require annual requests of external audit reports of JPMorgan Chase Bank and will review those reports for possible internal control weaknesses and proposed corrective actions.

ENCLOSURE II

Details on Audit Scope and Methodology

To fulfill our responsibilities as auditor of the financial statements of the two funds administered by FDIC, we did the following:

- examined, on a test basis, evidence supporting the amounts and disclosures in the financial statements;
- assessed the accounting principles used and significant estimates made by management;
- evaluated the overall presentation of the financial statements;
- obtained an understanding of internal controls related to financial reporting (including safeguarding assets) and compliance with selected laws and regulations;
- tested relevant internal controls over financial reporting and compliance, and evaluated the design and operating effectiveness of internal control;
- considered FDIC's process for evaluating and reporting on internal control based on criteria established by 31 U.S.C. § 3512 (c), (d), (commonly referred to as the Federal Managers' Financial Integrity Act); and
- tested compliance with applicable laws and regulations, including selected provisions of the Federal Deposit Insurance Act, as amended, and the Chief Financial Officers Act of 1990.

End Notes

[1] On February 8, 2006, the President signed into law the Federal Deposit Insurance Reform Act of 2005 (the Act). Among its provisions, the Act called for the merger of the Bank Insurance Fund (BIF) and Savings Association Insurance Fund (SAIF) into DIF. In accordance with the Act, the Federal Deposit Insurance Corporation merged BIF and SAIF into the newly established DIF on March 31, 2006. The financial results of the newly formed DIF were retrospectively applied as though they had been combined at the beginning of 2006, as well as for prior periods presented for comparative purposes.

[2] GAO, *Financial Audit: Federal Deposit Insurance Corporation Funds' 2006 and 2005 Financial Statements,* GAO-07-371 (Washington, D.C.: Feb. 13, 2007).

[3] A material weakness is a significant deficiency, or combination of significant deficiencies, that results in more than a remote likelihood that a material misstatement of the financial statements will not be prevented or detected.

[4] A significant deficiency is a control deficiency, or combination of deficiencies, that adversely affects the entity's ability to initiate, authorize, record, process, or report financial data reliably in accordance with generally accepted accounting principles such that there is more than a remote likelihood that a misstatement of the entity's financial statements that is more than inconsequential will not be prevented or detected.

[5] GAO, *Standards for Internal Control in the Federal Government*, GAO/AIMD-00-21.3.1 (Washington, D.C.: November 1999).

In: Financial Institutions in Turmoil
Editor: Carl D. Aspelin
ISBN: 978-1-60692-044-2

Chapter 7

FINANCIAL SERVICES INDUSTRY: OVERALL TRENDS IN MANAGEMENT-LEVEL DIVERSITY AND DIVERSITY INITIATIVES, 1993-2006*

U. S. Government Accountability Office

WHY GAO DID THIS STUDY

As the U.S. workforce has become increasingly diverse, many private and public sector organizations have recognized the importance of recruiting and retaining minority and women candidates for key positions. However, previous congressional hearings have raised concerns about a lack of diversity at the management level in the financial services industry, which provides services that are essential to the continued growth and economic prosperity of the country.

This testimony discusses findings from a June 2006 GAO report and more recent work on diversity in the financial services industry.

Specifically, GAO assesses (1) what the available data show about diversity at the management level from 1993 through 2006 and (2) steps that

* This is an edited, reformatted and augmented version of a U. S. Government Accountability Office publication dated February 2008.

the industry has taken to promote workforce diversity and the challenges involved.

To address the testimony's objectives, GAO analyzed data from the Equal Employment Opportunity Commission (EEOC); reviewed select studies; and interviewed officials from financial services firms, trade organizations, and organizations that represent minority and women professionals.

To view the full product, including the scope and methodology, click on GAO-08-445T. For more information, contact Orice M. Williams at (202) 512-8678 or williamso@gao.gov.

WHAT GAO FOUND

GAO's June 2006 report found that, from 1993 through 2004, overall diversity at the management level in the financial services industry did not change substantially, but some racial/ethnic minority groups experienced more change in representation than others. EEOC data show that management-level representation by minority women and men increased overall from 11.1 percent to 15.5 percent during the period (see figure below). Specifically, African-Americans increased their representation from 5.6 percent to 6.6 percent, Asians from 2.5 percent to 4.5 percent, Hispanics from 2.8 percent to 4.0 percent, and American Indians from 0.2 percent to 0.3 percent. In preparation for this testimony, GAO collected EEOC data for 2006, which shows that diversity at the management level in the financial services industry remained about the same as it had in previous years.

Financial services firms and trade groups have initiated programs to increase workforce diversity, but these initiatives face challenges. The programs include developing scholarships and internships, partnering with groups that represent minority professionals, and linking managers' compensation with their performance in promoting a diverse workforce. Some firms have developed indicators to measure progress in achieving workforce diversity. Industry officials said that among the challenges these initiatives face are recruiting and retaining minority candidates, as well as gaining the "buy-in" of key employees, such as the middle managers who are often responsible for implementing such programs. Without a sustained commitment to overcoming these challenges, diversity at the management level may continue to remain generally unchanged over time.

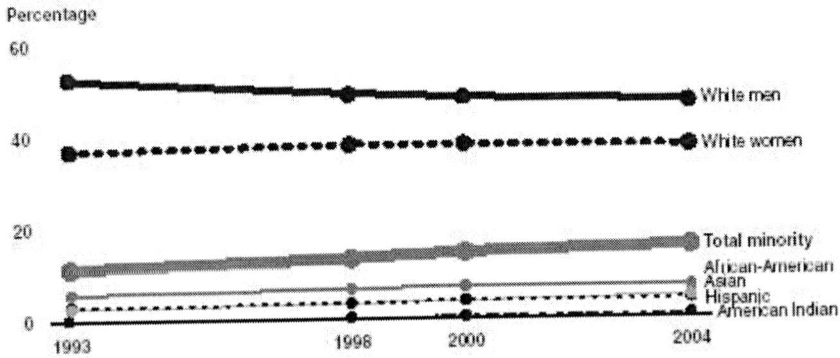

Source: GAO analysis of EEOC data.
Note: Percentages may not always add up to 100 due to rounding.

Workforce Representation in the Financial Services Industry at the Management Level by Racial/Ethnic Group and Gender (1993, 1998, 2000, and 2004)

Mr. Chairman and Members of the Subcommittee:

I am pleased to be here today to discuss the results of our June 2006 study on diversity in the management level in the financial services industry, as well as more recent information that we have gathered on this important topic.[1] As you know, the U.S. workforce has become increasingly diverse over the last several decades. As the composition of the workforce has changed, many private and public sector organizations have recognized the importance of recruiting and retaining minority and women candidates for key positions. In a 2005 report on diversity management, we stated that workforce diversity can benefit organizations in a variety of ways, such as by allowing them to better meet the needs of a diverse customer base, reducing the costs associated with employee turnover, and increasing staff morale.[2] However, this subcommittee and others have raised concerns about workforce diversity in the financial services industry, which provides key services necessary to help ensure the continued growth and economic prosperity of the country. In hearings held by this subcommittee in 2004 and 2006, some witnesses stated that financial services firms— banks and securities firms, for example—have not made sufficient progress in recruiting and retaining minorities and women at the management level.[3]

In my testimony, I will summarize the key findings from our work, which has sought to collect, analyze, and report data and information that provide insights into diversity in the financial services industry. Specifically, I will discuss (1) what the available data show about diversity at the management level in the financial services industry from 1993 through 2006 and (2) the types of initiatives that the financial services industry and related organizations have taken to promote workforce diversity and the challenges involved.

To prepare our June 2006 report, we used the Equal Employment Opportunity Commission's (EEOC) Employer Information Report (EEO-1) data on financial services firms with 100 or more employees for the period from 1993 through 2004.[4] The EEO-1 data provide information on racial/gender representation for various occupations, including "officials and managers," for a broad range of industries, including financial services. In updating our work in preparation for this testimony, we collected and analyzed EEO-1 data for financial services firms with 100 or more employees for 2006. We cannot conduct a direct and continuous trend analysis of changes in the representation of minorities and women at the management level in the financial services industry between 2004 and 2006 because the 2006 data is based on an updated system for classifying industries.[5] However, the 2006 EEO-1 representation data for the financial services industry can generally be compared with the EEO-1 data for 2004 and prior years. Our work has also involved reviewing reports on the state of workforce diversity and initiatives to increase the representation of minority and women in financial services firms. We have also interviewed academics and officials from a variety of financial services firms and trade and professional groups.

We performed this performance audit in Washington, D.C., in January 2008, in accordance with generally accepted government auditing standards. Those standards require that we plan and perform the audit to obtain sufficient, appropriate evidence to provide a reasonable basis for our findings and conclusions based on our audit objectives. We believe that the evidence obtained provides a reasonable basis for our findings and conclusions based on our audit objectives.

In brief:

From 1993 through 2006, overall workforce diversity at the management level in the financial services industry did not change substantially, but some racial/ethnic minority groups experienced more change in representation than others. As described in our June 2006 report, EEO-1 data show that overall management-level representation by minority women and men increased from 11.1 percent to 15.5 percent from 1993 through 2004. Specifically, African-Americans increased their representation from 5.6 percent to 6.6 percent, Asians from 2.5 percent to 4.5 percent, Hispanics from 2.8 percent to 4.0 percent, and American Indians from 0.2 percent to 0.3 percent. Representation by white women remained constant at slightly more than one-third during this period, while representation by white men declined from 52.2 percent to 47.2 percent. EEO-1 data also show that representation by minorities and women at the management level was about the same in 2006 as it had been in previous years.[6] For example, African-Americans and Asians represented about 6.4 percent and 5.0 percent, respectively, of all financial services managers in 2006. Moreover, the EEO-1 data show that depository institutions, such as commercial banks and insurance companies, have generally been more diverse at the management level over the years than securities firms.

Although financial services firms and trade groups have initiated programs to increase workforce diversity, these initiatives face challenges that may help explain why overall diversity at the management level has not changed substantially. Officials at financial services firms said that diversity was an important goal and that top leadership was committed to recruiting and retaining minority and women candidates. Some financial services firms have established scholarship and internship programs or partnered with groups that represent minority professionals. Officials from a few firms told us that they had begun linking managers' compensation and performance in promoting workforce diversity, and some firms had developed indicators (e.g., representation by minorities and women in key positions) to measure progress in achieving workforce diversity. Industry officials said that, among the challenges these initiatives faced were recruiting and retaining minority candidates, as well as gaining the "buy- in" of key employees, such as the middle managers who were often responsible for implementing such programs. Without a sustained commitment to overcoming these challenges, diversity at the management level in the financial services industry may continue to remain generally unchanged over time.

BACKGROUND

We defined the financial services industry to include the following sectors:

- depository credit institutions, which include commercial banks, thrifts (savings and loan associations and savings banks), and credit unions;
- holdings and trusts, which include investment trusts, investment companies, and holding companies;

- nondepository credit institutions, which extend credit in the form of loans, and which include federally sponsored credit agencies, personal credit institutions, and mortgage bankers and brokers;
- the securities sector, which is made up of a variety of firms and organizations (e.g., broker-dealers) that bring together buyers and sellers of securities and commodities, manage investments, and offer financial advice; and
- the insurance sector, including carriers and insurance agents that provide protection against financial risks to policyholders in exchange for the payment of premiums.

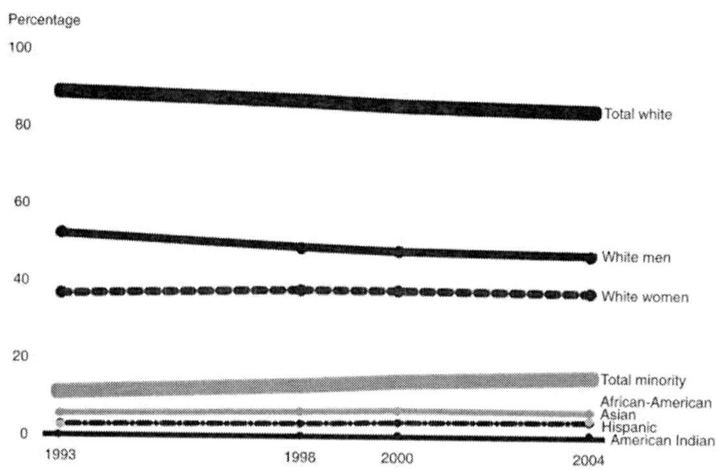

	1993	1998	2000	2004
Total white	88.9%	86.9%	85.7%	84.5%
White men	52.2	49.0	48.0	47.2
White women	36.7	37.9	37.8	37.4
Total minority	11.1%	13.1%	14.3%	15.5%
African-American	5.6	6.4	6.8	6.6
Hispanic	2.8	3.3	3.7	4.0
Asian	2.5	3.2	3.6	4.5
American Indian	.2	.2	.3	.3

Source: GAO analysis of EEOC data.

Note: Percentages may not always add to 100 due to rounding.

Figure 1. EEO-1 Data on Trends in Workforce Diversity in the Financial Services Industry at the Management Level, by Racial/Ethnic Group and Gender (1993, 1998, 2000, and 2004)

The financial services industry is a major source of employment in the United States. EEO-1 data showed that the financial services firms we reviewed for this work, which have 100 or more staff, employed nearly 3 million people in 2004. Moreover, according to the U.S. Bureau of Labor Statistics, employment in the financial services industry was expected to grow at a rate of 1.4 percent annually from 2006 through 2016.

Diversity in the Financial Services Industry at the Management Level Did Not Change Substantially

EEO-1 data for 1993 through 2006 generally do not show substantial changes in representation by minorities and women at the management level in the financial services industry, but some racial/ethnic minority groups experienced more change in representation than others. Figure 1, which is based on information that we obtained in preparation for our June 2006 report, shows that overall management-level representation by minorities increased from 11.1 percent to 15.5 percent from 1993 through 2004.[7] Specifically, African-Americans increased their representation from 5.6 percent to 6.6 percent, Asians from 2.5 percent to 4.5 percent, Hispanics from 2.8 percent to 4.0 percent, and American Indians from 0.2 to 0.3 percent. Management-level representation by white women was largely unchanged at slightly more than one-third during the period, while representation by white men declined from 52.2 percent to 47.2 percent.

As shown in figure 2, EEO-1 data also show that the depository and nondepository credit sectors, as well as the insurance sector, were somewhat more diverse at the management level than the securities and holdings and trust sectors. In 2004, minorities held 19.9 percent of management-level positions in nondepository credit institutions, such as mortgage banks and brokerages, but 12.4 percent in holdings and trusts, such as investment companies.

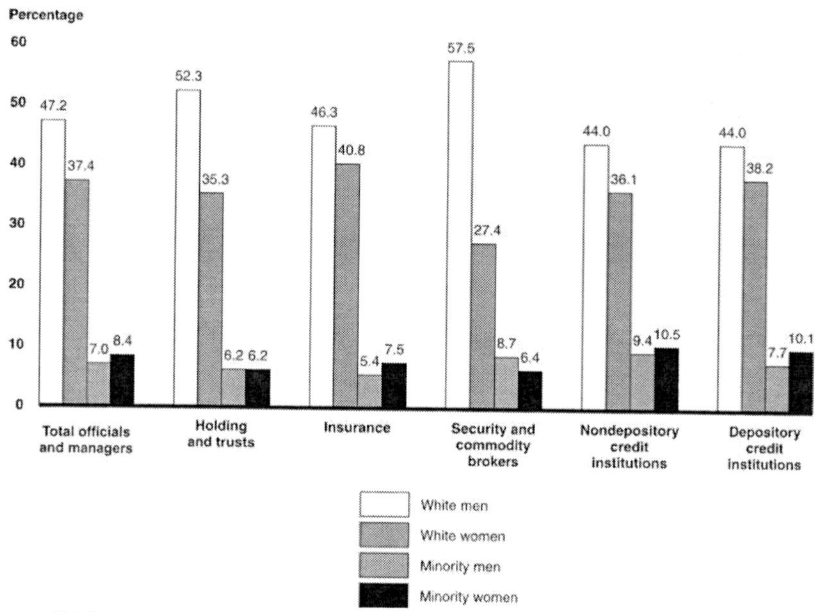

Source: GAO analysis of EEOC data.

Note: Percentages may not always add to 100 due to rounding.

Figure 2. EEO-1 Data on Workforce Diversity in the Financial Services Industry at the Management Level by Sector (2004)

In preparation for this testimony, we contacted EEOC to obtain and analyze EEO-1 for 2006 and found that diversity remained about the same at the management level in the financial services industry (see figure 3) as it had in previous years.[8] For example, the 2006 EEO-1 data show that African-Americans and Asians represented about 6.4 percent and 5.0 percent, respectively, of all financial services managers in 2006. In addition, the 2006 EEO-1 data show that commercial banks and insurance companies continued to have higher representation by minorities and women at the management level than securities firms.

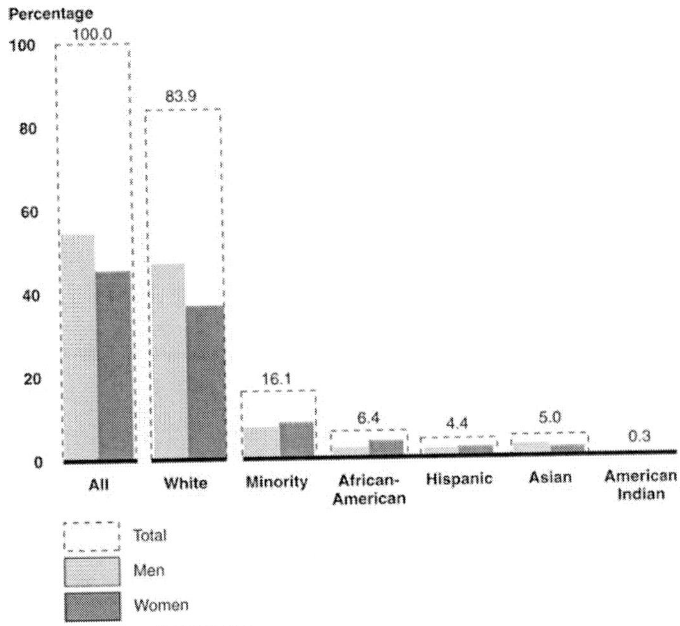

Source: GAO analysis of EEOC data.

Note: Percentages may not always add up to 100 due to rounding.

Figure 3. EEO-1 Data in Workforce Diversity in the Financial Services Industry at the Management Level by Racial/Ethnic Group and Gender (2006)

However, it is important to keep in mind that EEO-1 data may actually overstate representation levels for minorities and white women in the most senior-level positions, such as Chief Executive Officers of large investment firms or commercial banks, because the category that captures these positions—"officials and managers"—covers all management positions. Thus, this category includes lower-level positions (e.g., Assistant Manager of a small bank branch) that may have a higher representation of minorities and women. Recognizing this limitation, starting in 2007, EEOC revised its data collection form for employers to divide the "officials and managers" category into two subcategories: "executive/senior-level officers and managers" and "first/midlevel officials." We hope that the increased level of detail will provide a more accurate picture of diversity among senior managers in the financial services industry over time.

However, it is too soon to assess the impact of this change on diversity measures at the senior management level.

Initiatives to Promote Workforce Diversity in the Financial Services Industry Face Challenges

Officials from the firms that we contacted said that their top leadership was committed to implementing workforce diversity initiatives, but they noted that making such initiatives work was challenging. In particular, the officials cited ongoing difficulties in recruiting and retaining minority candidates and in gaining employees' "buy-in" for diversity initiatives, especially at the middle management level.

Financial Services Firms Have Implemented a Variety of Diversity Initiatives

Minorities' rapid growth as a percentage of the overall U.S. population, as well as increased global competition, have convinced some financial services firms that workforce diversity is a critical business strategy. Since the mid-1990s, some financial services firms have implemented a variety of initiatives designed to recruit and retain minority and women candidates to fill key positions. Officials from several banks said that they had developed scholarship and internship programs to encourage minority students to consider careers in banking. Some firms and trade organizations have also developed partnerships with groups that represent minority professionals and with local communities to recruit candidates through events such as conferences and career fairs. To help retain minorities and women, firms have established employee networks, mentoring programs, diversity training, and leadership and career development programs.

Industry studies have noted, and officials from some financial services firms we contacted confirmed, that senior managers were involved in diversity initiatives. Some of these officials also said that this level of involvement was critical to success of a program. For example, according to an official from an investment bank, the head of the firm meets with all minority and female senior executives to discuss their career development. Officials from a few commercial banks said that the banks had established diversity "councils" of senior leaders to set the vision, strategy, and direction of diversity initiatives. A 2005 industry trade group study and some officials also noted that some companies were linking managers' compensation with their progress in hiring, promoting, and retaining minority and women employees.[9]

A few firms have also developed performance indicators to measure progress in achieving diversity goals. These indicators include workforce representation, turnover, promotion of minority and women employees, and employee satisfaction survey responses. Officials from several financial services firms stated that measuring the results of diversity efforts over time was critical to the credibility of the initiatives and to justifying the investment in the resources such initiatives demanded.

Several Challenges May Have Affected the Success of Workforce Diversity Initiatives in the Financial Services Industry

While financial services firms and trade groups we contacted had launched diversity initiatives, officials from these organizations, as well as other information, suggest that several challenges may have limited the success of their efforts. These challenges include the following:

- *Recruiting minority and women candidates for management development programs.* Available data on minority students enrolled in Master of Business Administration (MBA) programs suggest that the pool of minorities, a source that may feed the "pipeline" for management-level positions within the financial services industry and other industries, is relatively small.[10] In 2000, minorities accounted for 19 percent of all students enrolled in MBA programs in accredited U.S. schools; in 2006, that student population had risen to 25 percent. Financial services firms compete for this relatively small pool not only with one another but also with firms from other industries.

- *Fully leveraging the "internal" pipeline of minority and women employees for management-level positions.* As shown in figure 4, there are job categories within the financial services industry that generally have more overall workforce diversity than the "official and managers" category, particularly among minorities. For example, minorities held 22 percent of "professional" positions in the industry in 2004 as compared with 15 percent of "officials and managers" positions. According to a 2006 EEOC report, the professional category represented a possible pipeline of available management-level candidates.[11] The EEOC report states that the chances of minorities and women (white and minority combined) advancing from the professional category into management-level positions is lower when compared with white males.

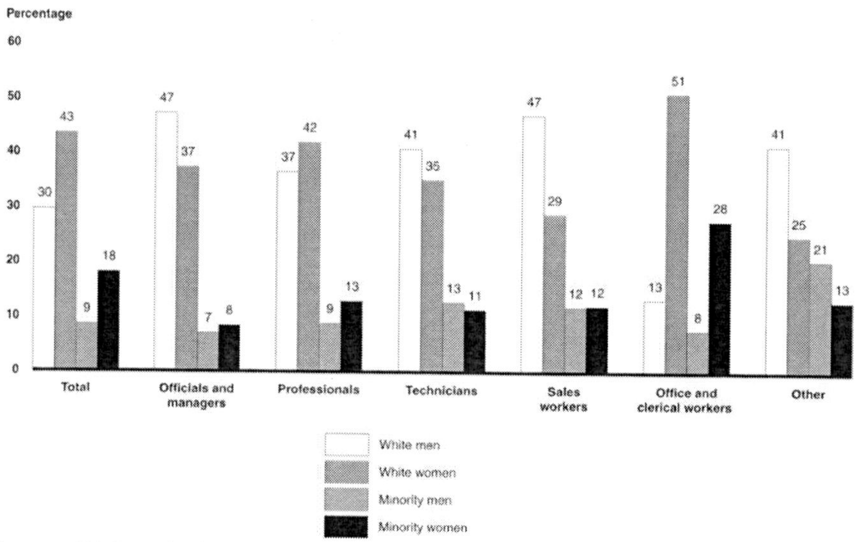

Source: GAO analysis of EEOC data.
Note: Percentages may not always add to 100 due to rounding.

Figure 4. EEO-1 Data (Percentage) on Workforce Diversity in the Financial Services Industry by Position, Gender, and Racial/Ethnic Group (2004)

- *Retaining minority and women candidates that are hired for key management positions.* Many industry officials said that financial services firms lack a critical mass of minority men and women, particularly in senior-level positions, to serve as role models. Without a critical mass, the officials said that minority or women employees may lack the personal connections and access to informal networks that are often necessary to navigate an organization's culture and advance their careers. For example, an official from a commercial bank we contacted said he learned from staff interviews that African-Americans believed that they were not considered for promotion as often as others partly because they were excluded from informal employee networks needed for promotion or to promote advancement.

- *Achieving the "buy-in" of key employees, such as middle managers.* Middle managers are particularly important to the success of diversity initiatives because they are often responsible for implementing key aspects of such initiatives and for explaining them to other employees. However, some financial services industry officials said that middle managers may be focused on other aspects of their responsibilities, such as meeting financial performance targets, rather than the importance of implementing the organization's diversity initiatives. Additionally, the officials said that implementing diversity initiatives represents a considerable cultural and organizational change for many middle managers and employees at all levels. An official from an investment bank told us that the bank has been reaching out to middle managers who oversaw minority and women employees by, for example, instituting an "inclusive manager program."

In closing, despite the implementation of a variety of diversity initiatives over the past 15 years, diversity at the management level in the financial services industry has not changed substantially. Further, diversity at the most senior management positions within the financial services industry may be lower than the overall industry management diversity statistics I have discussed today. While EEOC has taken steps to revise the EEO-1 data to better assess diversity within senior positions, this data may not be available for some period of time. Initiatives to promote management diversity at all levels within financial services firms appear to face several key challenges, such as recruiting and retaining candidates and achieving the "buy-in" of middle managers. Without a sustained commitment to overcome these challenges, management diversity in the financial services industry may continue to remain generally unchanged over time.

Mr. Chairman, this concludes my prepared statement. I would be pleased to respond to any questions you or other Members of the Subcommittee may have.

End Notes

[1] GAO, *Financial Services Industry: Overall Trends in Management-Level Diversity and Diversity Initiatives*, 1993-2004, GAO-06-617 (Washington, D.C.: June 1, 2006). For purposes of this testimony, we focused the diversity discussion on changes in management-level representation over time by gender and racial/ethnic minority groups, including African-Americans, Asians, Hispanics, and American Indians.

[2] GAO, *Diversity Management: Expert-Identified Leading Practices and Agency Examples,* GAO-05-90 (Washington, D.C.: Jan. 14, 2005).

[3] House Committee on Financial Services, Subcommittee on Oversight and Investigations, *Diversity: The GAO Perspective*, 109th Cong., 2nd session, 2006, 109-107; and House

Committee on Financial Services, Subcommittee On Oversight and Investigations, *Diversity in the Financial Services Industry and Access to Capital for Minority Owned Businesses: Challenges and Opportunities*, 108th Cong., 2nd Session, 2004, 108-10 1.

[4] We used the EEO-1 "officials and managers" job category as the basis for our discussion of management-level diversity within the financial services industry. EEOC defines the job category of "officials and managers" as occupations requiring administrative and managerial personnel who set broad policies, exercise overall responsibility for execution of these policies, and direct individual departments or special phases of a firm's operation.

[5] Our June 2006 report describes our approach to reporting the 1993 through 2004 EEO-1 data, which used the Standard Industry Classification System (SIC). In preparing for this testimony, EEOC said that the previous approach would not be reliable for the 2006 EEO-1 data because the SIC has become increasingly unreliable over time and has been replaced by the North American Industrial Classification System.

[6] As mentioned previously, it is not possible to directly conduct a trend analysis due to changes in collecting and reporting EEO-1 data from the 2004 to 2006 period. However, the 2006 EEO-1 data can generally be compared with the EEO-1 data from 2004 and earlier years.

[7] GAO-06-617.

[8] As mentioned previously, it is not possible to directly conduct a trend analysis due to changes in collecting and reporting EEO-1 data from the 2004 to 2006 period. However, the 2006 data can generally be compared with the financial services industry as a whole from 2004 and previous years.

[9] See Securities Industry Association (currently renamed Securities Industry and Financial Markets Association), *2005 Report on Diversity Strategy, Development and Demographics: Executive Summary* (November 2005).

[10] Association to Advance Collegiate Schools of Business, the world's largest accreditation association for business schools, conducts an annual survey called "Business School Questionnaire" of all its accredited schools. Participation in this survey is voluntary. For the year 2006, the most recent year, 94.3 percent of the accredited schools responded to the survey.

[11] Equal Employment Opportunity Commission, *Diversity in the Finance Industry* (April 2006).

INDEX

A

B

C

D

E

F

G

H

I

J

K

L

M

N

T

U

V

W